ANALYSIS AND ACTIVISM

Jungian psychology has taken a noticeable political turn in recent years, and analysts and academics whose work draws on Jung's ideas have made internationally recognised contributions in many humanitarian, communal and political contexts. This book brings together a multidisciplinary and international selection of contributors, all of whom have track records as activists, to discuss some of the most compelling issues in contemporary politics.

Analysis and Activism is presented in six parts:

- Section 1, *Interventions*, includes discussion of what working outside the consulting room means, and descriptions of work with displaced children in Colombia, projects for migrants in Italy and an analyst's engagement in the struggles of indigenous Australians.
- Section 2, *Equalities and inequalities*, tackles topics ranging from the collapse of care systems in the UK to working with victims of torture.
- Section 3, *Politics and modernity*, looks at the struggles of native people in Guatemala and Canada and oral history interviews with members of the Chinese/Vietnamese diaspora.
- Section 4, *Culture and identity*, studies issues of race and class in Brazil, feminism and the gendered imagination and the introduction of Obamacare in the USA.
- Section 5, *Cultural phantoms*, examines the continuing trauma of the Cultural Revolution in China, Jung's relationship with Jews and Judaism and German-Jewish dynamics.
- Finally, Section 6, *Nature: truth and reconciliation*, looks at our broken connection to nature, town and country planning and relief work after the 2011 earthquake in Japan.

There remains throughout the book an acknowledgement that the project of thinking forward the political in Jungian psychology can be problematic, given Jung's own questionable political history. What emerges is a radical and progressive Jungian approach to politics informed by the spirit of the times as well as by the spirit of the depths.

This cutting-edge collection will be essential reading for Jungian and post-Jungian academics and analysts, psychotherapists, counsellors and psychologists, and academics and students of politics, sociology, psychosocial studies and cultural studies.

Emilija Kiehl is a Jungian analyst in private practice in London. She is Chair of the British Jungian Analytic Association (BJAA) and member of the Executive Committee of the International Association for Analytical Psychology (IAAP). She is editor of a number of IAAP publications and Book Review Editor of *Spring Journal*. Before training in Jungian analysis, Emilija was a literary translator and contributor to cultural and informative journals in the former Yugoslavia. Her published translations include works by Noam Chomsky, Harold Pinter, Arthur Miller, John Updike and others. She teaches on the BJAA external courses and on the BJAA/Birkbeck, University of London MSc in the Psychodynamics of Human Development.

Mark Saban is a Jungian analyst working in Oxford and London. He also lectures on Jungian psychology at the Centre for Psychoanalytic Studies, University of Essex. He is the author of numerous journal articles and book chapters.

Andrew Samuels works internationally as a political consultant with politicians, parties and activist groups. He was co-founder of Psychotherapists and Counsellors for Social Responsibility in 1994 and chair of the UK Council for Psychotherapy 2009–2012, and is Professor of Analytical Psychology at Essex and Visiting Professor at New York, Roehampton, Macau and Goldsmiths, University of London. His books have been translated into 21 languages. Those published by Routledge include: *Jung and the Post-Jungians*; *A Critical Dictionary of Jungian Analysis*; *The Plural Psyche*; *The Political Psyche*; *Relational Psychotherapy, Psychoanalysis and Counselling* (with Del Loewenthal); and *Persons, Passions, Politics, Psychotherapy*.

ANALYSIS AND ACTIVISM

Social and political contributions of Jungian psychology

Edited by Emilija Kiehl, Mark Saban and Andrew Samuels

Сави и Лидији,
с љубављу,
Емилија
Лондон, јуна 2016

LONDON AND NEW YORK

First published 2016
by Routledge
2 Park Square, Milton Park, Abingdon, Oxon OX14 4RN

and by Routledge
711 Third Avenue, New York, NY 10017

Routledge is an imprint of the Taylor & Francis Group, an informa business

British Library Cataloguing in Publication Data
A catalogue record for this book is available from the British Library

Library of Congress Cataloging in Publication Data
Names: Kiehl, Emilija, editor. | Saban, Mark, editor. | Samuels, Andrew, editor.
Title: Analysis and activism : social and political contributions of Jungian psychology / edited by Emilija Kiehl, Mark Saban and Andrew Samuels.
Description: 1 Edition. | New York : Routledge, 2016. | Includes index.
Identifiers: LCCN 2015040431 | ISBN 9781138948099 (hardback) | ISBN 9781138948105 (pbk.) | ISBN 9781315669700 (ebook)
Subjects: LCSH: Jung, C. G. (Carl Gustav), 1875–1961. | Jungian psychology. | Psychology—Social aspects. | Psychology—Political aspects.
Classification: LCC BF173.J85 A53 2016 | DDC 150.19/54—dc23
LC record available at http://lccn.loc.gov/2015040431

ISBN: 978-1-138-94809-9 (hbk)
ISBN: 978-1-138-94810-5 (pbk)
ISBN: 978-1-315-66970-0 (ebk)

Typeset in Bembo and Stone Sans
by Florence Production Ltd, Stoodleigh, Devon, UK

Printed and bound in Great Britain by
TJ International Ltd, Padstow, Cornwall

We are living in times of great disruption: political passions are aflame, internal upheavals have brought nations to the brink of chaos. The analyst feels the violence even in the quiet of the consulting room. A psychologist cannot avoid coming to grips with contemporary history even if the very soul shrinks from the political uproar, the lying propaganda, and the jarring speeches of the demagogues. We need not mention duties as citizens which confront us with a similar task.

C. G. Jung (1946 Preface to *Essays on Contemporary Events*. *CW* 10, p.11)

CONTENTS

CONTRIBUTORS

Lawrence Alschuler is retired Professor of Political Science (University of Ottawa, Canada) now living in Switzerland. He taught also at the Universities of Hawaii and Zurich, and the Argentine Catholic University, and specialised in the political economy of Latin America. He studied at the C.G. Jung Institute-Zurich for four years in the 1980s, and has recently published on political consciousness, fanaticism, Islamism, and the welfare state, all from the perspective of analytical psychology.

Jerome S. Bernstein, MAPC, NCPsyA, is a Jungian Analyst in private practice in Santa Fe, New Mexico; a senior analyst on the teaching faculty of the C.G. Jung Institute of Santa Fe; the author of *Power and Politics, the Psychology of Soviet–American Partnership* (1989); *Living in the Borderland: The Evolution of Consciousness and the Challenge of Healing Trauma* (2005); the co-editor, along with Philip Deloria, of *C.G. Jung and the Sioux Traditions* by Vine Deloria, Jr (2009); the author of 'Healing Our Split: Participation Mystique and C.G. Jung' in *Shared Realities* (2014), and of numerous articles on international conflict, personal and collective trauma, and various analytical topics. He lectures and teaches internationally.

Walter Boechat, MD, PhD, trained at the C.G. Jung Institute-Zurich. He is a past member of the IAAP Executive Committee and a co-Regional Organiser (with Misser Berg) for the Latin American Developing Groups of IAAP. He is a founding-member of the Jungian Association of Brazil (AJB), and part of the staff in charge of the Brazilian edition of Jung's *Red Book*. He is the author of numerous scientific publications and of a comprehensive study on myth: *Mythopoesis of the Psyche: Myth and Individuation* (2012).

Stefano Carta is an analytical psychologist from AIPA, of which he has been President from 2002–2006; he is professor of Dynamic and Clinical Psychology at the University of Cagliari, Italy. He has contributed to the organisation of the Project of Ethno-psychology (ETnA) devoted to training and intervention in the field of ethno-psychological disorders. He has collaborated with the Centre for Trauma, Asylum and Refugees, University of Essex, UK. He is the deputy editor of the *Journal of Analytical Psychology* for Europe. He lives in Rome and Cagliari.

Angela Cotter is a Jungian analyst (GAP) in London UK, with a background as a nurse and health service researcher, manager and educator. Her PhD (1990) was an exploration of the wounded healer in nursing, and she has since researched this concept more widely in health and social care. She holds a certificate from the UKCP for her outstanding contribution to psychotherapy (2009). She is a Visiting Lecturer at Regent's University and Head of Research at the Minster Centre, London.

Peter T. Dunlap is a psychologist working in private and political practice. He is engaged in research at the interface between Jung's psychocultural and political thinking, group theory, and emotion-focused work in psychotherapy and groups. He currently leads a group for community leaders focused on cultivating activism with a psychological attitude. Peter is the author of *Awakening our Faith in the Future* (2008).

Roberto Gambini studied Law and Social Sciences and has an MA from the University of Chicago. He graduated from the C.G. Jung Institute-Zurich in 1981. His books are *Indian Mirror – The Making of the Brazilian Soul* (2006) and *A Voz e o Tempo*, a memoir of 35 years as a Jungian analyst (2008), which was awarded the Jabuti literary prize in Brazil. He has carried out several field researches among the Brazilian Indians.

Gottfried M. Heuer, PhD, is a Jungian training analyst and supervisor and neo-Reichian body-psychotherapist with over 35 years of clinical practice in West London. He is an independent scholar with more than 70 papers published in the major analytic journals. His books include ten volumes of congress proceedings for the *International Otto Gross Society* (which he co-founded), *Sacral Revolutions: Reflecting on the Work of Andrew Samuels* (2010) and *Sexual Revolutions: Psychoanalysis, History and the Father* (2011). In 2016 he published *Freud's 'Outstanding' Colleague/Jung's 'Twin Brother': The Suppressed Psychoanalytic and Political Significance of Otto Gross*. He is also a published poet, graphic artist, photographer and sculptor.

Toshio Kawai, PhD, is Professor at the Kokoro Research Centre, Kyoto University for Clinical Psychology. He is Vice-President of the IAAP. He was educated in clinical psychology at Kyoto University and in philosophical psychology at Zurich University where he received a PhD in 1987. He obtained a diploma from the C.G. Jung Institute-Zurich in 1990. He has published articles, books and book chapters in English, German and Japanese. His papers 'Postmodern Consciousness in Psychotherapy' (2006); 'Union and Separation in the Therapy of Pervasive

Developmental Disorders and ADHD' (2009) and 'The Red Book from a Pre-modern Perspective' were published in the *Journal of Analytical Psychology*. His work after the 2011 earthquake in Japan includes: 'The 2011 Earthquake in Japan: Psychotherapeutic Interventions and Change of Worldview', published in *Spring Journal* (2012), and 'Big Stories and Small stories in the Psychological Relief Work after the Earthquake Disaster' published in *Analytical Psychology in a Changing World*, edited by L. Huskinson and M. Stein.

Tom Kelly is current President of the IAAP. He is a senior training analyst and supervisor and past President of the Inter-Regional Society of Jungian Analysts (IRSJA) and of the Council of North American Societies of Jungian Analysts (CNASJA). Tom has been actively engaged in teaching and lecturing in many Developing Groups around the world for many years. He lives and has a private practice in Montreal, Canada.

Emilija Kiehl, MSc, is a Jungian analyst in private practice in London. She is Chair of the British Jungian Analytic Association (BJAA) and member of the Executive Committee of the International Association for Analytical Psychology (IAAP). She is editor of a number of IAAP publications and book review editor of *Spring Journal*. Before training in Jungian analysis, Emilija was a literary translator and contributor to cultural and informative journals in the former Yugoslavia. Her published translations include works by Noam Chomsky, Harold Pinter, Arthur Miller, John Updike and others. She teaches on the BJAA external courses and on the BJAA/Birkbeck University MSc program.

Sam Kimbles is a clinical psychologist, training analyst and member of the faculty of the C.G. Jung Institute of San Francisco as well as a clinical professor (VCF) in the Department of Family and Community Medicine, University of California, San Francisco. He is a former president of the C.G. Jung Institute, San Francisco. His published work on the cultural complex is a significant contribution of the application of analytical psychology to the study of groups and society. He is the author (with Thomas Singer) of *The Cultural Complex: Contemporary Jungian Perspectives on Psyche and Society* (2004) and *Phantom Narratives, the Unseen Contributions of Culture to Psyche* (2014).

Thomas B. Kirsch, MD, Jungian analyst, trained at the C.G. Jung Institute of San Francisco. He is a past President of the Jung Institute, San Francisco, past Vice-president and past President of the IAAP, author of *The Jungians*, the editor of many chapters on Jung and analytical psychology and the consulting editor for *The Jung–Kirsch Letters: The Correspondence of C. G. Jung and James Kirsch*. In 2014 he published *A Jungian Life*.

Ann Kutek, BA Hons Oxon, in Philosophy, Politics and Economics, Dip. Soc. Admin, Dip. SW (Edinburgh), CQSW, is a Member of BPF (BJAA), IAAP, and works in private practice. Her publications date from 1981. She spent many years as a social work manager and planner and was one of the original child protection officers in London. She was the first clinical director of an organisation offering therapeutic consultations to the commercial sector including engineering and banking. She translates analytic texts from the French mainly for the *JAP*. She presented a paper on climate change at the 2013 Copenhagen IAAP Congress. She teaches at Birkbeck, University of London, at BPF and in Poland where she supervises Polish Routers in analytic training.

Kevin Lu, PhD, is Director of Graduate Studies and Director of the MA Jungian and Post-Jungian Studies in the Centre for Psychoanalytic Studies, University of Essex. He is a former member of the Executive Committee of the International Association for Jungian Studies. Dr Lu's publications include articles and chapters on Jung's relationship to the discipline of history, Arnold J. Toynbee's use of analytical psychology, and critical assessments of the theory of *cultural complexes*.

François Martin-Vallas, MD, PhD, is a psychiatrist and Jungian analyst, and member of the French Society (SFPA). He works in private and institutional practice, with children in Public Consulting Centre, and with adults in a manufactory that offers jobs to persons with intellectual disabilities (most of them being former psychotic children and/or psychotic adults). He has published a number of papers in the *Cahiers Jungiens de Psychanalyse* and the *Journal of Analytical Psychology*. He is former member of the IAAP Programme Committee, a former editor of the *Cahiers Jungiens de Psychanalyse*, editor-in-chief of the *Revue de psychologie analytique*, and associated researcher at Lyon 2 University. He won an honorary prize of the National Association for the Advancement of Psychoanalysis in 2003 and the Special Fordham Prize for the 50th anniversary of the JAP in 2006.

Renos K. Papadopoulos, PhD, is Professor of Analytical Psychology at the Centre for Psychoanalytic Studies, Director of the Centre for Trauma, Asylum and Refugees, a member of the Human Rights Centre and of the Transitional Justice Network, all at the University of Essex; also, Honorary Clinical Psychologist and Systemic Family Psychotherapist at the Tavistock Clinic. In addition, he is a training and supervising Jungian psychoanalyst and systemic family psychotherapist in private practice. As consultant to the United Nations and other organisations, he has been working with refugees and other survivors of political violence, torture and disasters in many countries. He is the founder and director of the MA/PhD in Refugee Care that is offered jointly by the University of Essex and the Tavistock Clinic. He lectures and offers specialist trainings internationally and his writings have appeared in fourteen languages.

Eva Pattis Zoja (1952) is a clinical psychologist and Jungian psychoanalyst working in private practice in Milan, Italy. Her books in English are *Abortion, Loss and Renewal in the Search for Identity* (1997), *Sandplay Therapy: The Treatment of Psychopathologies* (ed.) (2002) and *Sandplay Therapy in Vulnerable Communities* (2011). She is currently working in Colombia, Argentina, Romania, South Africa and Palestine on projects in Expressive Sandwork (www.sandwork.org), helping neglected children in areas where psychotherapy is not available.

Joerg Rasche, Dr Med., is a Jungian analyst in Berlin, trained in the Berlin C.G. Jung Institute and with Dora Kalff in Zollikon (Sandplay therapy). He was for many years president of the German Association for Analytical Psychology (DGAP) and is a former vice-president of the IAAP (2007–10). Currently he is the liaison for the IAAP Developing Group in Kazakhstan and President of the German Society for Sandplay Therapy (DGST). He has given many seminars on Jungian Analysis and Sandplay Therapy in Riga, Krakow, Warsaw, Kiev and Almaty. In November 2012 he was honoured with the Golden Cross of Merit of the Republic of Poland for his work on the reconciliation of nations and for analytical training in Poland. He is an invited faculty member of the Transcend Peace University (Johan Galtung). Currently he is co-editing a book (with Thomas Singer) on *The European Cultural Complexes.*

Susan Rowland, PhD, is Chair of MA Engaged Humanities and the Creative Life at Pacifica Graduate Institute, California and formerly Professor of English and Jungian Studies at the University of Greenwich, UK. She is author of a number of books on literary theory, gender and Jung, including *Jung as a Writer* (2005); *Jung: A Feminist Revision* (2002); *C. G. Jung in the Humanities* (2010); *The Ecocritical Psyche: Literature, Evolutionary Complexity and Jung* (2012) and *The Sleuth and the Goddess in Women's Detective Fiction* (2015).

Mary-Jayne Rust is an art therapist, feminist therapist and Jungian analyst. Journeys to Ladakh in the early 1990s alerted her to the seriousness of the ecological crisis, and its cultural, economic and spiritual roots. Since then she has played a key role in the field of ecopsychology, an inquiry into our psychological relationship with the earth. Recent publications include *Vital Signs: Psychological Responses to Ecological Crisis*, which she edited with Nick Totton (2011).

Mark Saban is a Jungian analyst working in Oxford and London. He also lectures on Jungian psychology at the Centre for Psychoanalytic Studies, University of Essex. He is the author of numerous journal articles and book chapters.

Andrew Samuels works internationally as a political consultant with politicians, parties and activist groups. He was co-founder of Psychotherapists and Counsellors for Social Responsibility in 1994 and Chair of the UK Council for Psychotherapy 2009–12. He is Professor of Analytical Psychology at Essex and Visiting Professor at New York, Goldsmith's, Roehampton and Macau Universities. His books have been translated into 21 languages and include *Jung and the Post-Jungians* (1985); *The Plural Psyche* (1989); *The Political Psyche* (1993); *Politics on the Couch* (2001); *Persons, Passions, Politics, Psychotherapy* (2014) and *A New Therapy for Politics?* (2015).

Craig San Roque, PhD, is a psychologist and member of the Australia and New Zealand Society of Jungian Analysts. He currently works in remote Central Australia, engaged in a range of mental health and social action projects in Aboriginal affairs. Publications include *Placing Psyche, Exploring Cultural Complexes in Australia* (2011) and the almost cult classic graphic novel, *The Long Weekend in Alice Springs* (2013).

Joshua Santospirito is an Australian mental health nurse and a multimedia artist who has also worked on long-form comic-projects such as *Swallows* (which details Aeolian/Italian immigration to Melbourne) and *Sleuth*. He is currently working on *Sydney/Purgatorio* in collaboration with Craig San Roque.

Heyong Shen, PhD, is Professor of Psychology at SCNU (South China Normal University) and also at CUM (the City University of Macao). He is a Jungian analyst of the IAAP and an ISST sandplay therapist. He is Founding President of the Chinese Federation for Analytical Psychology and Sandplay Therapy and the principal organiser of the International Conferences of Analytical Psychology and Chinese Culture (1998–2013). He has spoken at Eranos Conferences in 1997 and 2007, is chief editor for the Chinese translation of the *Collected Works of C.G. Jung*, and chief editor of the Chinese *Journal of Analytical Psychology*. He was a Fulbright Scholar in Residence (1996–7) to research and give lectures on Chinese psychology at UNO/UCLA (USA). He was Visiting Scholar for the Research on Group Dynamics at Southern Illinois University (1993–4). He trained in Jungian analysis at the C.G. Jung Institute, Küsnacht and at the San Francisco C.G. Jung Institute (1997–2002). Heyong Shen has published 12 books and 50 papers in Chinese including, with Gao Lan in 2012, 'The Garden of the Heart and Soul: Psychological Relief Works in Earthquake Zones and Orphanages in China', *Spring: A Journal of Archetype and Culture*, Vol. 88, Winter. Also in 2012, with Gao Lan, 'The Beauty of Angels: Images and Symbol in the Garden of the Heart and Soul', *Journal of Sandplay Therapy*, Vol. 2.1

Thomas Singer, MD, is a psychiatrist and Jungian analyst (trained at the C.G. Jung Institute in San Francisco). He is editor of *The Analytical Psychology and Contemporary Cultural Series* for Spring Journal Books. He is current President of National ARAS, an archive of symbolic imagery (ARAS.org). He has written and/or edited the following books: *Who's the Patient Here?* (1978, with Stuart Copans), *A Fan's Guide to Baseball Fever* (1991, with Stuart Copans), *The Vision Thing* (2000), *The Cultural Complex* (2004, with Samuel Kimbles), *Initiation: The Living Reality of an Archetype* (2007, with Thomas Kirsch and Virginia Beane Rutter), *Psyche and the City* (2010), *Ancient Greece, Modern Psyche: Archetypes in the Making* (2011, with Virginia Beane Rutter), *Placing Psyche: Exploring Cultural Complexes in Australia* (2011), *Listening to Latin America* (2012) and *Ancient Greece, Modern Psyche: Archetypes Evolving* (2015, with Virginia Beane Rutter).

Tristan Troudart, MD, is a psychiatrist, psychotherapist and Jungian analyst, born in Chile, and lives in Israel, where he is a member of the Israel Institute of Jungian Psychology (IIJP). He was founder and former director of the Day Hospitalization Department at the Jerusalem Mental Health Centre, Kfar-Shaul Hospital. He is active in human rights work and has participated in projects of training and cooperation between Israeli and Palestinian mental health professionals, supported by Physicians for Human Rights-Israel, and in a project of documentation of torture, with the Public Committee Against Torture in Israel. He is currently in private practice in Jerusalem.

ACKNOWLEDGEMENTS AND PERMISSIONS

Emilija Kiehl: I am grateful to Andrew and Mark for their energetic and warm collegiality throughout this, our first collaboration, which made the project not only possible but hugely pleasurable too; to the IAAP Officers and Tom Kelly, IAAP President, for their enthusiastic support and participation in the Conference. Thanks to our London colleagues: Jay Barlow (SAP), Suzanne Bergne (GAP), Angela Cotter (GAP), Phil Goss (AJA), Tia Kuchmy (IGAP), Carola Mathers (AJA) and Vivien Zyms (BJAA), who worked tirelessly on all the intricate tasks involved in a project like this, and also to our wonderful audience. Special thanks to my husband, Frederick, for his unending support and participation in the conference and to my stepson, Alex, who generously contributed his time and professional skills by filming the opening panels of the Conference (the film can be viewed on the website of the International Association for Analytical Psychology: iaap.org).

Mark Saban: I owe a debt of thanks to both Emilija and Andrew for allowing me to help with both projects: co-organising the conference and co-editing the book. To work alongside them has been not only enormously enjoyable but hugely educational. Teamwork is a pleasure rarely enjoyed by the psychoanalyst. To operate as part of such a team has been a great privilege. Deep thanks too to Penny Boreham for everything.

Andrew Samuels: I'd like to salute and thank Emilija and Mark for all our great work together on this book (and also, with others mentioned elsewhere, on the conference). We took it in turns to get anxious and be calmed, though maybe I seized more turns than the others. Getting so many authors, from so many countries, and with so many different attitudes to writing into one volume – well, it needed a team. More widely, I owe a debt of gratitude to friends and colleagues in the Jungian world (and, as pertinently, outside it) who have been supportive of my work on politics and on Jung over many years. Sissy Lykou deserves a special thank you.

We acknowledge permission to print the images in the chapter by Walter Boechat received from Instituto de Pesquisa e Memória Pretos Novos – IPN Museu Memorial in Rio de Janeiro.

We acknowledge permission to publish the poem in the chapter by Heyong Shen: Su Tung-p'o, 'Ten Years – Dead and Living Dim and Draw Apart', translated by Burton Watson, from *Selected Poems of Su Tung-p'o.* Translation copyright © 1994 by Burton Watson. Reprinted with the permission of The Permissions Company, Inc. on behalf of Copper Canyon Press, www.coppercanyonpress.org.

We acknowledge the permission of the artist to utilise the image of the Chinese Opera masks designed by Chen Qiong in the chapter by Heyong Shen.

We acknowledge the permission of the artist to utilise the graphic image of the mask of a god designed by Li Yaping in the chapter by Heyong Shen.

We acknowledge permission to utilise the image of the ESAT factory in the chapter by François Martin-Vallas granted by AFIPaeim, association familiale de l'Isère pour enfants et adultes handicapés intellectuels dont le siege est au 3. Marie Renoard à Grenoble.

We acknowledge permission to use the image of 'Das Gerücht' (The Rumor) by Paul Weber from Bild-Kunst in the chapter by Thomas Singer.

We acknowledge permission of Macmillan Publishers Ltd to utilise the image of the coelacanth taken from *Nature* 143, 455–6 (18 March, 1939) in the chapter by Thomas Singer.

We acknowledge the open permission of the authors (Richard Wilkinson and Kate Pickett) to reproduce the graph taken from *The Spirit Level: Why More Equal Societies Almost Always Do Better* (London: Allen Lane, 2009) in the chapter by Thomas Singer.

We acknowledge the permission of the artist, Chester Arnold, for the one-time use of his painting *Thy Kingdom Come II*, oil on linen, 1999, held in the Collection of the DiRosa Preserve, Napa, California in the chapter by Thomas Singer. The image is used courtesy of the artist and Catherine Clark Gallery, San Francisco.

Permission from San Kessto Publications to republish extracts from Craig San Roque's *The Long Weekend in Alice Springs*, adapted and drawn by Joshua Santospirito (2013), in the chapter by Craig San Roque is gratefully acknowledged.

Despite exhaustive searching, it has not been possible to trace the copyright holder for the photomontage image of the Three Stooges plus President Obama in golf attire that appears in the chapter by Thomas Singer. Any omissions brought to the attention of the editors or the publisher will be corrected in future editions.

The image from the film *Coming Home* in the chapter by Heyong Shen was drawn from a DVD of the work and is included for the purposes of criticism and review. Attempts have been made to contact the copyright holder.

FOREWORD

Tom Kelly

It was my honour, as President of the IAAP, to welcome the participants of this very first conference on Analysis and Activism: Social and Political Contributions of Jungian Psychology.

Analytical psychology has traditionally been almost exclusively focused on understanding the inner world and the individual's process of individuation. While this is incontestably important, the shadow it constellates is the unfortunate consequence of unwittingly contributing to the strengthening of a disconcerting and disheartening collective attitude of narcissistic self-centredness. During my training in Zurich in the early and mid-eighties, group work of any kind was frowned upon by many Jungians at that time because what was considered of prime importance was *the individual*. The belief was that change in the collective could only come about through inner work and change on the individual level. Thanks to the courageous efforts of Dr Helmut Barz and his wife, Elynor Barz, group experience in psychodrama was introduced at the C.G. Jung Institute and continued to be offered long after my training.

In hindsight, this reluctance to give consideration to groups and to the collective is rather surprising when one considers how attentive Jung was to the impact of outer world events on his inner life and as an expression of the archetypal energies of the collective unconscious. Consider, for example, Jung's nightmarish dreams of Europe being flooded by a wave of blood prior to the outbreak of World War One. It seemed evident to Jung that individuation was not a uniquely inner process, but rather that it demanded and required active engagement and participation of the individual with the outer world. There was for him a clear distinction between individuation and individualism. His famous statement that one does not individuate by sitting at the top of Mount Everest further attests to this.

And yet, it has taken many Jungians a long time to move beyond the confines of their consultation rooms and to become actively engaged in sociopolitical issues affecting us all at the local, national and international levels. It is heartening to see that this is changing and that more and more Jungians are working to actively contribute to these pressing issues. This conference and the overwhelmingly enthusiastic response of the presenters to the invitation to participate is testimony to the increasingly active engagement of Jungians and to their willingness to contribute to finding novel approaches and innovative answers to the sociopolitical and environmental collective challenges we face.

Initially, the conference organisers, Emilija Kiehl and Andrew Samuels, proposed that any profit from the conference be donated to the IAAP. After reflection about this, however, and in keeping with the spirit of this conference, we decided that half of the profits of the conference would be donated to the International Red Cross and Red Crescent to help in their efforts to deal with the consequences of the many catastrophes they are called upon to respond to. The other half will be used in support of the Router programme of the IAAP to provide funds for training in countries where resources are otherwise severely limited or unavailable. In both of these initiatives, we felt we were truly honouring the spirit of the conference.

On behalf of the IAAP, I would like to extend my sincere and heartfelt thanks to Emilija Kiehl, Mark Saban and Andrew Samuels for their boundless enthusiasm and energy for this project from the very get-go and for all of the time and effort they have put into making this such a successful event. I would also like to extend my thanks to the five IAAP Group Member Societies from London – Association of Jungian Analysts (AJA), British Jungian Analytic Association (BJAA), Guild of Analytic Psychologists (GAP), Independent Group of Analytical Psychologists (IGAP) and Society of Analytical Psychology (SAP) – for their active support of and participation in the programming and planning of the conference.

May this conference be but the beginning of a long and creative effort to expand the boundaries and application of Jungian psychology!

Tom Kelly
President, IAAP

EDITORIAL INTRODUCTIONS

Emilija Kiehl

This book is the result of an unexpectedly enthusiastic response to what had started as an exchange of e-mails between Andrew Samuels and me about Andrew giving a talk on a political theme at British Jungian Analytic Association (BJAA). Soon after, we both attended the XIX Congress of the International Association for Analytical Psychology (IAAP) in Copenhagen where some of our colleagues' presentations inspired our renewed interest in pursuing the idea of a talk on politics in London. After the Congress, Andrew and I met in London to make a plan.

Little did we know what tremendous energy, of what was to become the first Analysis and Activism Conference under the auspices of IAAP, was already being generated. The original idea of a talk by Andrew at BJAA soon changed into thinking about a panel discussion with two or three colleagues. We drew a list of those we knew were interested and engaged in political matters, and came up with about thirty names, many from abroad. Would they want to travel to London for this event? Moreover, as we had no funds for the endeavour, anyone presenting would have to cover all their travel and accommodation expenses and there would be no fee! Instead of trying to guess who might and who might not accept these conditions, we decided to e-mail everyone on our list and hope for some positive responses.

Within a day or two, the replies started to pour in and our absolutely packed conference programme testified that almost everyone we invited said, yes! Needless to say, we were quite overwhelmed by such a positive response. Furthermore, once the word was out, more colleagues were contacting us offering to participate, but it was already clear that we were about to embark on a much larger event than we had anticipated and, regretfully, we could not include them.

The zeitgeist and other archetypal forces were playing a part in the tremendous momentum that our modest original idea was gathering.

We informed IAAP of what was happening, and they gave us seed money to secure a venue for the conference. The five IAAP London Jungian training organisations – AJA, BJAA, GAP, IGAP, SAP – delegated representatives for the conference organising team, and, only a year or so later, there we were, in the elegant nineteenth-century venue built by the British General Medical Council, partaking in an inspiring weekend of thinking, discussing and questioning together.

As the conference weekend was approaching, the twelfth-century Persian philosophical poem 'The Conference of the Birds' kept on appearing in my mind. It is a story about all the birds of the world, known and unknown, representing human vulnerabilities, who gathered together to decide who should be their ruler because, they said, 'no country can have a good administration and a good organisation without a king'. The wisest among them, the Hoopoe, came forward and told the birds about the mythological winged creature, *Simurgh*, 'the mysterious Being' and the true king of birds. According to Persian mythology, *Simurgh* is so old that he had seen the destruction of the world three times over. *Simurgh* can purify the land and waters and represents the union between the earth and the sky, serving as mediator and messenger between the two. *Simurgh* roosts in the Tree of Life, which contains the all-healing medicine, which can cure all the illnesses of mankind.

Having heard this, the birds felt longing in their hearts to see *Simurgh* and they set out on a pilgrimage to find him. What had started as a political cause was transformed into a spiritual quest for meaning, or in Jungian terms, individuation.

It might be that in today's world of relentlessly materialistic values, often ruthless exploitation of human, animal and other natural resources of the planet we all share, causing sharp socioeconomic inequality and unspoken class wars, being interested in the wellbeing of our fellow creatures and our planet brings a spiritual dimension into political concerns.

It is difficult to see on the present world political stage a leader deserving of our trust, and a growing number of groups are gathering internationally, around a shared hope that there may be an *idea* that could lead us through these times of apparent 'progress' but in whose shadow the primitive mentality of *'Homo homini lupus est'* (man is wolf to man) threatens to get us into another devastating war.

Perhaps nothing short of a collective transcendent function – Jung's concept for the mediating capacity of the psyche to bridge the gap between ego-consciousness and the unconscious, leading to a new point of view that transcends the conflicting opposites – could bring about the much needed peaceful sociopolitical change.

In the Persian poem, at the end of their perilous journey, out of many thousands who started the pilgrimage, only thirty birds survive and they do find *Simurgh*. They discover that *Simurgh*'s name means Thirty Birds. He is a mirror in whose reflection they see their bodies and their souls and, in each other's faces, they contemplate the face of the *Simurgh* of the inner world.

Deciding to spend a weekend contemplating the state of the outer world as a reflection of what goes on in the internal world of our species, I think acknowledges our sense of shared responsibility, and I feel honoured to have been part of such a gathering.

The authors of the chapters in this book are the presenters – the birds that flew from all over the planet to the conference, to gather together, listen and discuss the state of our world with each other and with the engaged and inspiring audience. I hope that, along with the thought-provoking ideas, thoughts and images, the following pages will convey to the reader at least some of the very special energy that was shared when the Spirit of the Times met the Spirit of the Depth that December weekend in London.

Mark Saban

It is not perhaps too provocative to remark (with Theodor Schieder) that there is 'a crucial interdependence between political action and historical consciousness' (Schieder, 1978, p. 1). However, for those of us who wish to explore a meeting place between analytical psychology and political activism, it is important to reflect upon what this 'crucial interdependence' entails. Such a reflection will take us in two related directions.

The first relates to the historical context of analytical psychology and indeed Jung himself. Generations of analytical psychologists have chosen sweet oblivion over painful awareness with regard to the actual historical setting of Jung's writings, and especially those of the 1930s. Everyone passing through a Jungian training should be encouraged to think long and hard on this question: why would the great Walter Benjamin have written in 1937 that Jung's 'auxiliary services to National Socialism [the Nazi Party] have been in the works for some time', and that he (Benjamin) was 'waging an onslaught on [Jung's] doctrines, especially those concerning archaic images and the collective unconscious' (Benjamin et al., 1980, p. 197)? This is not an issue that can be reduced to questions about Jung's presidency of the International General Medical Society for Psychotherapy or his personal anti-Semitism. Benjamin, reading Jung with a political eye, is claiming that the *fundamental ideas behind analytical psychology support Nazism*. In order to disagree, we are surely required at the very least to understand why Benjamin might have thought so.

To begin to answer Benjamin we would need to engage with our own relationship to our own past. This means, first, that we need to know our own history as Jungians. Defensive denial is not a promising first step in the direction of establishing a politics.[1] Our starting point needs to be a cool survey of Jung's conservatism: its *Völkisch* roots, its racism, its atavism. But then we need to go further and, through Benjamin's eyes, see that by prioritising the archaic (archetypal) image, and by allowing myth to trump history, Jung did indeed encourage the kind of mystification that will always lend support to irrationalist ideologies like fascism.

Only when we have seen and accepted this fact can we take the further step of pointing out that (as is often the case with Jung) to see through this one lens, however accurate, actually occludes a picture that is both more complex and more interesting.

In fact, Jung cannot be dismissed as a mere irrationalist: his psychology insists again and again upon the (albeit unsymmetrical) meeting of consciousness, reason and light with the unconscious, the irrational and the dark. And this is precisely where we find analytical psychology's untapped potential with regard to the historical/political. Jung's insistence upon a double perspective, applied to the historical/political, can offer us the means to unveil the shadowy underbelly of what we are generally presented with as history. But the crucial precondition for any analysis of this sort is that it *must stick rigorously to the historical image as it is*. All too easily the Jungian approach slips into an ahistorical archaism, whereby for example a political event will be subjected to an archetypal amplification with no care for (or knowledge of) the specific historical context that conditions this particular image. We may be able to get away with this kind of thing when it comes to the dreams of an individual but when it comes to constructing a historically responsible Jungian politics in the real world it becomes a serious problem, since, as Schieder says, all political consciousness is intimately bound up with a historical consciousness.

If we see a radical politics as primarily concerned with the liberation of persons or communities from a past or background experienced (not necessarily in consciousness) as limiting or constrictive, then what is essential is an in depth awareness of the precise nature of those limits and constrictions. This is why consciousness is so important: a clear consciousness of the past enables one to see through the invisible yet all-too-powerful shackles it imposes. Santayana is talking psychoanalysis as well as politics when he says 'Those who cannot remember the past are condemned to repeat it' (Santayana, 2011, p. 172).

The fact that, within the Jungian world, the importance of such an exercise is, generally speaking, rarely even acknowledged is further evidence of the resolutely ahistorical, free-floating perspective which is all too characteristic of the Jungian approach: an approach that invariably favours woolly abstractions about the archaic ('it's archetypal!') over a willingness to engage with the concrete complexity of events in history.

But this need not and should not be so. Jung's methodology (as in his insistence on sticking to the image, on the importance of 'not knowing', respect for the specific and personal context, and the necessity for the analyst to be engaged, as a whole person, with the image) offers an approach to the historical and political that could be enormously fruitful. It seems to me that the goal, both here and in psychological work with the individual, is to find the interface, the place of greatest tension, between the personal/historical and the collective/mythic, and to hold together or perhaps oscillate between the two perspectives, *without allowing either dimension to be subsumed into the other*, and without allowing the ego to already know what will unfold. In Jung's two personalities as he recounts them in *Memories, Dreams, Reflections* (1961), we have a model for what Jung describes as an ultimately interminable dialectic between these two positions – one collective/mythic and one personal/historical. Neither alone is enough. They need each other and they need to be in relation to each other. Keeping this conversation going is an ethical and political imperative.

This is not a passive process – as Jung emphasises again and again it requires the analyst, as whole person, in all her brokenness and vulnerability, to put herself on the line. This, it seems to me, is what makes it a true (and maybe the only true) activism.

Note

1 Putting to one side the numerous articles and books in which Samuels has overtly sought to establish a Jungian politics, one of his most important contributions in this area has perhaps been his dogged refusal to allow this subject to sink back into the oblivion which many (most?) Jungians would prefer.

References

Benjamin, W., Scholem, G. G. and Smith, G. (1980) *The Correspondence of Walter Benjamin and Gershom Scholem, 1932–1940*. Cambridge, MA: Harvard University Press.

Jung, C. G. (1961) *Memories, Dreams, Reflections*. New York: Pantheon Books.

Santayana, G. (2011) *The Life of Reason: Introduction and Reason in Common Sense*. Cambridge, MA: MIT Press.

Schieder, T. (1978) 'The Role of Historical Consciousness in Political Action'. *History and Theory*, 17: 1–18.

Andrew Samuels

In 2004, in a keynote at the Barcelona Congress of the International Association for Analytical Psychology, I said that we were witnessing a 'political turn' in Jungian analysis. Politics was being taken much more seriously as a matter for psychological reflection and analysis, and it was less plausible to reduce politics and the social to archetypal determinants than it had been previously.

I felt that Jung would have silently approved of this development. In 1946, he wrote:

> We are living in times of great disruption: political passions are aflame, internal upheavals have brought nations to the brink of chaos . . . The analyst feels the violence even in the quiet of his consulting room. . . The psychologist cannot avoid coming to grips with contemporary history . . . We need not mention his duties as a citizen . . .
>
> (p. 11)

This book, and the conference on which it is based that took place exactly ten years later, celebrates a further turn – the 'activist turn'. What I mean to say is that Jungian analysts are doing more than reflect on and analyse the political. Increasingly, they are working in a wide range of activities of a political nature. The scope of such activities can be directly assessed by studying the contents of the present book.

A Jungian book on politics inevitably brings up the question of Jung's politics, not so much in terms of what he supported or did not support at the time, but in terms of how his writings on the social realm have come to be received today. At the centre of this will be, of course, what has been written and said concerning Jung's political activities in the 1930s and, specifically, the allegation of anti-Semitism.

My personal and scholarly opinion (1993) has been that there was something going on during this period that should give cause for concern. It would follow that a Jungian project to engage with the political must needs repudiate some of Jung's positions and, in addition, offer itself as a kind of reparative process.

In my further opinion, the Jungian collective has done a good job in identifying problems, changing things, apologising and making reparation. That done, a space is cleared for an engagement with Jung's important ideas about the relations between the individual and the collective/society.

But we will still be far from 'so, that's all right then!' Those stringent critics of Jung won't be completely silenced and maybe that is a good thing. It is arguable that the intellectual climate that reinforces such criticisms won't change anyway. Yet there is still a problem when it comes to Jungian and post-Jungian political activism and analysis. It concerns our ethics, methods and epistemology. What follows is a sort of 'charter' for Jungian political contributions:

1 Engagement with the political is not new in psychoanalysis and psychotherapy. We've had more than 100 years of psychotherapy trying to change the world, but the world has stayed pretty much the same. I keep saying that the world didn't turn up for its first session with us, its putative political psychoanalysts. There are many reasons for this, for example to do with our record of heteronormativity and a seemingly incorrigible desire to get into bed with the powerful. We have to review our poor record and make changes in how we approach social and political issues.
2 We shouldn't attempt to do this alone – I would like to see a Jungian analyst on every government committee or commission, but, please God, not a committee of Jungian analysts! Every kind of interdisciplinary work should be pursued, in particular, finding activist groups and projects that might welcome the participation of an analyst or analysts. Even if there were to be a grouping of politically active analysts, along the lines of the UK's Psychotherapists and Counsellors for Social Responsibility, it should restrict its independent activities to the minimum, expending energy and resources instead on forging the kinds of links I am describing.
3 We should do our best to avoid reductive psychologising or triumphalist simple slogans (e.g. that 'the feminine' or 'the transcendent function' will sort everything out). Can you imagine how this is received by political activists? They suspect – and they are right – that they are in the presence of the analyst's 'maddening rectitude', to use a phrase of John Beebe's. For one often gets the impression that the hidden purpose of a Jungian analyst becoming involved in politics is to prove his or her theories correct. Other modalities of

psychotherapy, notably psychoanalysis, suffer from the same problem. I admit that sometimes I do myself. It needs watching.

4 We shouldn't ignore our professional situation today:

(i) The content of our trainings may need review from a political angle in terms of how supportive they are of inclusivity, diversity and equal opportunities.
(ii) Our professional politics are often cutthroat and unfeeling and play inclusion/exclusion games. There is a lot of cronyism in the Jungian world. This could be addressed more actively than is the case at present.
(iii) Clinical practice and the therapy relationship have markedly political dynamics on show – socioeconomic/class, gender, sexual, racial/ethnic politics (past, present and future) – and a clash of values between therapist and client. The desire to create a more diverse and more equal project of psychotherapy leads to working out the micro-politics of the therapy session itself – the power, vulnerability and differing experiences in the therapy and in the social world of both participants. Psychotherapy both operates in a sociocultural context and is itself such a context.
(iv) Being aware of the politics of the session and of the therapy relationship – not small matters – means that psychotherapists can't avoid struggling to devise new and responsible ways to engage directly with political, social and cultural material that appears in the clinical session. The fact is that the spirit is willing but the flesh is weak. Psychotherapists yearn to work with the social dimensions of their and their client's experiences. But they lack models and concepts that would enable them to do this.
(v) We need to remember how incredibly difficult it is to access psychotherapy, unless you are pretty wealthy, other than a particularly mechanistic kind of state therapy. It is equally difficult for members of ethnic minorities or working-class people to train as psychotherapist. These difficulties cover a wide range of concerns including the high cost of training, the Eurocentric cast of the ideas and concepts being taught, and the bourgeois and 'polite' atmosphere of many training institutes.
(vi) Finally there is the role of psychotherapy in developing critiques of the experience of the subject as a citizen in contemporary Western society. We lack texts on 'political development' or the 'political self'.

References

Jung, C. G. (1946) Preface to *Essays on Contemporary Events*. *CW*10.
Samuels, A. (1993) *The Political Psyche*. London and New York: Routledge.

SECTION 1
Interventions

1

OPENING OUR ROOMS

The ETnA projects for migrants in Italy

Stefano Carta

Introduction

Italy, as a country of emigration, has now rapidly become a country of immigration, which has enhanced the need to care for the people who have started to migrate from Africa, South America and Asia. In the last 25 years, this strong wave of immigration immediately has created a *sacred social space*, a Shadow projection, i.e. a scapegoating area (Girard, 1977), projected on the migrant, on the foreigner, on the refugee, who hence are often, if not always, seen as *bad* or *mad*. The migrant is *bad* because he is taking our jobs, imposing his point of view or menacing ours; or because he does not want to become like us, or because he actually *wants* to become like us too much, etc.

On the opposite side, the migrant is plainly incomprehensible and, therefore, he is *mad*.

It is this second, pathologising stigma, which, as psychotherapists, we need to be particularly aware of.

Due to this historical situation, 12 years ago, during my presidency of the Italian Association of Analytical Psychology (AIPA), a group of Jungian analysts began to get directly involved in social and anthropological matters regarding migrants and refugees.[1]

What do we do with them?

Perhaps the most fundamental tenet in our work with our foreign clients, which has guided us so far, is Jung's idea of countertransference and co-transference[2] and his view of psychotherapy as a dialectical process between patient and therapist:

> If I wish to treat another individual psychologically at all, I must for better or worse give up all pretensions to superior knowledge, all authority and desire to influence. I must perforce adopt a dialectical procedure consisting

> in a comparison of our mutual findings. But this becomes possible only if I give the other person a chance to play his hand to the full, unhampered by my assumptions.
>
> (Jung, 1935, para 2)

In such a situation it is impossible to influence someone if you are not influenced.[3]

For this (constructivist) Jung there is not only one form of consciousness, which may be assessed only in relation to its intensity.[4] For Jung, consciousness is an eminently *qualitative* phenomenon. Here Jung left behind the illuministic idea of a single form of consciousness (the illuminist *Reason*) in favour of a plural, constructed, and therefore *negotiated*, process of interpreting reality. The uncritical idea of consciousness as quantitative phenomenon represents an intrinsically positivistic and racist (I use this term in a general sense) realism, and would transform any encounter into a colonisation by the one who supposes to hold the 'higher', or 'truer' form of consciousness.

Unfortunately, in a multitude of passages, Jung also wrote about the 'primitive' mind (often referring to Lévy-Bruhl), *projecting* a less differentiated way of using one of the 'two forms of thinking' (Jung, 1911–12/1956) into those human beings that were more foreign to him: the Africans, but also, in different ways, the 'Eastern' cultures (as if these could really be subsumed into one category). Working with migrants, we constantly face these two sides of Jung. Nevertheless, this double nature of Jung paradoxically may help us, as if, by being so divided, he had highlighted for us in a clear form not just one opposite (the constructionist, dialectical, plural one), but also the other (the positivistic, culture-centred theoretical position).

The difficulty of integrating the 'two forms of thinking' and fostering a complex, plural form of consciousness, and therefore a complex identity, together with the risk of a regression towards a more undifferentiated, 'primitive' form of consciousness is obvious to all, although it does not involve any 'primitive people' at all (as there is not such an anthropological entity), but actually describes the 'primitive' way the psyche may function. And here I want to refer to *our own psyche* in the first place, of course. This inclusion of the European psyche among those that may function in a 'primitive' way is not based on the fact that at the very time that Jung was writing, Europe was regressing to the most undifferentiated and 'primitive' psychic condition in human history, but also because, in my opinion, we *function in a primitive way today and every day*. The penetrating persuasive force of publicity, the many hours lost commuting in our cars, the manic rhythms of our urban existences, hyper-capitalism and its reduction of everything to its quantitative (economic) 'value', the flat acceptance of the non-values of globalisation (for us psychotherapists the DSM is the most striking and poisonous example), and the way citizens are manipulated and form their political decisions are examples of the pervasive psychological slumber of the 'evolved' European – Western or Westernised – man.

Only if I, as a psychotherapist, am aware that I myself might be the (primitive) Other that I thought I was describing, can I make the imaginative step of comprehending my foreign client. And it is precisely this assumption that describes the constructionist, wholly symbolic and plural Jung that I am referring to. The Jung that advises us that in the dialectical analytical situation there are (at least, and *cum grano salis*, as the therapeutic relationship is a-symmetrical) two patients and two therapists at the same time:

> We could say, without too much exaggeration, that a good half of every treatment that probes at all deeply consists in the doctor's examining himself, for only what he can put right in himself can he hope to put right in the patient. It is no loss, either, if he feels the patient is hitting him or even scoring off him; it is his own hurt that gives the measure of his power to heal. This, and nothing else, is the meaning of the Greek myth of the wounded physician.
>
> (Jung, 1951, para 239)

How do we develop our work with our foreign clients?

Perhaps the best way to outline the basic attitude that guides us is to say that we try to apply the Socratic rule by which I, the analyst, do not know anything, except that I know that I do not know. This matters because I have in front of me a person who expresses his inner world with perhaps quite different cultural codes, therefore a person particularly fit to be an unknown. At the same time my client *does* know, but either does not know he knows, or he does not want to reveal to me what he knows. Migrants, refugees and asylum seekers have secrets that they keep within themselves, and rightfully so, because they need to protect their core identity through a natural process of concealment (Devereux, 1967; Jung, 1931; Winnicott, 1960/1965).[5]

In both situations, the non-expert is *I*, who must learn from the expert, who is my client. And this learning process will take place within the highly refined and peculiar environment of our inter-subjective relationship, which now defines a 'third area' between our two foreign cultural origins.

It goes without saying that I am describing a process in which I am constantly trying to understand something of *my own* unconscious – often a personal, and especially *cultural* unconscious content. Such unconscious contents often contain hidden, implicit, anthropological assumptions. This paradoxical process in which the analyst is the non-expert makes a true process of co-evolution possible – a process that binds the therapist to his patients. The nature of this 'third space', which I have mentioned before, is rooted in the pre-linguistic fundamentals of human experience, such as empathy, listening, recognising and mirroring – all striving to protect a sense of hope and trust, together with reparation and care. It is the analyst's fundamental ability to withstand and share his involved and self-reflective emotional stand towards the patient that forms the vessel, the holding environment, for this process.

Fostering this hybrid, complex vessel, this 'third space', is the fundamental aim of our encounter with our clients. In this regard we are comforted by the fact that a third space when two (or more) persons meet is *always* constellated. In this regard the references to Jung's highly differentiated theory of the therapeutic relationship, and therapeutic alliance and its various forms of transference, counter- and co-transference, is for us very important (Jung, 1946).

One interesting issue regarding the implicit relational structure that is spontaneously constellated between the Conscious and the personal, cultural and collective Unconscious of the therapist and those of his client, is the automatic tendency to constellate not only compensatory forms of relationships, but also hysomorphic[6] ones, in which one will resemble (mirror, in some way) the other. This was the case in the refugee camp in Dadaab, at the border between Kenya and Somalia, where both the refugees and the international personnel were in serious conflict, without realising that both of them were lamenting *similar* problems, such as that of 'having been away from home for too long'.

Again on depathologising

According to the structure that has been described as the 'triangle of violence' (Losi & Papadopoulos, 2004), if a 'saviour' is constellated, it will synchronically constellate a victim and a perpetrator. Therefore, paradoxically enough, when there is a clearly designated victim (and in the case of the migrant/refugee this is a strikingly constant occurrence), we should first of all 'work on' the perpetrator or the saviour. Therefore, in order to reach his foreign client, the therapist must once again first of all rescue *himself* from his own unconsciousness – from his blind faith in his personal (culturally personal, in this case) way of reducing the complexity of the world. This highly political process means that we abstain from considering our patients as weak psychiatric cases, but see them rather as resilient and strong human beings who have found themselves in this position as a result of their origins, their family, their value sets, their tribes, their countries, their ethnic groups, or by extreme adversities.

If we see our wounded and weakened clients as *healthy* human beings suffering from a sense of identity loss, and *nostalgic disorientation* (Papadopoulos, 2002), then the first thing to avoid is pathologising their condition, because these clients cannot be assumed to resemble patients with some 'narcissistic wound', or anything like that. As Hannah Arendt wrote: 'Refugees expelled from one country to the next represent the avant-garde of their people' (Arendt, 1943, pp. 69–77), i.e. the best ones, who have been sent in a mission to save themselves *and their world*. For Tobie Nathan, the symptom is *a text without a context* (Nathan, 1994). The suffering refugee is de-contextualised, psycho-culturally displaced, and we must help him to reconstruct a new context in which his text will regain its symbolic integrative meaning.

However, I disagree with Tobie Nathan's assumption (described as 'cultural fencing' (Fassin, 1999, pp. 146–71)) that *any* migration is *always* a traumatic wound for the subject's (cultural, i.e. personal) identity. While Nathan thinks the migrants' symptoms may reacquire a symbolic meaning only if he is reintegrated in his original cultural shell, I do not believe that a migrant (anyone, in fact) may 'really' go back. Like Ulysses, his Ithaca regained will never be the one that had been originally lost.

We are sons and daughters of Hermes, yet we are also sons and daughters of his companion Hestia, the immobile focal centre of the house, of home: we are at the same time natural dwellers and natural travellers. Therefore, at ETnA, we try not to impose our methods and knowledge on our clients, since this would be a sort of therapeutic colonisation, an assimilation into our cultural unconsciousness (i.e. into his implicit interiorised cultural complexes), even if done with 'the best of intentions'. At the same time, we also avoid trying to help our clients using *their* methods, as Tobie Nathan does at Centre Devereux in Paris. We believe that this would be a regressive attempt, a failure of the migrant's project, especially if he had somehow *decided* to leave.

The truly integrative context must be the third area, like that constellated by the encounter between the therapist and the patient. Therefore, for the way I see the 'analytical situation' in this context, the ethno-psychotherapist is not called to work just – or primarily – with his patient's identity issues, but – paradoxically enough – he must work on his own unconsciousness (his own memories and desires, as Bion would say) in the first place.

By systematically taking care of our countertransference we may safely neutralise the triangle of violence. Through a constant, systematic self-reflection, we assume ourselves to be 'wounded' and so devictimise the client, who may now be seen as the active, purposeful, resilient human being he is. And, illuminated by such a light, we may metaphorise his *telos* as that of a fairytale's hero.

As a matter of fact, our migrants, refugees or asylum seekers *have been sent* to do what all fairytale heroes do: to look for and refound their kingdoms and, more precisely: a) reacquire an identity, b) reacquire a 'Home' (Papadopoulos, 2002); c) take possession of a new language to share a common history and culture; d) integrate two (always complex) cultures; and e) keep memories alive.

Such an attempt entails the re-creation of new forms of relatedness. The migrant will have to re-create new relationship with his origins, his hopes. And, within a frame of an identity as a *process* of further integration, he will have to represent a living example of a multiple belonging and hybridisation.

This complex process challenges the migrant's *and the therapist's* identities seen as psychological *states*, and redefines them as *processes* of further dialectic co-integration between the same (myself, my own cultural assumptions) and the Other (see, for instance Waldenfels, 2011).

Complexity

In order to try to approach our foreign clients, we systematically try to foster our own complexity and transform our identity into an identity made by a plurality of parts. The more these parts are, the richer I am, although in working with them I may sometimes feel myself foreign *in my own culture* (for example in my *professional* culture) and feel uncertain about my own identity.

This fostering complexity through deconstructing our own identity-state means welcoming and integrating other theories, other points of view. Therefore, ETnA welcomes any psychotherapeutic approach which is open enough to critically accept our systematic method of deconstruction. Such a process tends to exclude as much as possible the use of interpretation, as interpreting may often mean reducing the object's world to that of the interpreter, which, in an intercultural encounter, is the worst thing that could happen.

Therefore, in order to find an area common with our clients, we refer to the Jungian fundamental operation that any analyst activates in front of something unknown and irreducible, yet universal (for Jung the archetype, in our case the Other): *amplification*.

Basically, our way for dealing with the therapeutic situation is to try to open up our imagination – to produce more and more hypotheses – yet always remaining firmly rooted in the emotional, empirical context of our specific therapeutic relationship. What we methodically ask ourselves by amplifying is: 'This seems so, but may we imagine it otherwise?'

Our settings are very variable. As I said before, we just opened up our methods and procedures, and we kind of let ourselves go, although always keeping a systematic relentless self-reflective attitude. What is crucial is that every method or procedure should be open to a negotiation, so to potentially be part of a third area between the analyst and the client.

In this multiple methodology we work individually, in couples, in families, in groups. Sometimes even in the presence of the client's friends or relatives if he/she asks us to do so (i.e. if it is within the client's context to cope with his problems with his friends or relatives). As a matter of fact, in many cultures psychotherapy is a very social matter, not a private issue between one person and another within socially sealed space. Sandplay, with some possible variations, is a great resource for us, as is any other expressive technique as long as it is negotiated.

In closing I would like to mention a key ingredient for our 'method': how we do intervision. Intervision is a process of reciprocal commenting on a session or a therapeutic process in which everyone is expected to 'crack open' what has happened and has been said or done in the course of the therapy. The goal of this device that we call intervision is to search for what has *not* yet been imagined.

A specific feature of our intervisions is what we have called 'the Thinking Mind'. The role of Thinking Mind is taken, in turn, by one of us, whose role is that of not saying anything during the intervision's discussion but to just think *about* what has been said, in order to write a report aimed at reopening up at a meta-level what has been already opened up by our divergent amplification process. Therefore, the focus of the Thinking Mind is not any more the relationship with the therapist and the patient, but the way we have discussed the case during the intervision. After this, the Thinking Mind reflections are discussed in a new intervision group.

At the 'end' of this progressive deconstruction and amplification process the therapist will go back to his client, hopefully with an increased plurality of possibilities, hypotheses and images, since the more possibilities there will be, the more will it be possible that the effort by the psychotherapist, rooted in the third, inter-affective area of the relationship, will promote a space of meeting which may represent a hybrid, complex, centred and yet displaced, new common home.

Notes

1 Throughout these years Renos K. Papadopoulos has always been a great help, and on this occasion I wish to thank him.
2 'The psychotherapist is no longer the agent of treatment but a fellow participant of individual development' (Jung, 1935, para 7). For a very good discussion on the topic of countertransference in Jung, see Sedgwick (1994).
3 'Psychic influence is the reciprocal reaction of two psychic systems' (Jung, 1935, para 1).
4 Here the Janetian key-concept of *abaissement du niveau mental* is a constant reference in Jung's writings.
5 For the double nature of the secret, as the foundation and warrant of any inner personal life and identity, and its opposite risk of an isolating, alienating factor, see, for instance, Jung (1931, paras 123–35); Devereux (1967, pp. 101–42) and Winnicott (1960/1965).
6 I am using this term as a general analogy of its use in biology, in which it describes a similarity of form or structure between organisms, generally between organisms with independent ancestries. In my example it would describe the tendency of two distinct (non necessarily biological) organisms in strict relation to each other for a certain time to resemble each other.

References

Arendt, H. (1943). 'We refugees.' *The Menorah Journal*, 31. New York: Intercollegiate Menorah Association.

Devereux, G. (1967) 'La renonciation à l'identité: défense contre l'anéantissement.' *Revue française de psychanalyse*, 31(1): 101–42.

Fassin, D. (1999) 'L'ethnopsychiatrie et ses réseaux. L'influence qui grandit.' *Genèses, sciences sociales et histoire*, 35.

Girard, R. (1977) *Violence and the Sacred*. Baltimore and London: Johns Hopkins University Press.

Losi, N. and Papadopoulos, R. K. (2004) 'Post-conflict constellations of violence and the psychosocial approach of the international organization for migration (IOM).' In *Book of Best Practices: Trauma and the Role of Mental Health in Post-conflict Recovery*. Rome: International Congress of Ministers for Mental Health and Post-Conflict Recovery.

Jung, C. G. (1911–12/1956) *Symbols of Transformation. CW5*.

Jung, C. G. (1921) *Psychological Types. CW6*.

Jung, C. G. (1931) 'Problems of modern psychotherapy.' *CW*16.

Jung, C. G. (1935) 'Principles of practical psychotherapy.' *CW*16.

Jung, C. G. (1946) 'The psychology of the transference.' *CW*16.

Jung, C. G. (1951) 'Fundamental questions of psychotherapy.' *CW*16.

Nathan, T. (1994) *L'influence qui guérit*. Paris: Editions Odile Jacob.

Papadopoulos, R. (ed.) (2002) *Therapeutic Care for Refugees: No Place Like Home*. London: Karnac.

Sedgwick, D. (1994) *The Wounded Healer: Countertransference from a Jungian Perspective*. London: Routledge.
Waldenfels, B. (2011) *Phenomenology of the Alien*. Chicago, IL: Northwestern University Press.
Winnicott, D. D. (1960/1965) 'Ego distortion in terms of true and false Self.' In *The Maturational Processes and the Facilitating Environment: Studies in the Theory of Emotional Development*. London: The Hogarth Press.

2

THERAPEUTIC ENCOUNTERS AND INTERVENTIONS OUTSIDE THE CONSULTING ROOM

Challenges in theory and practice

Renos K. Papadopoulos

Jung + activism = oxymoron?

This chapter attempts to address the conference theme, 'Jung and Activism', from one specific perspective based on my own endeavours, over many years, in working in contexts outside the analytical consulting room. At the outset, it is important to address the obvious question as to whether Jungian psychology and 'activism' are at all compatible. The question is appropriate because, *prima facie*, any connection between the two appears to be incongruous; if anything, 'Jungian activism' is an oxymoron because nothing about Jung could be construed as connected with activism, as it is commonly understood.

Without elaborating over the various definitions and forms of activism, I propose that we understand activism as the questioning of existing power relations and the contesting 'of regimes of authority that seek to govern us' (Rose, 1999, p. 60). Both the terms 'regimes of authority' and 'govern' should be understood in the widest possible way, to cover not only governmental politics but also societal discourses and professional ideologies with reference to theory and practice (Norris, 2002 and 2007).

Jung is known for his notorious conservative outlook with regard to his political and social views and, therefore, he can hardly be considered as an activist. During the cold war, he identified totally with the polarised view that everything that did not conform with the outlook of the 'free western world' was a product of 'communism', which he condemned outright (cf. Papadopoulos, 2002a). Uncharacteristically to the complexity of his thinking and cultural sophistication, he seemed to be incapable of affording any critique of his own political position. There is no evidence that he was involved in any movement for any consideration for social justice at any level – certainly, not in terms of any form of activism but not even at any theoretical or speculative level. Moreover, he used his own theories to support his conservatism. Characteristically, he argued that 'only those individuals can attain to a higher degree of consciousness who are destined to it and called to it from the beginning, i.e. who have a capacity and an urge for higher differentiation . . . Nature is aristocratic' (Jung, 1917/1943, para 198).

It should not be forgotten that the concept and very process of individuation, the cornerstone of his theory of personal development, is focused exclusively on the individual, despite his attempts to claim that (being) an individuated person does not exclude social awareness.[1] Jung's emphasis was almost entirely on the intrapsychic realm, arguing firmly for the simplistic formula that 'society is the sum total of individuals' (Jung, 1956, para 536). Moreover, he repeatedly maintained that 'every man is, in a certain sense, unconsciously a worse man when he is in society than when acting alone; for he is carried by society and to that extent relieved of his individual responsibility' (Jung, 1928/1953, para 240). This illustrates Jung's privileging the individual over any issues of social consideration.

I have long argued for the importance of realising and taking seriously the fact that Jung's view of the social realm was purely negative, and to consider studiously the multiple implications of this (Papadopoulos, 1997a, 1997b, 1998a, 1999a, 2000a, 2006a, 2009, 2011). Jung equated the societal dimension with the 'collective' that he simply considered negatively. The 'collective' he had in mind was identified with the amorphous masses that 'relieve' man 'of his individual responsibility'. This view represents the prevailing understanding of the time, propagated by the French writer Gustave Le Bon (1841–1931), who put forward the idea that in the crowd the individual loses his/her identity and becomes a small particle of the herd, which is led by unscrupulous demagogues. In the crowd, the individual becomes an anonymous entity, is prone to suggestibility and contagious negative influences (Le Bon, 1895). Jung was aware of the destructive effects of the masses not only in the context of the abhorrent fascist movements he experienced during his lifetime in Germany and Italy, but also in the 'collectivism' of the Soviet communism that he equally opposed, most vehemently.

No wonder that within this unfavourable perspective, Jung found it difficult to form any positive inclination towards anything associated with the social realm and one's involvement within it. Yet, it is important to remember that his actual theory of the collective unconscious clearly has a potentially positive and, indeed, rejuvenating role for the collective, when the individual integrates the archetypal elements in an appropriate way. Even on the seemingly destructive occasions when the collective unconscious 'floods' the individual psyche, Jung still saw its positive and renewing function, likening it to the 'flooding of the Nile' that 'increases the fertility of the land' (Jung, 1946, para 479).

At this point, it is instructive to pause and reflect on the significant confusion in distinguishing between Jung's attitudes towards the collective unconscious and towards the actual social collective. For Jung, the collective unconscious along with its archetypal elements has an unmistakably compensatory function, refreshing the withered psyche of the individual. Repeatedly, Jung lamented the current state of modern living that did not provide the vital connection with collective/archetypal forms that could nourish the modern person's psyche. In dramatic terms, he continually warned of the dangerous effects of this lack. At the same time, he expressed serious concern at people's attempt at resorting to fake substitutes for these positive archetypal forms. He drew a sharp distinction between appropriate and inappropriate expressions of these revitalising collective forms and it is telling of his mistrust for the social collective that he clarified this distinction as follows:

> Anyone who has lost . . . [the nurturing contact with these positive collective forms] and cannot be satisfied with substitutes is certainly in a very difficult position today: before him there yawns the void, and he turns away from it in horror. What is worse, the vacuum gets filled with absurd political and social ideas, which one and all are distinguished by their spiritual bleakness.
> (Jung, 1934/1954, para 28)

This typical quotation testifies to Jung's detesting of 'political and social ideas' that he considers 'absurd' and as characterised by 'spiritual bleakness', contrasting them to appropriate archetypal forms that are genuinely spiritual. This distinction is deeply rooted in Jung's own specific context, i.e. the historical times he lived in, the intellectual tradition within which he was educated, the sociopolitical realities of his time and his geographical location, and his own personal and family experience.

Accordingly, Jung seemed to idealise an intangible form of archetypal spirituality and demonise anything connected with the actual societal dimension. This sharp division was reflected in the way he conducted his psychotherapeutic/analytical practice: he worked exclusively with individuals in professionally delineated and defined settings (i.e. state mental health services and private practice) and did not engage with any group or family therapeutic activities, or even with individuals outside these settings. Admittedly, no models of such practices were available at the time and, therefore, one may argue that this is the sole reason why Jung did not extend his practice to those domains. Conversely, the claim of this chapter is that the main reason is not the lack of existing models of such practices but Jung's own firm prejudice against anything that he (mistakenly) considered was violating the sanctity of the individual. Jung was fairly iconoclastic in many respects and pushed many boundaries and applied his creativity in many spheres, so he could have done the same in relation to extending the range of his therapeutic practices. He was not able to do so, due to his own limiting specific context, but not due to any inherent limitations of his theory.

Therefore, my argument is that Jung's theories can be expanded to accommodate such extensions in practice, and I consider my own modest work with adversity survivors outside the consulting room as examples of such attempts. This would be in line with Jung's own dictum that the pupil serves the master better if he takes the master's work further and does not just keep imitating it.

In order to undertake this task, it is imperative to differentiate between what Jung himself thought and did and what one can develop on the basis of his theoretical premises and entire approach. Often this distinction is not made and, instead, analytical psychology tends to identify entirely with Jung the person, with what he said and what he did not say, and with what he did and what he did not do. Once this distinction is made (as well as some additional ones), it would be possible to illustrate that a connection between Jung and 'Activism' is not only feasible but also of considerable heuristic value.

Important differentiations

Traditionally, in contexts where so-called 'mental health' assistance is required, appropriately trained practitioners (analysts, psychotherapists, counsellors, et al.) provide their services in structured settings. However, in contexts where people experience various forms of human distress, disorientation, psychic ache, etc., due to being exposed to various forms of collective adversity (political/military conflict, involuntary dislocation, natural disasters, etc.), offering services that are conceptualised and developed for ordinary settings is inappropriate. Experience shows that even offering various forms of 'trauma counselling' is inappropriate as, inadvertently, they tend to fix a 'victim identity' on the persons they intend to assist; moreover, the epistemological basis of these types of 'counselling' is not culturally sensitive and it is not fitting for emergency situations or for unusual settings (e.g. refugee camps etc.). In these contexts, what is required is apposite response to the plight of the people who experience what is usually referred to as 'normal responses to abnormal circumstances'.

My own experiences in these contexts and settings has shown that what is required is not to offer psychotherapy or analysis or counselling but to provide contact with the adversity survivors that is essentially *therapeutic* (e.g. Papadopoulos, 1998b, 1999b, 2011). Thus, it is imperative to make a distinction between 'doing psychotherapy' and 'being therapeutic'. Whereas the former needs to be delivered by suitably trained analysts, psychotherapists, counsellors, the latter can be offered by anybody who has any type of contact with adversity survivors, as long as she or he is sensitised to the psychological complexities of the overall phenomena involved, and this is one of the main activities that I am engaged in: designing projects that enable workers to introduce a therapeutic dimension to whatever contact they have with adversity survivors.

An additional differentiation that needs to be made is between therapeutic ideologies, therapeutic techniques and therapeutic frameworks.

Therapeutic ideologies

Each school of psychotherapy or analysis is based on a set of theoretical presuppositions not only about their methods of intervention but also about the way they conceptualise the very phenomena they observe (in particular, the way they identify what is 'the problem') as well as, directly or indirectly, shaping the stance of the therapist. For example, Cognitive Behaviour Therapy focuses on the interactions between behaviour, thinking and feeling, and, therefore, the way they would conceptualise both their identification of the problem, as well as the methods of treatment and stance of the therapist, would be in line with this theoretical schema. Comparably, a psychodynamically oriented therapist would consider the unconscious as central to any understanding of the problem and the method of treatment as well as the way the therapist would relate in order to access and address unconscious material.

Inevitably, these therapeutic ideologies are present, explicitly or implicitly, in all forms of interventions with adversity survivors, thus imposing their assumptions onto every situation, especially when they are applied to 'trauma' intervention contexts.

Therapeutic techniques

By and large, these techniques are specific applications of therapeutic ideologies, e.g. free association (psychoanalysis), active imagination (analytical psychology), empty chair (Gestalt), writing self-statements to counteract negative thoughts (CBT), etc. However, what is of great significance is that, almost imperceptibly, the landscape of psychotherapy has been changing, and whereas before the profession was dominated by established schools of psychotherapy or analysis, now there is an endless plethora of specific therapeutic techniques, seemingly independent of therapeutic ideologies. Propagators of these techniques (some of them are even called 'therapies') claim that it is not necessary for one to embark on a long, arduous and expensive form of training, but, instead, a few weekend trainings would suffice to enable one to apply these techniques. Examples of these techniques include Mindfulness, Narrative Expressive Therapy, Tree of Life, Acceptance and Commitment Therapy, Coherence Therapy, Eye Movement Desensitisation and Reprocessing (EMDR), Mode Deactivation Therapy, Nonviolent Communication, etc.

Often, the most successful and most enduring of these techniques, eventually, develop theoretical perspectives to support them and, consequently, they extend and formalise the training they offer to the prospective of these techniques. Thus, gradually, these techniques begin to resemble the traditional schools of psychotherapy.

When applied to working with adversity survivors, these forms of therapeutic interventions tend to be more rigid insofar as they apply the set technique to any given situation, regardless of the setting and complexity.

Therapeutic frameworks

Different from the above, a therapeutic framework consists of a set of basic principles, not at a theoretical or applied/practice level but, instead, aimed at providing an epistemological perspective that can then be used with, almost, any theoretical ideology and/or theoretical technique. It is this that emerged from my experience in working with adversity survivors, in unusual settings outside the consulting room and away from traditional mental health services, as the most useful set of guidelines for this work. The advantages of therapeutic frameworks are that, free from therapeutic ideologies and fixed techniques, they are adaptable to any situation and they can be used by persons of any cultural, educational or work background.

The present therapeutic framework

The basic elements of the therapeutic framework that emerged during my work with adversity survivors in non-traditional settings and outside the consulting room include the following:

(a) Conceptualisation of 'the problem'

The predominant way of perceiving human distress in the face of any forms of adversity has been in terms of trauma. My investigations into this field revealed that trauma is an inaccurate and crude term to capture the fine shades and uniqueness that each individual, family or community respond in, in each given adverse situation (Papadopoulos 2000b, 2002b, 2006b, 2007, 2010, 2013). There is a persistent but erroneous assumption that all phenomena of human distress involve psychological trauma and, moreover, most traumatic experiences are equivalent to Post Traumatic Stress Disorder (PTSD).

It should not be forgotten that the prevalence of PTSD following exposure to most forms of adversity is not much more than 10% (Arnberg et al., 2013; Berger et al., 2012; Zhang et al., 2012). This means that the overwhelming majority of people respond in non-pathological ways. Yet, this fact is hardly addressed in the literature. This does not mean that they do not suffer or do not experience forms of distress and disorientation; certainly, they do and it is our responsibility to develop ways of grasping the specificities of these phenomena without confusing them with psychopathological or psychiatric conditions.

It is within this perspective that my experiences led me to develop the concepts of 'nostalgic disorientation' and 'onto-ecological settledness' (Papadopoulos, 2012, 2015) to account for non-pathological ways of responding to adversity. Under ordinary circumstances, people experience a state of relative stability where life is fairly predictable. I call this state 'onto-ecological settledness', referring to the familiar arrangement and relationship 'between the totality of one's being and the totality of one's environment' (Papadopoulos, 2015, p. 40). This is not an ideal state but it is predictable and creates a sense of settledness that is disrupted once adversity strikes. Then, people experience a sense of disorientation that includes a strong nostalgic element in it, insofar as it creates a yearning for returning to the disrupted state of settledness, and this is what I call 'nostalgic disorientation'. Although 'nostalgic disorientation' is not a psychiatric disorder, the felt discomfort and distress are real and should not be underestimated.

(b) Conceptualisation of the intervention

Consequently, it is inappropriate to offer psychotherapy to the overwhelming majority of adversity survivors because of the nature of their suffering, and the cultural and situational contexts. Therefore, what is required is to provide 'therapeutic input' via suitable 'therapeutic encounters' within the existing settings. Short and focused trainings can equip all who work with adversity survivors to add a 'therapeutic dimension' to the work they already do, by becoming sagaciously aware of the *psychological complexities* of

1 the relevant phenomena (definition of 'the problem')
2 the beneficiaries (clients) and their contexts
3 the workers themselves and their contexts
4 the interaction between them
5 the organisational/systemic and sociopolitical contexts within which the encounters between them take place
6 the epistemological assumptions and methodology that are used in these encounters, and
7 the interaction of all the above.

(Papadopoulos, 2013)

Finally, instead of focusing exclusively on the negative responses to being exposed to adversity, this therapeutic framework is drawing from the obvious reality that, in addition to (not instead of!) their pain and suffering, persons do retain some of the positive functions, characteristics, abilities, relationships, qualities they had before their exposure to adversity, as well as developing new positives as a direct result of the fact that they were exposed to adversity. The existing positives I call 'resilience', and the new positives that are activated by the very exposure to adversity, I call 'adversity-activated development' (AAD). The three groups of responses to adversity (i.e. negative, resilience and AAD) are accounted for in the 'Adversity/Trauma Grid' that represents a formalisation of my experiences and it is now used widely (Papadopoulos, 2002b, 2006b, 2007, 2010, 2011, 2012, 2013).

These are the key ingredients of the framework that I use to design consultancies and interventions at both macro and micro levels in various contexts with adversity survivors. The framework is, essentially, an explicit epistemological perspective to conceptualising all the relevant phenomena (including the 'identification of the problem') in situations of societal adversity and all the required interventions.

Jungian reflections

This framework was not intended to apply Jungian theories, instead, it evolved from my experiences in the field; however, some key Jungian themes are easily discernible in it (Papadopoulos, 2009, 2012, 2013).

Jung encouraged creative ways of conducting therapy beyond the traditional frame of verbal exchange. Known for his attempts at depathologising psychological difficulties, he 'emphasised the transformative function of suffering and its renewing effect. In this way, he appreciated the complexity of individuals having more than one response to painful events and experiences' (Papadopoulos, 2013).

Finally, this framework includes a not-so-obvious but still extremely significant contribution by Jung to these situations – the multiple implications of *polarisation*. Situations of adversity in mass catastrophic contexts create polarised phenomena at all levels, where Jungian reflections can be most fruitful.

Under ordinary conditions, with our 'onto-ecological settledness' relatively stable, we experience archetypes in their bi-polarity, in a balanced and 'human' way, i.e. 'in forms that combine not only the two polarities (positive and negative) but also both collective and personal dimensions'. However, under polarised conditions, archetypes tend 'to lose their flexibility and nourishing abilities' and, instead, 'pure archetypal dazzling energy' is released that 'can exert an irresistible fascination, often of a numinous nature' resulting in individuals and groups becoming 'totally gripped by their power', losing their ability to bear complexity and resorting to crude and destructive oversimplification at all levels (Papadopoulos, 2013).

This framework illustrates an approach that includes 'activism' not only in terms of engaging within the social realm, but also in terms of contesting the 'regimes of authority' that 'govern' conceptualisations and work in this field. Moreover, it illustrates how Jungian theories, once extended, can be used fruitfully in 'activism' endeavours.

Note

1 'As man is not only an individual but also a member of society, these two tendencies inherent in human nature can never be separated, or the one subordinated to the other, without doing him serious injury' (Jung, 1912/1955, para 441).

References

Arnberg, F. et al. (2013) 'Prevalence and duration of PTSD in survivors six years after a natural disaster.' *Journal of Anxiety Disorders*, 27(3): 347–52.

Berger, W. et al. (2012) 'Rescuers at risk: a systematic review and meta-regression analysis of the worldwide current prevalence and correlates of PTSD in rescue workers.' *Social Psychiatry and Psychiatric Epidemiology*, 47(6): 1001–11.

Jung, C. G. (1912/1955) 'The theory of psychoanalysis.' *CW*4.

Jung, C. G. (1917/1943) 'On the psychology of the unconscious.' *CW*7.

Jung, C. G. (1928/1953) 'The relations between the ego and the unconscious.' *CW*7.

Jung, C. G. (1934/1954) 'Archetypes of the collective unconscious.' *CW*9i.

Jung, C. G. (1946) 'The psychology of the transference.' *CW*16.

Jung, C. G. (1956) 'The undiscovered self.' *CW*10.

Le Bon, G. (1895, trans. 1947) *The Crowd: A Study of the Popular Mind*. London: Ernest Benn.

Norris, P. (2002) *Democratic Phoenix: Reinventing Political Activism*. Cambridge: Cambridge University Press.

Norris, P. (2007) 'Political activism: New challenges, new opportunities.' In *The Oxford Handbook of Comparative Politics*. Oxford: Oxford University Press, pp. 628–52.

Papadopoulos, R. K. (1997a) 'Individual identity and collective narratives of conflict.' *Harvest: Journal for Jungian Studies*, 43(2): 7–26.
Papadopoulos, R. K. (1997b) 'Archetypal Family Therapy: developing a Jungian approach to working with families.' In *Psyche and Family*, edited by L. Dodson and T. Gibson. Wilmette, Il: Chiron.
Papadopoulos, R. K. (1998a) 'Jungian perspectives in new contexts.' In *The Jungians Today*, edited by A. Casement. London and New York: Routledge.
Papadopoulos, R. K. (1998b) 'Destructiveness, atrocities and healing: epistemological and clinical reflections.' *The Journal of Analytical Psychology*, 43(4): 455–77.
Papadopoulos, R. K. (1999a) 'Analytical psychology and cultural sensitivities'. In *Destruction and Creation: Personal and Cultural Transformations*, edited by M. A. Mattoon. Einsiedeln, Switzerland: Daimon Verlag.
Papadopoulos, R. K. (1999b) 'Working with families of Bosnian medical evacuees: therapeutic dilemmas.' *Clinical Child Psychology and Psychiatry*, 4(1): 107–20.
Papadopoulos, R. K. (2000a) 'Factionalism and interethnic conflict: narratives in myth and politics.' In *The Vision Thing: Myth, Politics and Psyche in the World*, edited by T. Singer. London and New York: Routledge.
Papadopoulos, R. K. (2000b) 'A Matter of shades: trauma and psychosocial work in Kosovo.' In *Psychosocial and Trauma Response in War-Torn Societies: the Case of Kosovo*, edited by N. Losi. Geneva: I.O.M.
Papadopoulos, R. K. (2002a) 'The other other: when the exotic other subjugates the familiar other.' *Journal of Analytical Psychology*, 47(2): 163–88.
Papadopoulos, R. K. (2002b) 'Refugees, home and trauma.' In *Therapeutic Care for Refugees: No Place Like Home*, edited by R. K. Papadopoulos. London: Karnac, Tavistock Clinic Series.
Papadopoulos, R. K. (2005) 'Political violence, trauma and mental health interventions.' In *Art Therapy and Political Violence: With Art, Without Illusion*, edited by D. Kalmanowitz and B. Lloyd. London: Brunner-Routledge.
Papadopoulos, R. K. (2006a) 'Jung's epistemology and methodology'. In *Handbook of Jungian Psychology: Theory, Practice and Applications*, edited by R. K. Papadopoulos. London and New York: Routledge.
Papadopoulos, R. K. (2006b) 'Refugees and psychological trauma: psychosocial perspectives.' Invited contribution to 'Good Practice Website Project'. Can be accessed at http://www.ncb.org.uk/dotpdf/open%20access%20-%20phase%201%20only/arc_1_10refandpsych.pdf.
Papadopoulos, R. K. (2007) 'Refugees, trauma and adversity-activated development.' *European Journal of Psychotherapy and Counselling*, 9(3), September: 301–12.
Papadopoulos, R. K. (2009) 'Extending Jungian psychology: Working with survivors of political upheavals.' In *Sacral Revolutions*, edited by G. Heuer. London: Routledge.
Papadopoulos, R. K. (2010) *Trainers' Handbook: Enhancing Vulnerable Asylum Seekers' Protection*. Rome: International Organisation for Migration. Available at http://www.evasp.eu/TrainersHandbookOnline.pdf.
Papadopoulos, R. K. (2011) 'The Umwelt and networks of archetypal images: a Jungian approach to therapeutic encounters in humanitarian contexts.' *Psychotherapy and Politics International*, 9(3): 212–31.
Papadopoulos, R. K. (2012) 'Jung e l'approccio allo straniero. Alcune considerazioni storiche e applicative' ('Jung and the approach towards the stranger. Some historical and applied considerations'). *Rivista di Psicologia Analitica*. Nuova serie n. 33, 85: 15–36.
Papadopoulos, R. K. (2013) 'Ethnopsychologische Annäherungen an Überlebende von Katastrophen. Prolegomena zu einer jungianischen Perspektive.' *Analytische Psychologie. Zeitschrift für Psychotherapie und Psychanalyse*, 172(44) Jg. 2/2013, 134–71.

Papadopoulos, R. K. (2015) 'Failure and success in forms of involuntary dislocation: trauma, resilience, and adversity-activated development.' In *The Crucible of Failure*. Jungian Odyssey Series, Vol. VII, edited by U. Wirtz et al. New Orleans, LA: *Spring Journal, Inc.*, pp. 25–49.

Rose, N. (1999) *Powers of Freedom: Reframing Political Thought*. Cambridge, UK: Cambridge University Press.

Zhang, Z. et al. (2012) 'Prevalence of post-traumatic stress disorder among adolescents after the Wenchuan earthquake in China.' *Psychological Medicine*, 42(8): 1687–93.

3

AFTER MASS VIOLENCE AND DISPLACEMENT – HOW A 'SAFE PLACE' EMERGES THROUGH SYMBOLIC PLAY

Eva Pattis Zoja

We humans are social beings, and we need each other in order to maintain our physical and emotional balance.

Perhaps psyche is not just hidden inside us, perhaps it is precisely *between* us that the soul is formed. From a mentalisation concept perspective one would say: we recognise and experience ourselves emotionally not from within ourselves, but only through another person.

Expressive sandwork (Pattis Zoja, 2011) – the method that I will be presenting in this chapter – has to do with just such an invisible and effective bond between people. Over the past ten years, volunteers from various professions have made expressive sandwork an efficient psychosocial tool for assisting children who suffer from neglect, violence and abuse. These volunteers aren't psychologists, pedagogues or therapists: they are empathetic humans who offer time and energy for others. Expressive sandwork takes place in situations where almost no psychological assistance is available: in Chinese and Romanian orphanages, makeshift settlements in Africa and in the slums of Latin America.

The first expressive sandwork project in Colombia began in 2008 in a part of Bogotá known as 'el Bronx' where drug and weapons dealing, contract killings and child pornography are part of everyday life. The civil war, which has been ongoing in Colombia for 50 years, has not only led to massacres and the mass displacement of two million refugees, who now live without work at the edges of the larger cities: the decade-long fighting has also altered the social fabric. War has a lasting effect on habits and behaviour, and raw violence can take effect all the way down to the family level. On a 'small scale', a similar war is being fought in the poverty-stricken 'barrios' compared to the 'large scale' civil war: enemy gangs of youths terrorise and murder the population in endless acts of revenge. In Barrio Norte, where sandwork had commenced in 2010, the project had to be ended after just a few months because the driver of one of the buses that brought children to the sandwork sessions had 'accidentally' been shot at. Sandwork could be resumed in 2014, once there were almost no gang members left alive. Today, one of our projects attends to some of the children of those who had been killed, themselves still minors. They live in constant fear of being followed by the enemies of their murdered fathers.

What is expressive sandwork?

Expressive sandwork is a supra-cultural, largely non-verbal method based on Sandplay Therapy, which was developed in the 1930s by British paediatrician Margaret Lowenfeld (1890–1973) (she named her technique the 'World Technique') and advanced in the 1960s by Dora Kalff (1904–90), a student of C. G. Jung's (Kalff, 2000). A child plays with sand and little figures in a sandbox. Margaret Lowenfeld was the first child therapist to assume that play in itself is therapeutic and does not require interpretation (Lowenfeld, 1979). She was criticised, for this reason, by Melanie Klein (see Davis, 1991 and Frank, 1999).

The psyche's tendency towards self-regulation and the genetic predisposition to attachment as theoretical premises

Two theoretical premises, both emanating from a teleological point of view, are combined in expressive sandwork. First, C. G. Jung's 'natural tendency of the psyche towards self-regulation' (Jacobi, 1973, p. 150), which describes how the psyche continuously produces spontaneous, emotionally loaded images and entire image processes with the purpose of counteracting existing mental and emotional imbalances. We adults know these image processes from our dreams; in children, there is also imaginative play.

John Bowlby – the second premise – illustrated the significance of the primary relationship for the development of internal working models of attachment (Bowlby, 1983).

Assuming that the psyche is able to 'regulate itself', it follows that this form of regulation must be geared to attachment and relationship, since this corresponds to our biological needs as mammals. In order to develop, we require others. We could also say: development and relationship are the two great motivating factors of our human existence.

This leads us to one of the central effect factors of sandwork: it takes place in a group. The fact that children and adults share a large room creates a feeling of security (i.e. decrease of fear), which in turn promotes explorative play. One advantage of the group, for example, is that a very inhibited child can afford to do nothing at first – can simply stand and watch what the others are doing for a few sessions. The group signals that nothing else is expected of the child. This offers the child a 'safe place', which is the precondition for self-regulating psychological processes to work.

One could even say that collective traumas, such as are known from war zones, can *best* be healed through and in a group. When a village community is massacred – as happens in Colombia – then not only is every individual survivor traumatised to the core, but the community of individuals, the 'collective soul', is also injured. Each individual's faith in human togetherness is broken. We shall see how this healing of an entire community is depicted by children in sandplay time and again: first destruction and then healing through the depiction of shared meals and the celebration of feasts – as if the children understood the importance of rituals.

What do we actually mean by the term 'trauma'? We describe as a traumatic experience something which exceeds the ability to be processed psychologically: the psyche then produces modalities for experiencing the world which protect against renewed injuries (e.g. apathy). But this brings the grave disadvantage that, from then on, the individual lives 'on low flame' as far as relationships and emotions are concerned: possibilities of experiencing life are extremely limited; the very situations in which self-efficacy could be rehearsed are avoided; in children, this is precisely imaginative play. This is a vicious circle. Despite all this – and in defiance of all biological regulatory circuits of cortisol release – there is a lasting psychological, archetypically predetermined willingness to gain new experiences of relationship. In other words: because we are social beings, something deep within us never gives up the search for others.

Expressive sandwork makes use of this self-regulatory function of the psyche, directed at attachment. Children play in a sandbox without any instructions whatsoever; two months later, their improved social competence is noticeable. Nobody showed them how to achieve greater self-confidence, nobody taught them that it is better to cooperate than to take away each other's toys. Where did they learn this? During their own play in the sandbox, in the presence of a reference person.

The three factors of expressive sandwork

Three factors are needed for psychological conflicts and traumatic experiences to be processed by children with the help of expressive sandwork, and these factors must remain constant for a period of at least three months: the offer of imaginative play, one adult who is responsible for the child during this period, and the group.

In practice, the setting is the following: there is a group of children and adults – we call them volunteers – in a large room. Each child sits or stands in front of a sandbox and is busy creating his or her own world; the adult sits alongside and observes. The room is silent. Countless miniature figures and objects are set up in the centre of the room and sorted by categories: people, animals, houses, cars, trees, shells, marbles. The children switch back and forth between the play items and their sandboxes, fetching small animals, soldiers, building blocks or toy cars. They do not disturb each other but appear to be busy with their own imaginations. Some of the adults sitting next to the sandboxes are so discreet, one hardly notices them. Taking a closer look, however, one can sometimes see their expressions changing unexpectedly. This reveals how deeply affected they are. A very special psychological space is created between each child and 'his' or 'her' adult during the sessions. If there is any speaking at all, then only in such hushed tones as not to disturb the others. Communication happens via body language, mostly through eye contact. Between 12 and 20 sessions are offered a week, each lasting an hour. Children can also finish sooner, if they wish, and leave the room while the others finish playing.

Now, what do the adults do, who – this must be added – do not have any psychological training? Or – more to the point – what don't they do? They do not ask any questions and do not comment. They try to observe what is happening in a child's play, and what emotional effect this is having on the child and on themselves. Of course they also notice changes in the contents of play. If most of the last sessions were marked by confrontations and fighting, before the next session a volunteer may well think to himself, 'Here we go again. . .' But if he then sees the child carrying a handful of football players instead of soldiers to the sandbox, and a referee and two goals, then the volunteer will likely be astounded. He will not only take rational note that the conflict appears to have shifted to a new level: since he himself spent session after session in a war, as it were, he might well now breathe a sigh of relief.

But how is this play related to the theme of attachment?

Let me illustrate this with an example: since early childhood a girl has been insecure and reserved. She is now offered the opportunity to do sandwork: she is overjoyed with all the toys and about having her own sandbox! But she doesn't know what to think about this empathetic adult who appears to be 'part of the package'. 'He should just leave me in peace,' her body language appears to say. In the first session, the girl might even begin to play with her back turned to the adult. Meanwhile, in the sandbox, this avoidance is also depicted with the use of the play figures; but so is, very cautiously, a desire for attachment. This needs to be tested slowly and carefully: the girl places a mother pig and her piglets in the sand, for example; then a mother horse and her foals, and also a little child in a chair and a dog looking at the child.

During play, the children are constantly busy 'having their own effect' on things. These tend to be things that they could never have effectuated in their often hostile environments. This nurtures confidence in themselves and in the world. And then, at some point during play, a short glance is cast in the direction of the adult: 'Is she actually watching what I'm doing?' And again, a little bit later, a second almost involuntary glance: 'Oh, now I've gone and collapsed the tunnel!!' The adult was watching and did not only see the tunnel collapse, she also experienced it with the child. By and by, the adult's presence will be 'used' by the child emotionally with the very intensity that the child requires at the time. The child himself can regulate the level at which he would like to test attachment: on the symbolic level in play, or on a concrete level. One can almost watch as the two levels build up on each other: play becomes more intense because an adult is present; and because play becomes more intense and emotionally challenging, the adult will be drawn in more closely. The child looks at the adult more often, play becomes more differentiated and the shared presence becomes stronger, much like the case of good attunement during infancy: together, they create a pre-lingual, active form of togetherness. And since this form of togetherness might be entirely new and never before experienced for some children, it will establish itself in their psyche as a new working model in the sense of John Bowlby (Bowlby, 1983).

Examples of expressive sandwork

If children are allowed to play long enough and regularly enough in this way, then play contents will spontaneously be depicted from those phases of development which still require some degree of 'saturation' because children may have suffered from neglect at that time.

Such contents can be read in the play sequences over and over again: feeding, eating, caring, even 'playing' is played in the sand. And then: finding friends, fighting, conquering, owning and sharing something, etc. An inner wealth of experience and emotions is created; a solid emotional base, as it were, from which children can then dare to deal with the traumatic experiences of their more distant past: unpleasant, painful memories appear by and by, which are depicted scenically in the sandbox. A child's psyche alone knows when the time is right.

Here is but one example of a series of sandworks by a nine-year-old girl from Colombia. Maria Camila had to witness an armed attack on her village in the Amazon region. She saw people lose their lives, including small children. Her own family was spared, but the leader of the guerrilla troops offered her father money if he would hand over his daughter to be trained as a guerrilla fighter. That same night her family fled to Bogotá, and since then has lived in el Bronx.

Maria Camila was timid and suffered from poor sleep. During numerous sessions from the beginning of the project, she had made sand images depicting a peaceful world where people and animals lived together. There were farms and cultivated fields, the adults worked, the children played, and ducks and fish swam around the lake. The animals lived in protected enclosures and each had enough space and plenty of food. It was plain to see that the girl relaxed while putting together these scenes. She clearly found pleasure in repeatedly depicting the peaceful farming life in great, lovingly chosen detail. The fifth sand image, for example, included five little children on five little chairs, each child with a bottle of milk.

The sixth session brought about a sudden change – something entirely unexpected for the volunteer: war (see Plate 1). A pink tulle fabric, which the girl spread over the sand and on which the scene of war took place, as it were, appears like a desperate attempt to soften the horror of the scene at least a little bit. There were soldiers fighting in a jeep. The glass marbles in the bottom of the picture were bombs, the girl explained. In the top right of the image, these same marbles represented water: this was a place of resilience, with a well, flowers and four cats. In the top left stood a house, remindful of a peaceful world; on the ground, a flock of white birds. The five chairs, where five little children had sat with their milk bottles in the previous picture, were now empty.

'Self-regulation of the psyche' also means that the child knew by herself when and how the traumatic experience was to be represented and processed. In the following session, the girl apparently felt an urge to protect herself. There were lots of vehicles, as if to be able to escape quickly from a situation. This sand image was like a pause for breath before processing of the trauma continued. In the following picture, the conflict took place in prehistoric times as if brutality and inhumanity would then be easier to bear. Dinosaurs were fighting in pairs. But the scene also contains a protected area, an enclosed pen with little pigs, a place of resilience.

The theme of 'brutality in prehistoric times' was continued in the next sandwork session. A Tyrannosaurus is attacking a young woman. One can well imagine that the girl would already have experienced the brutality that girls and women can be subjected to. It didn't get any easier in the next image. Life in el Bronx is portrayed in detail: piled-up houses and flats. There are wild animals down below who – according to the girl – eat human cadavers. A child is fair game on the streets of such a place. Things seem to be more peaceful inside the houses. The people are praying, says Maria Camila. There followed further attempts of the girl to portray peaceful life in her sandwork, including numerous images of copious shared meals. Then the sequence of trauma processing is repeated on a new level: another sudden and unexpected depiction of war. This time the scene was not underlaid with a pink tulle fabric. Houses and people are interspersed with soldiers and tanks. Unfortunately, this photo is quite poor. The volunteer accompanying Maria Camila was himself a displaced person and would have experienced similar things in his own youth. Perhaps he was so taken by the sand image emotionally that he didn't take a better photo.

Acts of war and motherly love (mothers with their prams) are very close to each other in this image: trauma and the overcoming of trauma. There followed another series of conciliatory sandworks in which harmonious togetherness and shared meals were portrayed in loving detail (see Plate 2). Today, the girl is doing well.

Imaginative and symbolic play is already an expression of self-regulation of the psyche. Even if volunteers may not yet understand the symbolic or metaphoric meaning of the play contents, they will be able to observe that children depict not only the trauma itself, but also hope, protection and resilience, and that this slowly becomes reality in the children's own lives. The adult's function comes down to being an emotional resonator – something for which the majority of people are probably naturally gifted. This explains the effectiveness of the volunteers and also the low cost of the projects.

Back to theory: why should attachment styles change through imaginative play?

One concept is provided by Jaak Panksepp (Panksepp & Biven, 2012), who has studied play behaviour in mammals for 20 years. Panksepp showed that play not only fulfils an affect-regulating function, it primarily targets the development of social competence. The unfortunate play-deprived rats with which he worked not only showed general deficits in their development, but above all they displayed blatant social incompetence. Since the human brain is more of a symbolic organ – compared to the brains of Panksepp's rats, which engage in very boisterous play – it is safe to say: in humans, learning about relationship and also making up for relationship deficits takes place also, or above all, on an imaginative and symbolic level. And in children, this level is play. What was imprinted on us in earliest childhood can be changed *because* we are able to represent and experience things on a symbolic level. Fortunately, we humans are not trapped in an irreversible biological imprinting like Konrad Lorenz's geese. An ill-fated primary relationship can be 'repaired' because an autonomous symbol-producing function of the psyche continues to try and achieve whatever may have worked out so badly until that point.

References

Bowlby, J. (1983) *Attachment: Attachment and Loss, Volume One*, 2nd edition. New York: Basic Books.

Davis, J. M. (1991) Foreword to M. Lowenfeld, *Play in Childhood*. Cambridge: Cambridge University Press.

Frank, C. (1999) *Melanie Kleins erste Kinderanalysen – die Entdeckung des Kindes als Objekt sui generis von Heilen und Forschen*. Stuttgart: Frommann und Holzboog.

Jacobi, J. (1973) *The Psychology of C. G. Jung*. New Haven: Yale University.

Kalff, D. (2000) *Das Sandspiel*. Basel: Ernst Reinhard Verlag.

Lowenfeld, M. (1979) *The World Technique*. London: George, Allen & Unwin.

Panksepp, I. and Biven, L. (2012) *The Archaeology of Mind*. New York: Norton.

Pattis Zoja, E. (2011) *Sandplay Therapy in Vulnerable Communities: A Jungian Approach*. London: Routledge.

4

THE LONG WEEKEND IN ALICE SPRINGS

Craig San Roque and Joshua Santospirito

Introduction

This 30-page sequence is selected from the 140-page book covering one long weekend of activity in the town of Alice Springs, central Australia. This isolated, unique, arid land town is located in Aboriginal territories, 1,500 km from the nearest city. As narrator, my alter ego recounts incidents in local life and death. This is a case history and a history of events depicting relationships between Aboriginal families and my own. Beginning Friday night in the back yard, we move through streets, hospital, country, history, travelling time zones, mythic locations, thoughts. I return to the yard, alone, late on Monday night. I tell a story to show psychic life as we experience it. Josh Santospirito is intimately familiar with the complex intersecting realities of Aboriginal and Australian European mentality in our place. He has taken my original essay and, with cinematic skill, has constructed a graphic account.

This extract follows the video version shown at the conference. You will be missing scenes, linking threads, reflective reverie, but will gather impressions of relationships and events in an interracial borderzone.

Hunger is a daily concern for many Aboriginal people. This selection follows a thread of food, allowing me to introduce the idea of cultural cannibalism – the experience many of us have within Aboriginal territories, of being entrapped in a muddled yet relentless enculturating drive by both peoples to incorporate the other. On one hand, the 'White' majority, supported by politicised administrative systems of power, continue the mentality of (colonising) incorporation. Australia, once the most rebellious young country, has reconstructed itself into the most regulated bureaucratic nation under democratic governance in the world. On the other hand, indigenous psychic resistance, though not armed, is a fact of life, a fact of behaviour and a fact of subliminal refusal to become what 'White' expectations expect. The cross currents are bewildering, barely acknowledged, yet psychosomatically experienced in the transference/countertransference. Some of this crossing current is conveyed in the *Long Weekend*.

In the story it is Amos, who introduces a connection between food, cannibalism and the determination of the indigenous (incumbent) and nonindigenous (invader) to gobble each other. In the *Long Weekend* I wanted to hint at the horror and the banal ordinariness of the experience of people, especially young people, being dragged (taken down) into a strange derangement. They do not actively resist. They do not take up arms. Suicide is preferred. You see an indication of this in the scene in the psychiatric ward.

The cannibalism idea is metaphor, tagging the experience of being chewed up by collective mental paralysis, a mixed-up recurring experience, which the term 'cultural complex' helps identify. The mix for us here has humour and the absurd and psychotic dream like entrapments in which one 'cannot sleep and cannot awake'. It is this atmospheric flavour that is depicted in the Santospirito graphic style, a primal bewilderment and disgust at being eaten alive by something you cannot quite identify, which might, however, turn out to be doing its best to love you.

Beauty outshines the psychotic.

I can see a campfire in our backyard.

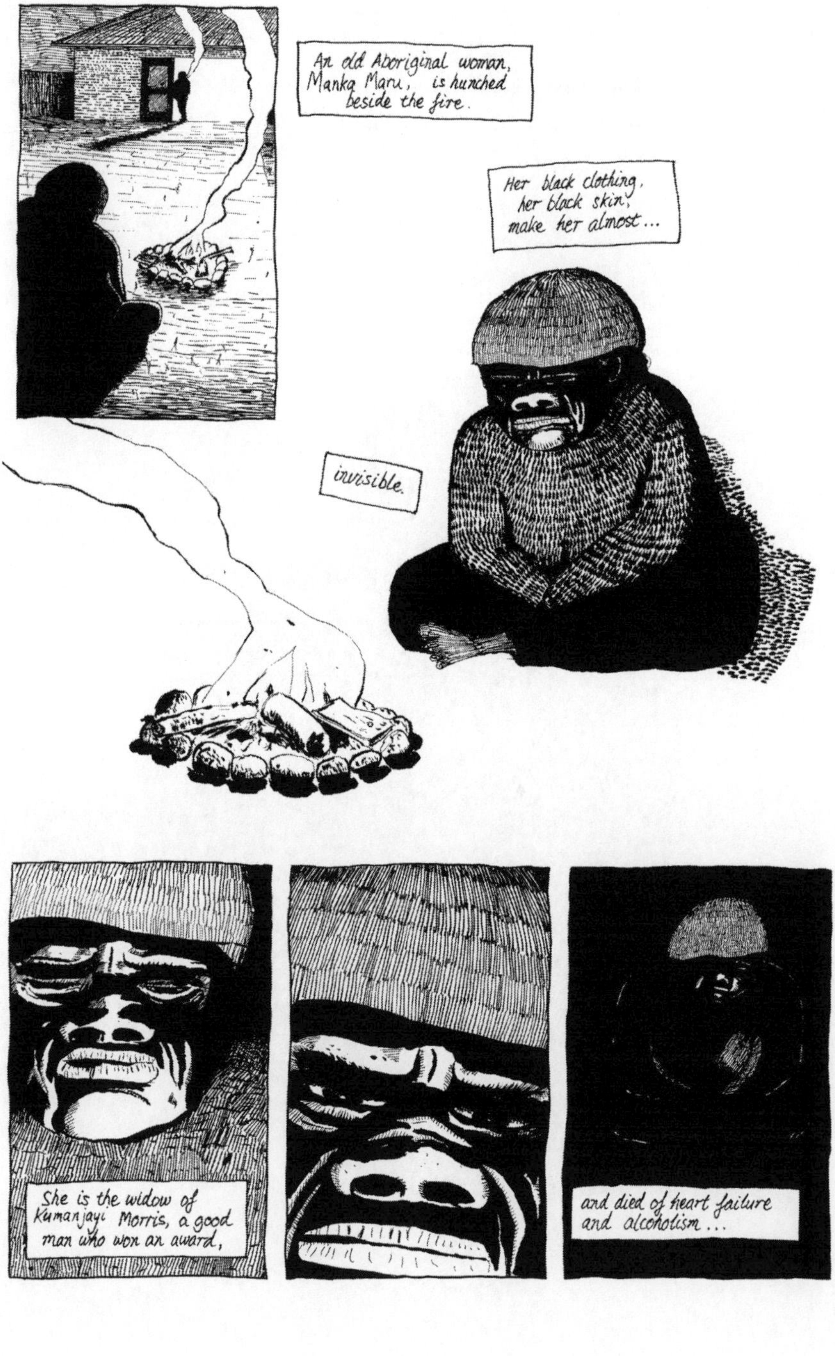

An old Aboriginal woman, Manka Maru, is hunched beside the fire.

Her black clothing, her black skin, make her almost...

invisible.

She is the widow of Kumanjayi Morris, a good man who won an award,

and died of heart failure and alcoholism...

She hasn't spoken about her deceased husband.
She will not mention his name.
There's a clutch of polaroid photos in her plastic handbag.
In the mornings, sometimes, she takes them out and ponderously gazes into the images of her husband.
She fondles them,
then slips them back into her bag.

Now the cooking has hold of her attention
lamb chops, tomato sauce.
chicken nuggets, hot tea.
comfort in a life that has no forseeable development,
no progress.
no economic vitality.

FRIDAY

My name is Craig.
An American editor named Tom Singer has asked me to write a chapter on the idea of cultural complexes...
an old idea of Jung's: it was a bit controversial at the time.
I'd like to finish this by the end of this long weekend.

In his psychological languages Tom writes -

Cultural Complexes
structure emotional
experience,
tend to be repetetive,
autonomous,
resist consciousness
and collect experience
that confirms their
historical point of view
... automatically take on
shared body language...
express their distress
in similar somatic complaints

...provide a simplistic
certainty about the
groups place in the
world in the face of
otherwise conflicting
and ambiguous
uncertainties.

I don't know how to think about these things

I do not really know how to represent the action of a 'cultural complex' to myself.

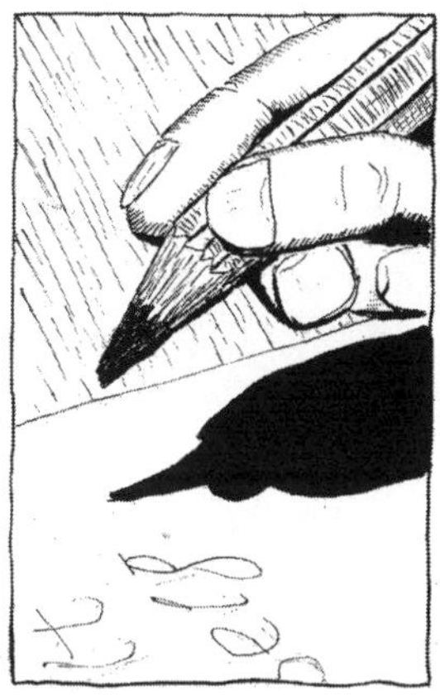

I can look at what goes on in other countries: observe the incredibly stupid things that one mob of people does to another ... and I can say

AH! THERE'S A CULTURAL COMPLEX IN ACTION

with the wisdom of distance I can point out the mote in another's eye BUT the really hard thing is to see the mote in my own eye.

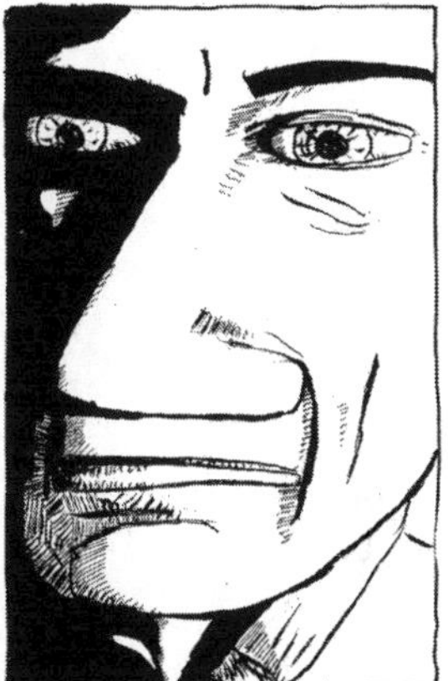

Something seems to happen to my consciousness when a complex operates: self-awareness becomes less sharp.

On a mob level it is as though a population becomes dazed and addicted to a state of intoxication – a sleepwalk that silences voices of contradiction as well as revelation.

Perhaps I can discover where a complex operates by noting when and where I am most ... inarticulate.

When I am fascinated by something but am almost unable to think about it

and almost unable to speak.

This weekend I sat down to think and it was as though shades came to visit with a purpose.

There are others around the fire.
It is Friday – the beginning of a long weekend.

There are six or seven bush people down from Warlpiri country for the football.

Beth is an Aboriginal health worker She talks to her mother about computers and blood pressure ...
KFC
and the health hazards of fried chicken.

who played with a can of petrol over a campfire.

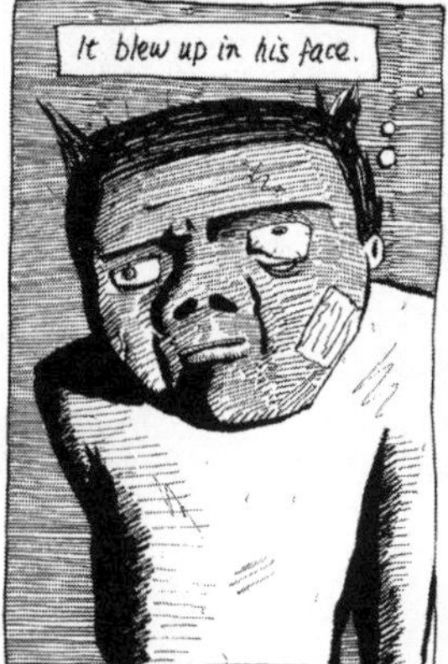

I have a list of boys like this,
looking after them is my work.

Celine found him tonight in another camp being tormented by drunks.
With uncharacteristic consideration she brought him here to be looked after.

That's her mother and sister sitting over by the fire ...

She wants her mother to see her display of care.

She won't stay herself...

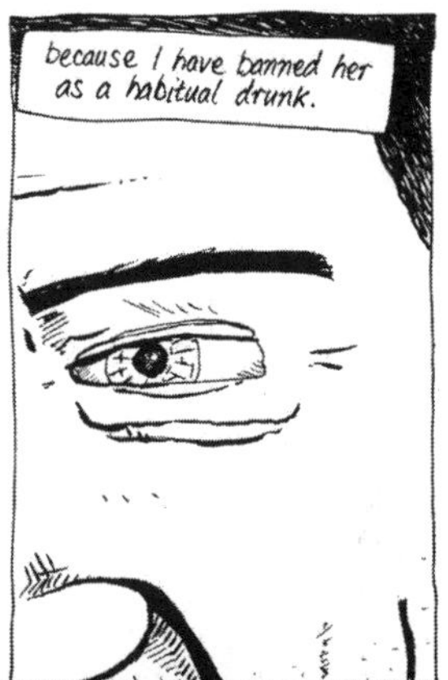
because I have banned her
as a habitual drunk.

BUT SHE SEEMS SOBER ENOUGH
THIS EVENING...

and her care for this boy
seems authentic enough.

I try to stay at my table,
the doors opened out
onto the scene.

I'm trying to develop a theme for this essay that I'm writing…
but I feel interrupted by these…
incidental…

bacchic…
visitations.
Suddenly, I realise…

I don't have to THINK any more about the problem that Tom troubles me with.
I just have to sit here and describe what is happening around the fire…
and in my mind's eye.

Therefore I set myself a boundary.

I will write no more than it is possible to describe in this weekend in Alice Springs.
BLACK

I will set down what the place makes me think.

There will be a lot happening as people from the bush converge on the town.

Stories will unfold.
FOOTY
SOME FAMILY BUSINESS
MAYBE SOME FIGHTS

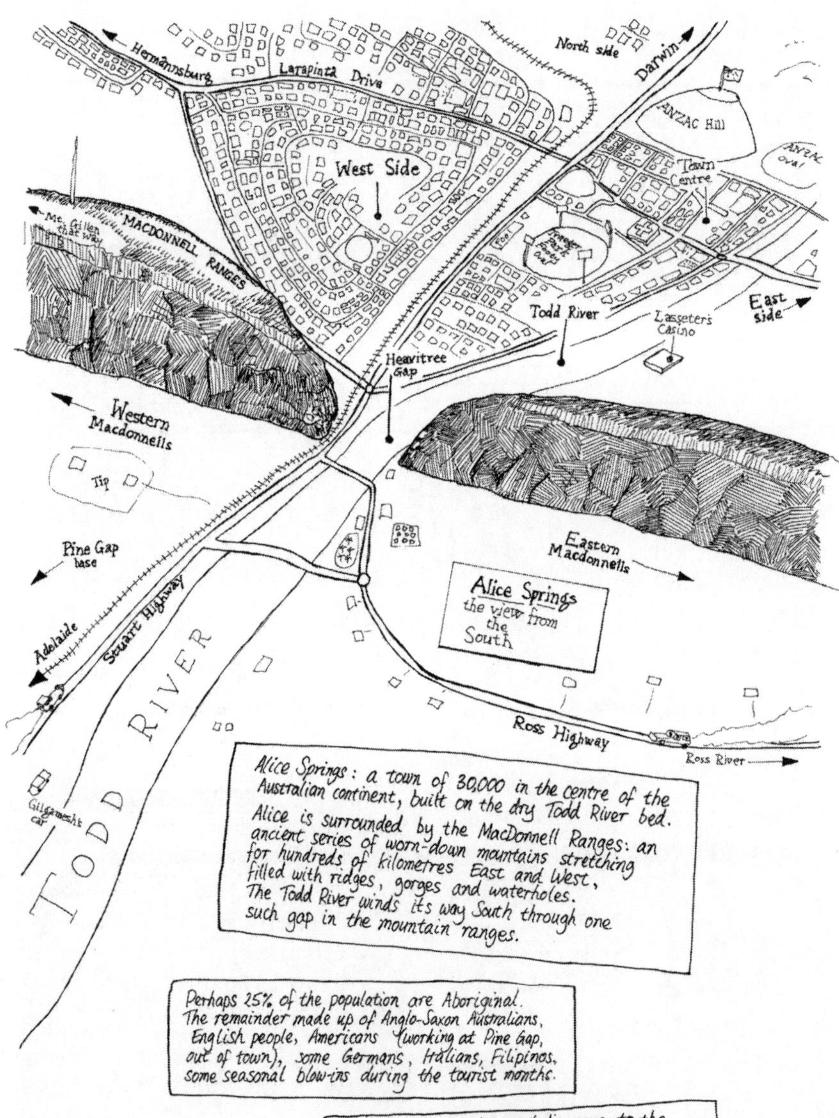
Hermannsburg
Larapinta Drive
North side
Darwin
ANZAC Hill
ANZAC oval
Town Centre
West Side
MACDONNELL RANGES
Mt. Gillen that way
Todd River
Lasseter's Casino
East side
Heavitree Gap
Western Macdonnells
Tip
Pine Gap base
Eastern Macdonnells
Alice Springs
the view from the South
Adelaide
Stuart Highway
TODD RIVER
Ross Highway
Ross River
Gilgamesh's car
Alice Springs: a town of 30,000 in the centre of the Australian continent, built on the dry Todd River bed. Alice is surrounded by the MacDonnell Ranges: an ancient series of worn-down mountains stretching for hundreds of kilometres East and West, filled with ridges, gorges and waterholes. The Todd River winds its way South through one such gap in the mountain ranges.
Perhaps 25% of the population are Aboriginal. The remainder made up of Anglo-Saxon Australians, English people, Americans (working at Pine Gap, out of town), some Germans, Italians, Filipinos, some seasonal blow-ins during the tourist months.

The Arrernte people are Indigenous to the immediate area, though in Central Australia there are many desert tribal cultures and languages that have lived in the region for thousands upon thousands of years.

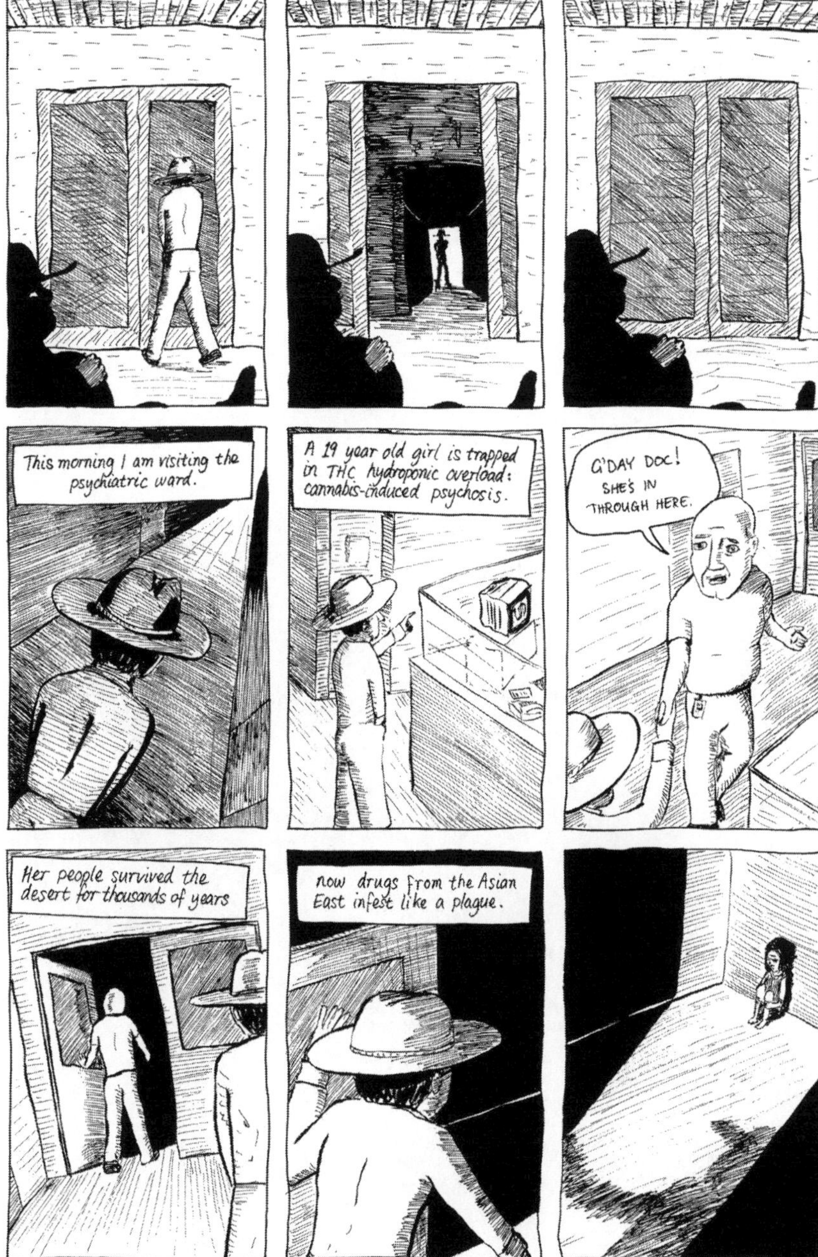
This morning I am visiting the psychiatric ward.
A 19 year old girl is trapped in THC hydroponic overload: cannabis-induced psychosis.
G'DAY DOC! SHE'S IN THROUGH HERE.
Her people survived the desert for thousands of years
now drugs from the Asian East infest like a plague.

The girl in the hospital is confused. Her eyes roll, she clutches at her stomach and says 'I have a bellyache!'

evil

bad girl

She looks with a dumb kind of appeal, almost like an animal which is trapped, expecting death.

girl

evil

piece of shit

devil's child

ick

evil

evil

shit

dirt

bad girl

nothing

She has a white plastic crucifix hanging from her dark-skinned, velvet neck . . .

It catches the attention of the nurses.

COME ON TERESA. WE DON'T WANT YA TO HURT YOURSELF. YA'LL GET IT BACK WHEN Y'GO HOME.

Teresa has spent years sniffing petrol out of a can. She has refused her mother's entreaties to put it aside. Her younger brother and her young husband still fondle the can with dedication, ignoring all urgencies and urgings to stop.

It is not so much suicide

more a rejection of the responsibility of being human.

A possessive and inevitable force that does not allow insight.

autonomic...

insistent...

Dust and country music roll through the darkened streets of Teresa's home community.
Much like any other one: badly designed, badly built, badly serviced...
subject to idiosyncratic heroes and missionaries of one ideology or another - an expression of the pathology of the Australian psyche.
These people will be saved through the WORD!
through artistic expression I think Aboriginal people will be given the opportunity to
Through EDUCATION we will raise the standard of living etc.
Sermons on salvation and eternity have had little impact on Teresa.
She's witnessed hundreds of funerals. The spectre of death is no deterrent.
Oi
HEY!! T'resa, you gotta throw away that can. STOP Dat sniffing! If you DON'T throw it out you'll fry your BRAIN! You'll DIE like your brother Done! They'll take you to Ward One!!
You don't wanna DIE! LISTEN!

ABORIGINAL
LAND
NO PORN!
NO GROG

The alcohol keeps coming to town.
HEY
NO BLOODY
GROG!
XXX

The police do what they can.

AND I CAN'T DO NUTHIN'! IT'S A FAMILY PROBLEM.

IT'S UNSATISFIED LOVE
He's right
XXX

The tragedy here is not about massive conflicts and brutal bloody invasion,

The tragedy is about experiencing self-decomposition through the erosion of access to loving bonds with family, country and integrity of cultural practice.
The human psyche loves processing its own thoughts and indigenous Australians have developed an artful way of doing this,
but when the form is lost ...
psychic integrity falls helplessly out of being.
XXX

your mother, it's your mother...
It welcomes it.
Something in the cultural lobe of her brain allows her psychic demise...
you'll never go back
Her psychic immune system is down.
shit
black
worthless
piece of
they won't let you go
bad girl
going to kill you
It's not just cannabis.
evil
nothin' but dirt!
they're coming
slut
kill her
worthless
evil
Teresa has no conceptual frame for what is troubling her... nor does her mother.
sick
die die die

FUKKEN KILL YOU

LET'S TAKE HER DOWN QUICK TIM!

It is this multiple collapse which has reached the proportions of a cultural complex.

We can see the complex in the interactions...

of two cultures that don't...
Y'GOT THAT JAB READY CAROL?

have the slightest notion of how to deal with each other's presence.

In the clash of cultures we see embedded 'complexes' exposed.

Perhaps the evolution of a new complex ...

one that is born out of the legacy of the British empire and Jesus' kingdom in Central Australia.

SUNDAY

Early morning mugs of tea,

Bits of white bread crushed into sand,

And then a FLURRY! as another branch of the Warlpiri family converges...
Nakamarra
Napaltjarri
from three places
Katherine
Lajamanu
and the hospital
No one told us they were coming... we were sort of planning other things. Some of them go along with my wife for a picnic.
It is not always like this.
Perhaps it's because people are coming to tell Tom Singer something?

The visitors have no blankets, no food, little money,
no prior arrangements to get the next 400 k's home.
MEBBE THE LAND COUNCIL TOYOTA ON TUESDAY
Travellers here rely on family obligation, concrete floors, food and tea from someone else.
HEY JUNGERAI!
Napaltjarri wants to go hunting for echidna or lizard OR HONEY-ANT!!!
COME ON JUNGERAI TAKE US!!
HM, OK. BUT I NEED A MAN FOR COMPANY.
I'M PICKING UP AMOS.

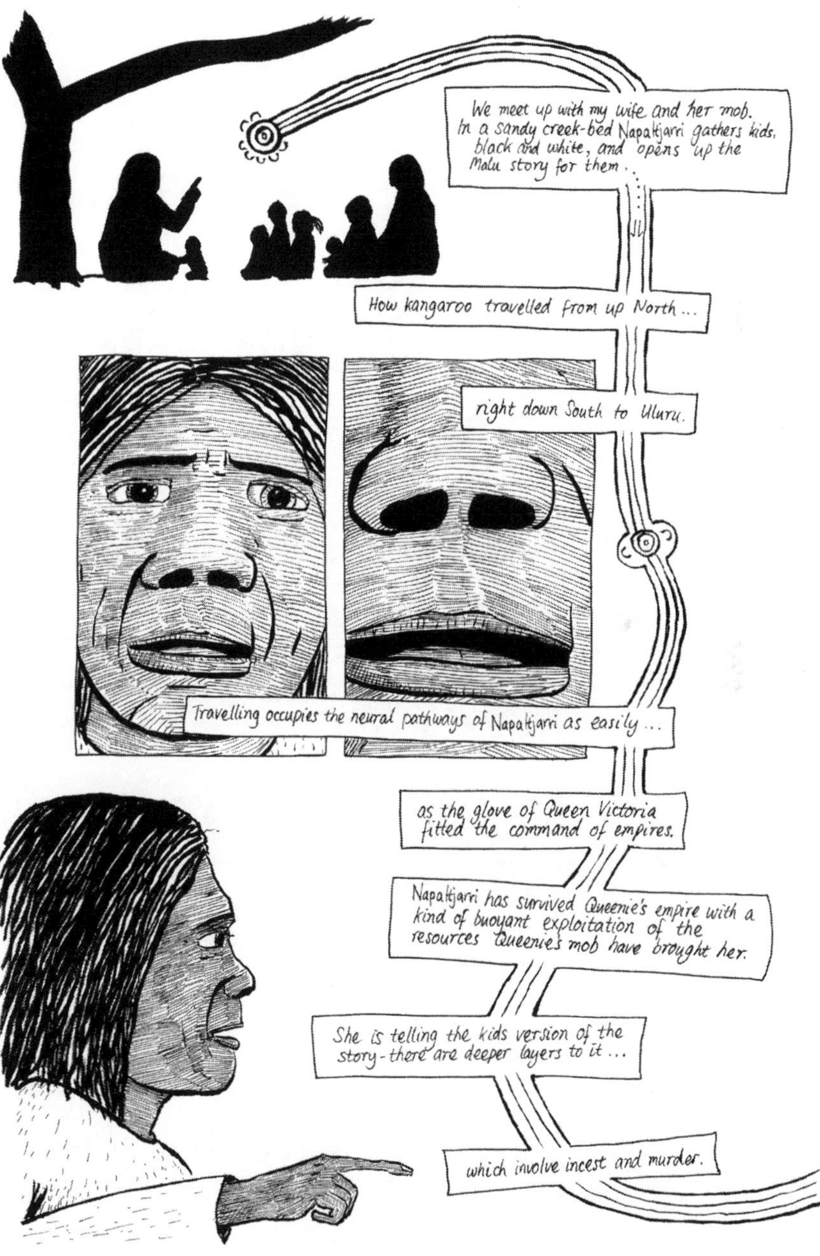
We meet up with my wife and her mob. In a sandy creek-bed Napaltjarri gathers kids, black and white, and opens up the Malu story for them . . .
How kangaroo travelled from up North . . .
right down South to Uluru.
Travelling occupies the neural pathways of Napaltjarri as easily . . .
as the glove of Queen Victoria fitted the command of empires.
Napaltjarri has survived Queenie's empire with a kind of buoyant exploitation of the resources Queenie's mob have brought her.
She is telling the kids version of the story - there are deeper layers to it . . .
which involve incest and murder.

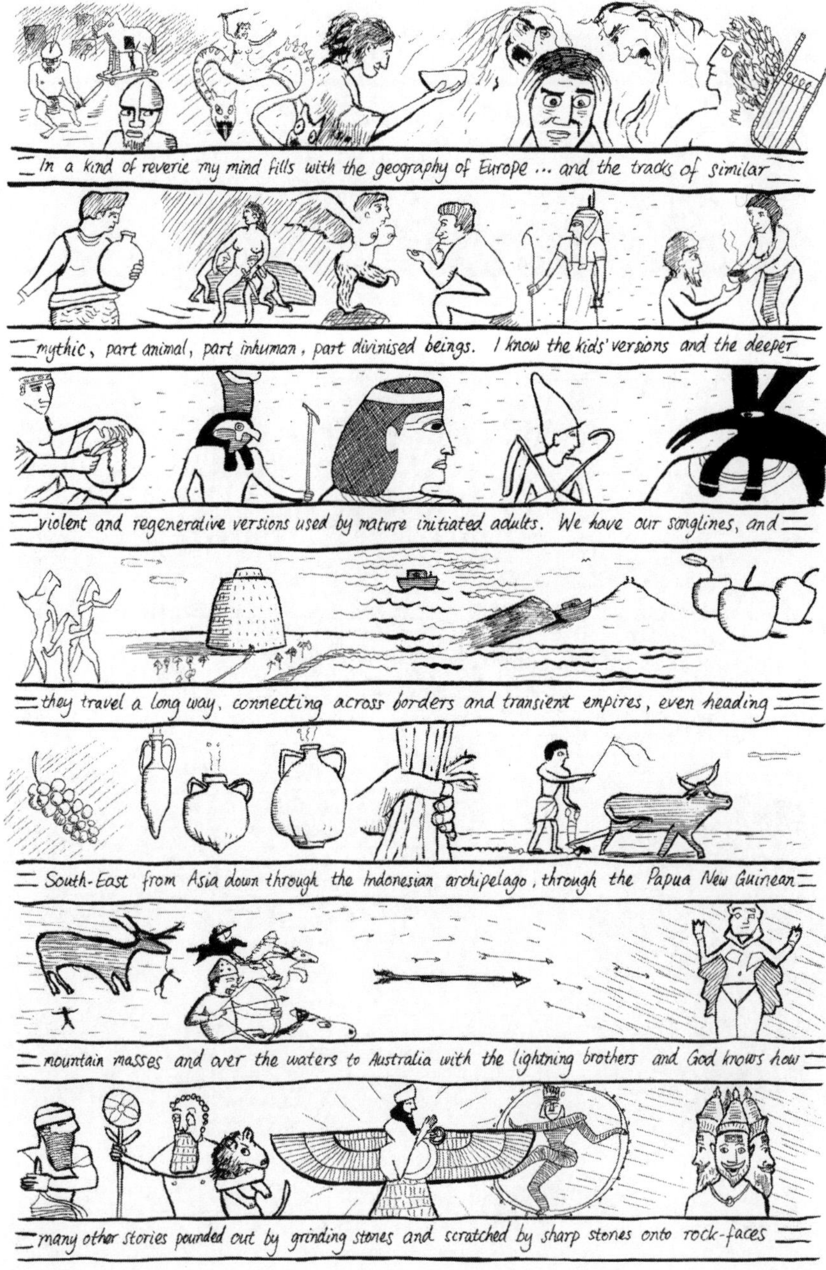
In a kind of reverie my mind fills with the geography of Europe ... and the tracks of similar
mythic, part animal, part inhuman, part divinised beings. I know the kids' versions and the deeper
violent and regenerative versions used by mature initiated adults. We have our songlines, and
they travel a long way, connecting across borders and transient empires, even heading
South-East from Asia down through the Indonesian archipelago, through the Papua New Guinean
mountain masses and over the waters to Australia with the lightning brothers and God knows how
many other stories pounded out by grinding stones and scratched by sharp stones onto rock-faces

NOW THE GOVERNMENT IS SENDING FUNDS TO REPAIR THE DAMAGE....
INCOMPETENTLY OF COURSE, WHICH IS THE SUBCONSCIOUS INTENTION.
SITES HAVE BEEN TURNED INTO COMMODITIES.
THESE ARE CULTURAL PROCESSES SET GOING BY THE BIG GUYS
WITH THE PSYCHOLOGICAL PURPOSE OF BREAKDOWN
AND
ASSIMILATION
OF THE LITTLE GUYS
IT'S A FORM OF CANNIBALISM.

Hey guys, check out the Aborigine!
CHOMP chomp
Daddy? Mummy?
What are you doing?
Lunch darling?

MY FAMILY ARE POLISH AND JEWISH: WE ARE ALWAYS BEING EATEN.
SO WE INVENTED WAYS TO MAKE US TASTE NASTY AND PRESERVE OUR STRUCTURE SO AS TO MAKE US INDIGESTIBLE TO THE CANNIBALS.
WE LIVE IN THE BELLY OF NATIONS BUT THEY DON'T CONSUME US...
KOSHER FOOD IS TO REMIND US NOT TO BE EATEN!
YOUR QUEEN VICTORIA TOOK OUR GOD YAHWEH AND MADE HIM INTO A CANNIBAL FATHER TOO...
THAT IS WHY THE PRIMAL CHRISTIAN CEREMONY IS ABOUT EATING THE BODY OF THE SON!
QUEENIE SAYS IT IS GOOD TO BE EATEN BY THE FATHER - THAT IS LOVE! AND THAT'S HOW AFRICA GOT EATEN UP BY EUROPEANS POSING AS CHRISTIANS.
SLOP
YOU SEE, THE PRIMAL COMPLEX IS ABOUT EATING OTHER PEOPLE OR THEIR COUNTRY.
Hmm.

This dog will outlive the generations of humans.

It is now Monday night, the long weekend is over.

The lizards have been eaten, the Warlpiri have all left...

... the ashes are cold,

there is no food in the house.

We believe we are individuals...

but we have already been swallowed by stomachs bigger than ourselves.

These are the cultural complexes.

SECTION 2
Equalities and inequalities

5

THE POLITICS OF CARE AND CARING

One UK perspective

Angela Cotter

The argument of this chapter is that the healthcare professions as articulated and delivered in the UK now face a metamodernist (Vermeulen & van der Akker, 2010) dilemma, articulated for some years as the conflict between humanity and bureaucracy (Cotter, Meyer & Roberts, 1998). Approaching this subject as a second-wave feminist, I remain convinced that the 'personal is political'. On the first night of the Analysis and Activism conference, two questions from the floor asked the presenters about their own stories, wishing to know what led them to become involved in their moving work in different settings. This chapter sets out an unashamedly personal perspective, the story of how a well-meaning activist can become co-opted into meeting the neo-liberalist agenda. It also contains threads indicating resilience and hope for the future.

Firstly, it sets out relevant lessons from my nursing experience, involvement in health service policy-making and then psychotherapy policy-making. The chapter finishes with a short polemical statement for the future. Like the current auto-ethnographic turn in social science research (Adams, Holman Jones & Ellis, 2015; Denzin, 2014), building on the earlier biographical turn (Chamberlayne, Bornat & Wengraf, 2000), it seeks to illuminate the cultural context through the lens of individual experience; in this case, aiming to turn on its head the dominant evidence-based research focus in healthcare policy. Additionally, my own cultural background is Celtic, where story telling has been an essential aspect of the transmission of culture, social connection and political implications.

I entered nursing in the late 1970s as a graduate in philosophy and politics, with a socialist feminist perspective. Working as a care assistant in a community-based hospital while at university, I had grown to respect and love the fundamentals of nursing care as skilled and relational work. By 'fundamentals of nursing care' I am referring to what is now called personal care, e.g. assisting with washing, dressing, walking, moving around and eating. The older patients I encountered often had several co-existent medical conditions, which meant working with them to gauge how their self-care could be maximised. At those times when they needed help, preserving their dignity and self-esteem meant working empathically. In both cases, attunement was an important aspect.

Having a background in philosophy presented a tension in nurse training, which came to a head when I was told by the Director of Nurse Education that if I wanted to 'think', I should have stayed doing what I was doing before I became a nursing student. The controversy was caused by my wish not to participate in ECT on my mental health placement – I had studied Laing (2010) and Szasz (1971) at university. What seemed intolerable was that my reaching this conclusion was informed neither by personal experience of ECT nor by any direct experience of family members or friends but by academic study and reflection. On a bad hair day, I rather believe that if I were training now, I might be told that if I wanted to 'feel', I should have stayed doing what I was doing before I entered nursing!

As a member of the Radical Nurses Group, I studied the professionalisation of nursing, beginning with Florence Nightingale (Salvage, 1985). The lady with the lamp was a very clever strategist, who could also lay claim to being the first public health specialist. She saw what was in the wind in relation to the development of medicine and healthcare, and brought nursing in Britain into a subservient role vis-à-vis doctors, which strategy included vilification of the old Poor Law Nurses, arguably more autonomous descendants of the traditional women healers in this country (Davies, 1981). She did this, I believe, for nursing to survive, but there was a cost, which has been handed down the generations, and is one strand of the humanity and bureaucracy conflict. However, reclamation of the humanity pole is seen recently in a movement towards humanisation of healthcare, which has resulted in, for example, the setting up of dedicated research at Bournemouth University. The Centre for Qualitative Research (https://research.bournemouth.ac.uk/centre/centre-for-qualitative-research) includes a linked page which records the impetus behind its inclusion as a strand of research from 2013:

> research is particularly topical and relevant following the Francis report which considered appalling standards of care at the Mid Staffordshire NHS Foundation Trust. The Francis report heralds an overdue 'wake-up' call to the realisation that 'something important is missing' in current health and social care practices and systems. There are debates about what this 'something missing' is, and Galvin and Todres [the lead researchers] characterise this as 'humanly sensitive care'.
>
> (Bournemouth, 2013)

In a book published contemporaneously, Galvin and Todres (2014) state that humanisation of healthcare calls for, among other things, open-heartedness.

Back to my own story, the first reason for my inclusion in policy-making was that I had managed an NHS nursing home that was seen as delivering high-quality care. It was a significant fact that, in an attempt to pacify the community, this home was set up as part of an agreement to build a new centralised hospital. A nowadays unimaginable skill mix was therefore allowed, i.e. a skill mix and number of staff that would now sadly be seen as appropriate for running a home of perhaps three times the size. A three-week induction was accepted, in which we set our own standards and principles for care, prior to moving residents of an old workhouse NHS hospital into the home. These included the aim of working to deinstitutionalise residents from the workhouse setting, so that the staff team would, for example, address issues directly with each other rather than complaining behind each other's backs, and importantly would look at the demands placed on us by caring in the home. We wanted to provide an atmosphere of caring for ourselves as we wanted to care for others. We found particularly informative Menzies Lyth's seminal paper (1960) about the way that task orientation, uniformity of nurses and depersonalisation of patients within nursing functioned as a defence against anxiety, as well as the work of the Tavistock consultants to institutions (Obholzer & Zaghier Roberts, 1994). My PhD (Cotter, 1990) about the wounded healer in nursing highlighted individual and organisational transference and countertransference issues, as seen in nurses who experienced either severe acute or enduring illness (either physical or mental health). At this time, I had also started Jungian training and had begun to realise that working in care settings often meant being surrounded 24/7 by people (i.e. service users) going through traumatic experiences. As a defence or survival strategy, staff sometimes unconsciously resorted to seeing themselves as different, i.e. as strong and capable, over against the 'patients' as weak and vulnerable. If they then contracted a significant illness, they often experienced themselves as being rejected by other staff within the system.

The staff team of the nursing home comprised people from 18 different national/cultural backgrounds and this led to an enriching and stimulating environment. To give one example, I overheard two staff members – a member of catering staff from Northern Ireland and a nursing assistant from the Philippines – discussing the fact that one had sworn at the other, who had found that intolerable. The former said that in Northern Ireland you defend yourself by being aggressive, and the other said that in the Philippines at that time if you swore at the wrong person you were apt to disappear for ever. The standard of the quality of care resulting from such openness to the 'other' was dramatically demonstrated by an incident where a resident one night requested four changes of nightdress to wear in bed. She was very ill, with little movement, so this took considerable effort from her and the nursing staff. She died that night.

Eventually, the skill mix and number of staff began to be eroded (for example, the care assistants were downgraded). The resultant effect on morale was palpable. I left and became a senior manager in another NHS Trust with responsibility for management, research and development in the care group for older people. I was seconded to the then NHS Executive and trained in evidence-based medicine at its inception. I soon became aware that quantitative research dissemination does not change clinical practice on its own. Following this, I worked as the lead action researcher on a multi-agency, multi-sector project trying to change the patchwork quilt of discharge of older people from acute care into something more seamless (Marks, 1994). The university research team began by interviewing older people in acute care and soon learnt that they did not want to answer structured interview questions but rather to tell us about their experience. The resultant narratives became incorporated in learning packages to inform care delivery. The advantage here was that the narratives did not blame and judge (and therefore evoke resistance in) care staff. Often the patients took responsibility on themselves. For example, one participant, on being discharged from hospital and then seen again in A&E following a fall where her new hip fracture went undiagnosed, stated that perhaps it was her fault because she did not tell the A&E staff how much pain she was in. Members of staff reading this, instead of feeling blamed, began to say: Why didn't we ask you how much pain you were in? What was wrong with our assessment?

As a result of this experience I was asked to be involved in two policy initiatives. One was the National Service Framework for Older People (Department of Health, 2001a), and the second was Standards of Acute Nursing Care for Older People in Hospital (Department of Health, 2001b). Both are still referenced and used.

My experience of this involvement in policy-making was that the 'softer' elements, valued by the working groups of 'experts' in high-quality care delivery, were written out as the documents progressed. For example, in my group of the National Service Framework, we all emphasised the importance of the development work needed to establish a functioning multi-disciplinary team in community care. Dedicated team-building over time could lead to sharing of skills so that risk was not a one-profession province but rather a decision that was reached in collaboration, in such a way that trust operated between different disciplines. This background relational work did not appear in the final document. What was left, therefore, were the standards expected of good quality care, though without the processes needed to attain it.

Now on to psychotherapy: in 2007–8, I was managing a PhD programme in an integrative psychotherapy training setting and represented that training at the UKCP.

I then found myself part of the debate in relation to setting evidence-based National Occupational Standards (NOS) in the UK in relation to humanistic and integrative psychotherapy. NOS are statements of the standards of performance individuals must achieve – the skills needed – when carrying out functions in the workplace, together with specifications of the underpinning knowledge and understanding. Although many psychotherapists practise integratively nowadays (in that, whatever approach we start out from, we have usually integrated new approaches to psychotherapy), within the NOS work there was an emphasis that the integrative approach was not amenable to research within the current demands of evidence-based practice, demands which required therapies to be manualisable, i.e. reducible to standards that can be demonstrated across the patch. This emphasis works against an individual approach where needs are geared to each client. Clearly, integrative work was never going to enter into this debate. So the resultant standards that were set were 'humanistic' because there was good, largely randomised controlled trialled (RCT), evidence about person-centred care and its adaptations. Integrative psychotherapy could not be included, because there was not seen to be common manualisable integrative work researched within the post-positivistic framework. Although I accepted that the humanistic NOS were good (see http://nos.ukces.org.uk), I was nonetheless disillusioned.

So far, I have given two examples of policy involvement where the work has involved exclusion of that which does not fit the model. I want now to consider a clinical guidelines example, namely, the National Institute for Health and Care Excellence guidelines on care of people with dementia (NICE, 2006). NICE provides national guidance and advice to improve health and social care, and the dementia guidelines present a very positive but telling set of principles, emphasising, for example, the human value of people with dementia, regardless of age or cognitive impairment, and those who care for them, and the individuality of people with dementia. However, the actual guidance contains the word 'should' in every section. Two examples from the guidance on the principle concerning diversity, equality and language are illustrative:

> 1.1.1.1 People with dementia should not be excluded from any services because of their diagnosis, age (whether designated too young or too old) or coexisting learning disabilities.
>
> 1.1.1.2 Health and social care staff should treat people with dementia and their carers with respect at all times.
>
> (NICE, 2006, p. 11)

These guidelines offer less help with how to achieve these standards, particularly the relational aspects, beyond the need for training in communication skills. Yet those of us who work with people with dementia recognise that one of the most crucial aspects is to look at our own countertransference, meaning here our own fears about losing our mind or brain in a society that arguably over-values cognition. Yet this is discussed in one of two key references for the guidelines (Kitwood, 1997).

The problem with all the 'shoulds' is that the clinician can get 'hardening of the oughteries'. The critical superego has a field day with what can seem like a counsel of perfection, fuelled by a belief in the 'even better if' principle ('That was very good but it would have been even better if . . .'). Kalsched's (2013) description of Dis as the tyrannical negative voice/s within the self-care system, as a personification of the psyche's dissociative defences, is apposite. Yet what is the collective trauma that is being defended against? Setting up guidelines is apt to increase the belief in a perfectible world. Theoretically, they reduce risk and create the illusion of safety. It seems that having policy standards protects government by devolving responsibility for quality of care onto clinicians and protects workers from the impact of being surrounded by people like them experiencing trauma, since they have to focus on the bureaucracy as much as the humanity of care delivery.

On a more positive note, they may also protect service users, since they set out the expectations of services. However, these policy documents can become whipping posts for practitioners, as, arguably, without the provision of in-depth support, they can overload their defensive system. Anecdotally, the four healthcare workers I have known, or known of, who committed suicide were all seen as highly diligent and successful in their disciplines, yet felt that they were not good enough, which three of them mentioned in their suicide notes.

What has happened to the qualities that belonged to the older women healers who had often to rely on being alongside people in the absence of sophisticated curative interventions? Is it not time to bring back a focus on the fundamentals of human care, together with a recognition of the inherent vulnerability of being human, whether client or practitioner? That the relational aspect of care is skilled affective and effective work, needing in-depth support, which cannot be replaced by a focus on technique alone, is one that we must continue to champion in psychotherapy.

References

Adams, T., Holman Jones, S. and Ellis, C. (2015) *Autoethnography: Understanding Qualitative Research*. Oxford: Oxford University Press.

Bournemouth (2013) *About Humanising Health and Social Care at BU, Bournemouth University*. Downloadable at https://research.bournemouth.ac.uk/2013/11/about-humanising-health-and-social-care-at-bu/ (accessed 14 September 2015).

Chamberlayne, P., Bornat, J. and Wengraf, T. (eds) (2000) *The Turn towards Biographical Methods in Social Science: Comparative Issues and Examples*. London: Routledge.

Cotter, A. (1990) *Wounded Nurses: Holism and Nurses' Experiences of Being Ill*. PhD Thesis held at London South Bank University.

Cotter, A., Meyer, J. and Roberts, S. (1998) 'Humanity or bureaucracy? The transition from hospital to long-term continuing institutional care.' *Nursing Times Research*, 3(4): 247–56.

Davies, C. (ed.) (1981) *Rewriting Nursing History*. New York: Barnes & Noble.

Denzin, N. K. (2014) *Interpretive Autoethnography. Second edition*. London: Sage.

Department of Health (2001a) *The National Service Framework for Older People*. London: Department of Health.

Department of Health (2001b) *Standards of Acute Nursing Care for Older People in Hospital*. London: Department of Health.

Galvin, K. and Todres, L. (2014) *Caring and Well-being: A Lifeworld Approach*. Routledge Studies in the Sociology of Health and Illness series. London: Routledge.

Kalsched, D. (2013) *Trauma and the Soul: A Psycho-spiritual Approach to Human Development and its Interruption*. London: Routledge.

Kitwood, T. M. (1997) *Dementia Reconsidered: The Person Comes First*. Buckingham: Open University Press.

Laing, R. D. (reprinted 2010) *The Divided Self: An Existential Study in Sanity and Madness*. London: Penguin Classics.

Marks, L. (1994) *Seamless Care or Patchwork Quilt? Discharging Patients from Acute Hospital Care (Research Report)*. London: King's Fund.

Menzies Lyth, I. E. P. (1960) 'A case-study in the functioning of social systems as a defence against anxiety: A report on a study of the nursing service of a general hospital.' *Human Relations*, 13: 95–121. London: Sage Publications.

National Institute for Health and Care Excellence (2006) *Dementia: Supporting People with Dementia and their Carers in Health and Social Care*. CG42. Manchester: NICE. Downloadable at https://www.nice.org.uk/guidance/cg42/chapter/introduction (accessed 14 September 2015). (NB: This Guideline is currently being updated to incorporate new evidence, which is, however, unlikely to change the aspects mentioned here.)

Obholzer, A. and Zagier Roberts, V. (eds) (1994) *The Unconscious at Work: Individual and Organisational Stress in the Human Services*. London: Routledge.

Salvage, J. (1985) *The Politics of Nursing*. London: Heinemann.

Szasz, T. S. (1971) *The Manufacture of Madness*. London: Routledge & Kegan Paul.

Vermeulen, T. and van der Akker R. (2010) 'Notes on metamodernism.' *Journal of Aesthetics and Culture*, 2: 1–14.

6

TAKING CARE OF PSYCHOTIC PATIENTS BY GIVING THEM A JOB

An analyst in a French social institution

François Martin-Vallas

Translated from French by Ann Kutek

It is well known that Jung began his psychiatric practice at the Burghölzli Hospital whose then director was Eugen Bleuler (Jung, 1961, chapter 4). In those days the choice of interventions for psychotic patients was pretty modest. Thus, one of the components of treatment was the rhythm of a very well-ordered existence, one we could today consider stereotypical, where work activity formed an important aspect: the patients were put to work on a farm which produced most of their food.

In terms of each member of society, Jung quickly discerns two dimensions he regards as quintessential. The first is around the importance of rhythm, as an organiser of human relationships. The second is each person's obligation to give back to society some of what she/he has gained from it, by contributing the fruit of their labour. Although, to my knowledge, he never developed these two points as specific issues, I think they are today very specifically part of his thought. He never went along with the Freudian idea prevalent at the time, that rhythmic activity was essentially sexual in character. He explains this line of thought in the metamorphoses (Jung, 1950, para 219). Neither did he ever accept, as far as I know, the idea often prevalent today, not least in our analytic institutions, which holds that anyone who wishes to contribute to society from her/his own work, does so merely out of a thirst for power.

I have personally rediscovered the importance of these two dimensions in social life, through my work in an 'Etablissement et Service d'Aide par le Travail – ESAT', a type of sheltered work scheme. This scheme is part of the French social insurance system for disabled people, giving them the opportunity to be gainfully employed, in a setting that takes account of the limitations they may have as a result of their disability. Some of them live in sheltered housing, some with their families and a number have their own independent accommodation. An important proviso: for those who need or wish for any medical or psychiatric supervision, it is provided to each outside the ESAT set-up; ESAT is a work setting, not a social care setting.

The ESAT where I work[1] numbers 250 adult workers with mental disability; almost 80% have significant deficits as a result of childhood psychosis or have been diagnosed as autistic and could be deemed, in today's parlance, to be suffering from a Pervasive Developmental Disorder. Half of them are not stabilised, and my task, with a psychologist colleague, is to support the social work teams in their efforts to address the problems of their charges as and when they arise. It should be noted that I am only available to the project for not quite a full day a week.

A word about definitions: when I speak of psychosis,[2] I subscribe to the twentieth-century French psychiatric tradition, notably that of Henri Ey *et al.* (1960), who followed in the footsteps of the French and German schools of the late nineteenth and early twentieth centuries, which integrated psychodynamic thinking out of psychoanalysis. Therefore, to speak of psychosis does not mean focusing on a dysfunction or an anomaly to be corrected, rather it is to refer to a form of pervasive psychological functioning, potentially present in each one of us, but which in the case of some people holds such permanent sway that the projections it engenders can utterly obscure the reality of an object.

The workshop set-up

The workers are divided into three workshops: two of 100 employees each and one smaller one. Within each workshop they are split into teams of 15, each group being overseen by a monitor. It is the monitor's job to allocate work, to supervise and to support the workers. Hence each monitor is the first to feel the impact of any psychological problems among the workers, despite the fact that she/he has no specific training in how to deal with psychotic dynamics. Each monitor is a referral point for the workers in his team.

In terms of economics, the project gets a government subsidy to cover the costs associated with the support required by the workers, but their productivity is expected to have a direct bearing on the economic viability of the project, since it pays their salaries. So their work is not just a pretend occupation, but is an actual revenue stream. This is very important for most of them and enables them to feel as fully participating citizens and to regain a sense of self.

One peculiarity of our ESAT is that it has a wide range of provision to ensure that workers stay in work even if/as their mental state deteriorates or to help those who have not yet achieved a level of stability.

There is a legal requirement (France, Service-Public.fr, 2015) that an annual case conference be held about each worker, with the participation of the monitor, the head of the workshop, the social worker, the psychologist, the nurse and the director of medical and social provision. The outcome of the conference is a report that both audits and suggests possible alterations to each individualised professional plan. I participate in conferences for about 100 workers, according to a selection

FIGURE 6.1 One of the ESAT factories

made by the psychologist. Prior to the meeting, the worker is obviously involved in the editing of her/his plan, with their monitor, and is free to attend at the end of the conference. This is the only legally binding provision.

Workers who experience unusual difficulties are able to use one of two sheltered spaces away from the main body of the workshops. There they can be supported in their work by two specialist social workers who have at least some background in psychopathology. These social workers have twice-monthly supervision with the psychologist.

For workers in less acute difficulty, we have a process of Reinforced Support, which involves twice-monthly supervision of the monitor by the psychologist, tracking the worker's progress by the psychologist, and a quarterly audit meeting. It is important to note that the focus of the reinforcement by these provisions is not merely the support offered to the most vulnerable workers but, as a matter of priority, support for the monitors who are directly engaged with the workers.

Containment and self-organisation

Neither Jung nor, for that matter, Freud rely directly on ideas of containment or self-organisation. Nevertheless, they are the premise of a number of their concepts. In the case of Freud, it is his notions of narcissism and protective shield, which are presumed to act directly as containers. Then, less obviously, there is his idea of Oedipal organisation, which can be seen as adumbrating the process of self-organisation.

In Jung's case, things appear to be more straightforward: his notion of the archetypes can be seen as a self-organised dynamic (Knox, 2003; Hogenson, 2004; Martin-Vallas, 2005, 2013a, 2013b). About the notion of containment he hardly ever mentions a container, but in relation to the transference he has no trouble talking about content. As if it were possible to have content without a container. I have already dealt with this issue in my work on the transferential chimera (Martin-Vallas, 2006, 2008, 2014, 2015), so I shall tackle it here from a slightly different angle.

In fact, whereas Freud was enquiring into the existence of the unconscious and how its potential contents might be brought into consciousness, Jung was asking a virtually opposite question. For him the existence of the unconscious was not a question, it was self-evident. But the existence of a conscious, of something upon which existence is predicated, as is the continuity of will, or a certain level of energy in order to power consciousness, these were the fundamental questions for him (Jung, 1928; Martin-Vallas, 2013c). Here we have the source of conceptions that are quite specific to him, such as the idea of ethics as inherent in the 'I–self' relationship, and furthermore, that it is inextricably bound up with his notion of the transcendent function (Solomon, 2000). This is what enabled him to regard the 'I' simultaneously as a complex and therefore boundaried as a psychic object, and as the centre of consciousness, in the sense that it is like a geometrical figure in being purely abstract.

It now becomes clear how for a population of women and men who present with the active consequences of childhood psychosis, the question of maintaining a centre of consciousness and of the 'I' comes into focus. For them, as was the case for Jung and doubtless for many of us, the issue of repressed content comes as secondary to the issue of being: surely, the idea of repressed content can have no meaning if it is not predicated upon a boundary that differentiates the inner from the outer – in other words, upon a container?

It becomes possible, in this train of thought, to consider the institution where I work as a succession of containers which emerge and self-organise with the help of one another. Some of the containers are purely static, such as the internal rules of the institution that determine precisely the limits of what is permissible and what is forbidden. Other containers are by nature dynamic, as for instance the quality of the relationship that each worker develops with her/his peers or with the support staff. This is the area where people's toxic attitudes or past traumas often emerge and replay, but it is likewise the opportunity to resolve some of them, as it is in the transference with the emergence of the transferential chimera (Martin-Vallas, 2015).

The question of meaning

Yet, be they static or dynamic, such containers can only fulfil their role of containing each person's humanity if they make sense explicitly in the case of the support staff and, at the very least, implicitly for the workers. In the absence of meaning, a container can contain behaviour, and to an extent can transform disabled workers into perfect little craftspeople for their employer. Moreover, this transformation can be deceptive! In turn the deception can make some sort of sense even if it is itself illusory! So the question of meaning becomes an ethical issue in a very Jungian sense; that is to say the 'I' has to deal with the reality of the person, with his/her self: the point is not to 'behave properly', but to be real. However, in the case of profoundly mentally scarred workers there is a problem in that their defences, the very mechanism which prevents their disintegration into psychosis, are not defences of the 'I' but rather, as Fordham (1974) had it, they are defences of the self. It is worth recalling that the conundrum of the psychotic patient is not so much how to become who I am, but more how *not* to be who I am, in order to continue being, in the hope of one day becoming who I am.

Psychosis is paradoxical, as Gregory Bateson (et al., 1956) demonstrated with his double bind theory; but long before that, Jung had already noted that the archetype is psychotic. On the one hand an archetype can be viewed as ignoring its objective reality, and on the other, it can be regarded as being permanently in a double bind with its object, arising out of creativity and out of destructiveness, which gives the impression at once of love and of hate and so it appears to be in perpetual paradox. Furthermore, the paradoxical nature of psychosis is contagious, transforming the psychotic patient's environment – an environment which itself becomes paradoxical – into a genuinely toxic pool for the patient and for everyone else overcome by it. It is easy to see how the environment may be accused of being the source of the psychosis, since its behaviour towards the patient is permanently paradoxical, when like the patient himself, it is the victim of psychosis. This type of dynamic has been demonstrated many times in the family environment of psychotic patients and it is also demonstrable in professional settings. This dynamic, with its tendency towards psychosis, is the challenge which my psychologist colleagues and I are called to rise to.

Then again, it is not a question of being prescriptive, nor, if one prefers, trying to cure anything. It is only about detoxifying, attempting to lower the level of paradox inherent in psychotic processes in order to release some meaning out of the relationships among the workers or from how they relate to the support staff, as usually happens spontaneously among human beings who are not overly crazy – the people to whom we refer as normal.

This then is the objective of the case conferences relating to our disabled workers, that are attended by the multidisciplinary team, and that consider the different levels of difficulty encountered by each of the workers concerned. The workers are obviously informed about the conferences, and if they are willing, they may attend at the conclusion of the meeting. These meetings take place at least once every 18 months for workers who present fewer problems, but their frequency can be raised to four or five times a year if the situation demands it. They enable the support staff to express their experience with each worker, so that the psychologist and I can suggest interpretations about the underlying dynamics, not as if instigated by the worker (which would place him more or less in the shoes of the accused), but more in terms of his psychological functioning and his history, as it can emerge in the group psychic apparatus (Kaes, 1976) as well as in the transferential chimera (Martin-Vallas, 2015).

The aim of the interpretations is not to explain, even if frequently they add to understanding, but to help each member of the support staff to detach her/himself from the role they have been assigned by the psychological dynamics of any particular worker. In fact, such introjective effects among the support staff are very common, whether it is about being cast as a good or bad object, as an aggressor or victim, which naturally tends to evoke a defensive attitude from the staff, leading to apotropaic denial, or to actions that could descend into ill treatment of the disabled worker. Since these defensive dynamics manifest themselves permanently, our influence likewise needs to be permanently in operation, so that, *by the grace of God*, chaos does not prevail over meaning, that there is a sufficient gap between chaos and meaning to allow the latter to fulfil its socially containing function for these disabled workers who, otherwise, would be left as a burden on the social exchequer.

FIGURE 6.2 . . .left as a burden on the social exchequer

Photo: François Martin-Vallas

Notes

1 The 'Ateliers Nord Isère' administered by the AFIPAEIM (Association familiale de l'Isère pour enfants et adultes handicapés intellectuels).
2 People who in the English-speaking world could be termed as the long-term mentally ill or mentally fragile.

References

Bateson, G., Jackson, D. D., Haley, J. and Weakland, J. (1956) 'Towards a theory of schizophrenia.' *Behavioral Science*, 1: 251–64.

Ey, H., Bernard, P. and Brisset, C. (1960) *Manuel de psychiatrie*. Paris: Masson.

Fordham, M. (1974) 'Defences of the self.' *Journal of Analytical Psychology*, 19(2): 192–9.

France, Service-Public.fr (2015) *Emploi et handicap: établissements et services d'aide par le travail (Esat)*, 18 February 2013. Available at service-public.fr http://vosdroits.service-public.fr/particuliers/F1654.xhtml (accessed on 13 April 2015).

Hogenson, G. (2004) 'Archetypes: emergence and the psyche's deep structure.' In J. Cambray and L. Carter, *Analytical Psychology Contemporary Perspectives in Jungian Analysis*. New York: Brunner Routledge, pp. 32–55.

Jung, C. G. (1928) 'La structure de l'âme.' *Revue métapsychique*, Paris, 6, 472–90. second edition: *La structure de l'âme*. Paris: L'esprit du temps, 2013.

Jung, C. G. (1950) *Symbols of transformation*. *CW*5.

Jung, C. G. (1961) *Memories, Dreams, Reflections*. New York: Pantheon Books.

Kaes, R. (1976) *L'appareil psychique groupal*. Paris: Dunod.

Knox, J. (2003) *Archetype, Attachment, Analysis: Jungian Psychology and the Emergent Mind*. New York: Brunner Routledge.

Martin-Vallas, F. (2005) 'Towards a theory of the integration of the Other in representation.' *Journal of Analytical Psychology*, 50(3): 285–93.

Martin-Vallas, F. (2006) 'The transferential chimera: a clinical approach.' *Journal of Analytical Psychology*, 51(5): 627–41.

Martin-Vallas, F. (2008) 'The transferential chimera II: some theoretical considerations.' *Journal of Analytical Psychology*, 53(1): 37–59.

Martin-Vallas, F. (2013a) 'Are archetypes transmitted or emergent? A response to Christian Roesler.' *Journal of Analytical Psychology*, 58(1): 277–84.

Martin-Vallas, F. (2013b) 'Quelques remarques à propos de la théorie des archétypes et de son épistémologie.' *Revue de psychologie analytique,* 1: 99–134.

Martin-Vallas, F. (2013c) 'Une préface à 'La structure de l'âme' de C.G. Jung.' *Revue de psychologie analytique*, 1: 163–76.

Martin-Vallas, F. (2014) 'The transferential chimera and neuroscience.' In M. Winborn, *Shared Realities: Participation Mystique and Beyond*. Skiatook: Fisher King Press, pp. 186–219.

Martin-Vallas, F. (2015) La chimère transférentielle. Proposition épistémologique, neuroscientifique et clinico-théorique du transfert psychanalytique comme système complexe. A thesis submitted in fulfilment of the requirements of Lumière Lyon 2 University for the Degree of Doctor of Clinical Psychology. Lyon: Université Lumière Lyon 2. Available at http://chimere.martin-vallas.fr (accessed on 21 December 2015).

Solomon, H. (2000) *Jungian Thought in the Modern World*. London: Free Association Books.

7

INTERVIEWING PEOPLE COMPLAINING ABOUT TORTURE

The interpersonal and inner experience from a Jungian perspective

Tristan Troudart

Documentation of torture

As a volunteer with the Public Committee Against Torture in Israel, together with a group of physicians, psychologists, social workers, Israelis and Palestinians from Israel and the West Bank, I am participating in a project of Documentation of Torture, based on the Istanbul protocol.[1] The victims are mainly Palestinian detainees, called officially 'security detainees', and popularly referred to as 'terrorists', as well as African refugees, called in Hebrew 'infiltrators', a word with an intentionally negative meaning, reminiscent of the incursions of the *feddayun*' fighters, armed Arab groups that crossed the border in the fifties and caused Israeli deaths. Palestinians' complaints of torture are directed towards Israeli security forces, generally in the occupied West Bank, while in the case of African (generally Sudanese or Eritrean) refugees, the perpetrators are generally Bedouins in the Sinai desert or soldiers of the Egyptian Army, with Israel adding a dosage of harsh treatment, with internment in detention camps in the desert and sometimes forced deportation. Most of the people interviewed by us are Palestinians, and they will be the focus of this chapter. On the other hand, Israeli Human Rights NGOs work actively and at times influentially against torture, and promote a humanistic response to the refugees' distress in Israel.

Often, the detainees that we interview complain that they have been severely beaten by soldiers during their detention at home, late at night. Commonly, in Palestinian villages, extended families live together in a housing complex, or close by in neighbouring flats. The beatings are frequently directed towards all the adult men, sometimes in front of the women and children in their family. Then they are transferred often to a jail for high-security prisoners, from where they are taken to be interrogated by the GSS (the General Security Service). In this case the interrogations are prolonged and systematic and can reach levels of severe violence, through tying the detainee to a chair in painful positions for long periods, pushing him, shouting, beating him, sometimes causing temporary or permanent physical damage. Torture can go on for days or weeks, with constant psychological pressure, sleep deprivation, solitary confinement and use of sexual threats and humiliation.

I have brought some of my impressions to bear on this chapter, and tried to understand and formulate the processes I could identify, in terms of Jungian analytical psychology.

It became clear to me that during the torture experience powerful archetypal processes are activated, which affect both the victims and the perpetrators, who sometimes use them with premeditation to influence the victims. In fact, I believe that they are also present in the internal world of the professionals conducting the interviews and the persons being interviewed, and in the relationship that develops between them.

The relationship of torturers and victims transcends the scope of this article. In this project, our source of information originates only in the detained person. Despite their testimonies about the behaviour of the interrogators, an assessment of their motives or their personality would be one sided and biased and would not allow us to really understand the inner world of the perpetrators.

I will focus on some of the interpersonal processes that took place during the interview between us and some Palestinian detainees who complained that they had suffered from torture. To explain some of these processes, the source of information was our group. I asked our group members to tell me briefly what were their main emotional experiences during the interviews, and I selected some of their impressions, choosing those that seemed to be more representative. I also based my account on my own immediate experience of documenting torture complaints, sometimes as the sole interviewer and at other times together with another team member, in both cases with the help of a translator. All those who answered were Israeli Jewish members of the group (who are the majority), to which I also belong. This means that the relationship with the persons being interviewed was, we may assume, more complex and tense than what would have been expected in the case of Palestinian interviewers.

Developing a trustful relationship

Perpetrators often use the skills of the archetype of the Trickster. They might work in teams, playing the good cop and the bad cop, expressing roughly the archetype of Good and Evil, with the conscious goal of psychologically manipulating the detainee, obtaining his trust, and promising relief if he collaborates.

The process of documentation can parallel the interrogation. Being Israelis, we have to make clear to the detainee that we are not interrogators trying to find out what he did or investigating where his relative, who has been accused of armed activities, is hiding, but that we are professionals trying to document his complaints of torture.

We have to make clear what our role is, and to try to develop a trusting relationship as members of a human rights organisation. Although we are considered to be 'good Israelis', we are also part of the society that is oppressing and depriving the person interviewed of his freedom. This can be confusing and be perceived by him as yet another trick by the interrogators. I learned during the interviews that our strongly Hermes-like psychological skills can unwittingly lose their way into the shadowy side of the Trickster archetype, or can become an object of negative projection by the victims, leading them to misinterpret our efforts to diagnose and discover the truth of their complaints. Paradoxically, our guilt can lead us to over-emphasise our efforts and therefore increase the suspiciousness of the victim. However, our experience is generally positive, and the Palestinians express deep gratitude because of our willingness as Israelis to help them to present their complaints.

The Victim Perpetrator archetype

Being a victim is a situation that is deeply rooted in us and evokes strong emotions, especially in two peoples like Israelis and Palestinians, who live under the shadow of collective trauma: the Holocaust *(Shoah)* and the 1948 Palestinian exodus (the *Nakba*). We also live under the collective trauma of continuous violent conflict, and our peoples often shift their roles between being a victim or a perpetrator. Paradoxically, the right to apply force towards those who threaten the security of the nation is frequently justified by the Israeli government as the consequence of a sort of entitlement, based on the experience of victimhood, racial persecution and murder that the Jewish people suffered during the Holocaust.

The detainee tries to develop a closer relationship and to gain our empathy by telling us the story of his suffering. At the same time sometimes he tells us with subtlety that he was not involved in violence against Israelis, even if we, unlike the interrogators, do not generally ask details about what he is accused of doing. This kind of dialogue permits us to develop a positive countertransference and can allow him to trust us and to feel safe.

Another point that sometimes is brought up by the victim is 'I did not break down under torture; I have not become a traitor.' At this point, our feelings can be ambivalent and either cause admiration for his resilience in resisting torture, or on the contrary, they can provoke a negative countertransference; 'I did not fail' could mean, in my fantasy, 'I did not disclose to my torturers plans for violence against you Israelis.'

A member of our group, a psychologist, discovered that somebody whom he interviewed was apparently involved in violent armed attacks against Israelis. Our colleague felt that until then he had perceived his interviewees as passive and innocent victims, and realised that was a distortion of reality, that the interviewee probably was a perpetrator and we could have been his victims. Being on either pole of the archetype, the victim can become subjectively or objectively a perpetrator.

Our team member was confused, realising that he found this person, allegedly responsible for many killings, likeable, and our team member tried to make sense of the discrepancy between his feelings and the severe accusations against the prisoner. It was clear that we could be defending somebody who somehow had participated in a process that targeted people like us. A passionate discussion in our group followed about what to do, about violence, justice and human rights, about what we should know, and if we should know at all about the reason for the person's detention. At the end, we were left with a deep feeling of ambivalence.

This same member felt that it is difficult to remain objective and not identify with the victims of torture. I would add that at the same time he can identify with the victims of violence in the society to which we belong in Israel. In this case, it could be helpful to use the transcendent function that permits us to hold opposite feelings and avoid splitting.

Surprisingly, a detainee told me a dream related to grief, which was emotionally very important to him. This unexpectedly created a therapeutic situation, activated by the detainee, who related to the interview as a healing experience. I felt hampered in my efforts to document his complaints and to examine him as thoroughly as possible.

I could feel how difficult it was to hold the opposites and behave as an interviewer documenting torture objectively, while at the same time keeping an empathic therapeutic approach. This involves also maintaining a certain degree of suspicion towards a person whose credibility could be in doubt, while the documentation should be complete and truthful, so as to be presented in court. The answer to this situation could be again the utilisation of the transcendental function, and the understanding that in this act of balance we could somehow harm the development of trust between the interviewer and the person being examined.

Secondary traumatisation

At the beginning of the training I did not realise how difficult it could be to remain as objective as possible in the documentation process, and somehow cope with the emotionally disturbing narrative to which we are exposed during the interview. In archetypal mythological language, I feel we need all the lucid rational consciousness of Apollo to think clearly, while at the same time when we listen to the stories of torture we immerse ourselves in the dark world of Hades, the god of the Underworld, together with the victim we are interviewing. This can be done only with the mobilisation of the Hermes principle within us, who can guide us in this visit to the darkness, while flexibly keeping in sight the upper world of objective assessment and documentation.

These archetypal forces are essential also to deal with a possible secondary traumatisation as a result of the interview. The emotional burden can be extremely heavy after being exposed to a story of somebody who claims that he underwent severe torture. It is also difficult to witness emotional reactions, for example the grief for the death of a relative or the sadness and anger at the demolition of their common house. Personally, all my long experience in psychiatric interviewing was not enough to help me cope with the unprecedented emotions that built up gradually during long hours of an interview that was full of disturbing details of intentionally inflicted pain, humiliation and fear. For the first time in my life, I found myself having a tearful sensation of choking, and being on the verge of not being able to continue. I was there, in the Underworld with him, sharing his grief and his suffering. After a few minutes, I pulled myself together and could continue. I experienced secondary traumatisation, which may be reflected in a written report coloured with extra depth. An intimate environment with a safe Temenos is essential for creating a dignified and respectful space. This is almost impossible in military prisons, where these requirements are utopian, as a result of limitations on privacy by the placement of a guard near the room, or shackling imposed by the authorities. On the other hand, intimacy and secrecy can be quite real in the conditions of a planned interview after the victim has been freed. At this stage it can be carefully planned and the space can be designed accurately.

Interviews in teams can also be of great help, by providing mutual counselling and most of all mutual emotional support.

Confronting the Israeli collective

Another colleague, a physician, was concerned with her encounter with the side of the Israeli society that expresses hostility and suspicion towards our work, because people do not want to admit to themselves that they support torture – they have to say that 'she' or 'the Committee against Torture' supports terrorists. In this case we have to cope with collective projections that demonise not only the Palestinians, but also Israeli human rights organisations, attitudes that are supported by the present government. In the context of the confrontation between the Israelis and the Palestinians, and from the perspective of the 'war against terror', the argument of the 'ticking bomb', that legally allows forms of torture to be applied in order to prevent immediate danger, is widely used by the security services. The application of harsh measures, even torture, is seen by the Israeli collective as a necessary measure to protect itself from Palestinian violence, and part of a warlike situation. In a community that lives in a mixture of archetypal demonic projections against 'the enemy', and real danger of politically motivated violence, those of us who are Israeli Jewish human rights activists are seen in the best case as a proof of the democracy of Israeli society, and in the worst case as traitors and fifth columnists or self-hating Jews supporting the Palestinians. However, there are beams of light, and as an example, the Israel Medical Association instructed its members not to comply with the law that allows forced feeding of Palestinian hunger strikers who protest against administrative detentions, seeing it as a form of torture.

The Wounded Healer

One of our colleagues, a psychologist, was himself a prisoner of war during the October War in 1973 and his fellow prisoners cannot understand how he could overcome his anger and feel solidarity with enemies accused of terrorism against Israelis. In fact, his way of coping with trauma was to become a therapist and a human rights activist.

This last example can show us that the archetype of the Wounded Healer is very present in our soul. In this case it means that the main energy of healing comes from an internal psychological wound. This wound is also collective, motivated in the case of the Jews by the Holocaust, and possibly by guilt for the *Nakba* inflicted on the Palestinians. The situation of the interview, which requires a cognitive process of objective documentation, can lead us to take up an emotional distance from the interviewee, and become the 'paternalistic doctor' who strengthens feelings of impotence and passivity. Only if we connect ourselves with our internal wound and adopt, at least partially, a therapeutic position, can we avoid this destructive development and potentiate the internal healing energies of the persons being interviewed, in parallel to people in therapy.

The lesson I learned is that while we try to objectively document torture, we are willingly or not participating in a therapeutic process.

In this region we are all wounded individually and collectively. Some of us become healers, therapists, human rights activists. In the sense of depth psychology, the potentiation of the Wounded Healer in us is probably the main tool that can help us build a bond with the Other who is bleeding together with us in this land.

Epilogue

A friend in Jerusalem, who is a psychodynamic, non-Jungian psychotherapist, asked me if there is an archetype of Hope. I told him that as a result of Pandora emptying the contents of her jar, Hesiod tells us, 'earth is full of evils and the sea is full' (Hesiod, 1914, p. 9). One item, however, did not escape the jar. It was Hope *(Elpis)*.

'Only Hope was left within her unbreakable house, she remained under the lip of the jar, and did not fly away' (ibid.).

Note

1 Istanbul protocol: Manual on Effective Investigation and Documentation of Torture and Other Cruel, Inhuman or Degrading Treatment or Punishment (a set of international guidelines for documentation of torture and its consequences, adopted by the General Assembly and the Commission on Human Rights in the year 2000). United Nations, New York and Geneva, 2004.

Reference

Hesiod (1914) 'Works and days.' In *Hesiod, the Homeric Hymns and Homerica*, translated by H. G. Evelyn-White, Cambridge, MA: Loeb Classical Library.

SECTION 3

Politics and modernity

8

THE PSYCHOPOLITICS OF LIBERATION

The struggle of native people against oppression in Guatemala and Canada

Lawrence Alschuler

Forty years ago Paulo Freire, a Brazilian educator, gave us insights into the psychology of the oppressed. Twenty years ago I translated Freire's insights into the language of analytical psychology (Alschuler, 1992 pp. 14–15). Ten years ago Thomas Singer and Samuel Kimbles introduced the concept of cultural complexes that deepens our understanding of social groups in conflict. Seven years ago I put all of this together in my book, *The Psychopolitics of Liberation: Political Consciousness from a Jungian Perspective* (2007). In this chapter I will present the highlights of my book.

During my 34 years as Professor of Political Science, I specialised in the study of political change in Latin America. After an interruption of my career for four years of study at the C.G. Jung Institute in Zurich, I was struck by the idea that analytical psychology might contribute to an understanding of political change. A major question persisted: *why do the oppressed so seldom revolt against their oppressors?* I was not satisfied by the usual answers, including the ineffectiveness of their leadership, the lack of appealing ideologies of change, and military repression. I answer this in my book in terms of the stages of political consciousness, viewed from a Jungian perspective.

The structure of oppressed consciousness

Freire's insights translated smoothly into a language of complexes once I found the relevance of John Perry's formulation. According to Perry, complexes always appear in pairs, one of which is ego aligned and the other ego projected (Perry, 1970 p. 9). Think of the persona and the shadow in this sense as paired. Perry gives the example of a young man who has a problem with men in authority. The young man's ego is aligned with a rebellious son complex while his unconscious authoritarian father complex is projected onto any man who exercises domination over him. Whenever the father complex is constellated, the young man over-reacts in some form of rebellion. This is what Perry calls *split bi-polarity*, in other words, one-sidedness. When the young man assimilates certain aspects of adult male authority, he ceases to project this image and moves towards wholeness.

From a careful reading of Freire on the psychological nature of oppression, I realised that Perry's ideas would enhance our understanding of the *depth psychological basis of oppressed consciousness*. I condensed the many attributes of the oppressed, found in Freire's writings, in terms of a pair of complexes that I labelled 'paternalism' and 'dependence'. The oppressed readily identify with their own dependence (inadequacy, childishness, ignorance, weakness, inferiority), thus making them inauthentic persons, not their true selves. To be authentic would mean that their egos were relatively free of the 'illusory' images with which they identify. Instead, they suffer from split bi-polarity. They view their oppressors as having positive qualities that I call 'paternalism'. They believe that they need the oppressors, need to follow their dictates, need even to become more like them. In terms of complex theory, the oppressed have dependence as an ego-aligned complex and repress their positive qualities (self-reliance, power, maturity, knowledge, superiority) that they encounter as paternalism projected onto the oppressors. This summarises the structure of oppressed consciousness.

Freire is eloquent in describing the *dilemma of the oppressors*, who also are not truly themselves, suffering from split bi-polarity. Their egos live under a 'veil of illusion', attributing to themselves certain 'mythical' images that do *not* belong to them: being superiors, protectors and civilisers. They have the same complexes as the oppressed, only here the oppressors' ego aligns with paternalism while they project dependence onto the oppressed. They project their own repressed childlike traits onto the oppressed, whom they view as immature, needing the protection and guidance of the oppressors. The split bi-polarity of the oppressors and the oppressed complement and reinforce each other. As a consequence, their interaction creates a vicious circle that sustains oppressed consciousness. The first answer to the question of why the oppressed so seldom rebel against the oppressors is that they feel inferior and dependent. I will return to this question in greater detail in the context of the stages of political consciousness.

The origin of oppressed consciousness

We can move easily from a description of typical oppressed and oppressor consciousness to a societal perspective where their two subcultures continue to be in conflict. Thomas Singer tells us that a historical trauma is often at the origin of a *cultural complex* that is experienced by an entire society (Singer, 2004, pp. 19, 32). This supports my view on the historical nature of oppressed and oppressor consciousness. I believe that the cultural complex of the Native people of the Americas originates in the *trauma of colonial conquest* by Europeans. The Post-Traumatic Stress Syndrome has been perpetuated over the centuries of colonisation and independence by subjecting Native people to *oppression*, understood as military repression, economic exploitation, ethnic discrimination and the denial of human rights.

The trauma of colonial conquest created a *collective psychic wound*, dissociation in the form of split bi-polarity that characterises oppressed consciousness. Two distinct subcultures formed, that of the oppressors and the oppressed. The attitudes each subculture has towards itself and towards the other express the cultural complexes (Singer and Kimbles, 2004, pp. 6–7). We are compelled to ask, then, how these cultural complexes might be resolved. The stages of political consciousness offer some answers.

Stages of political consciousness

Perry tells us that when a person overcomes split bi-polarity the personality moves towards wholeness. For subcultures, when large numbers of oppressors and oppressed overcome their split bi-polarity, they may be able to transform an oppressive society into a democratic one. How that transformation takes place is the subject of Paulo Freire's *Pedagogy of the Oppressed* (1972).

To understand the *subjective* conditions of oppression, I have reformulated Freire's ideas on the stages of political consciousness in terms of Perry's model. At each successive stage the oppressed react in distinctly different ways to the *objective* conditions of oppression: exploitation, repression, denial of human rights, and discrimination.

First stage: naive consciousness

The oppressed identify with the dependence complex; they are one sided. Since their ego-aligned complex largely contains 'inferior' traits such as laziness, childishness, dependence and weakness, they are most likely to find fault in themselves for not living up to the expectations of the oppressors. As a consequence, they want to become someone other than this 'inferior' being. Since they deplore being 'inferior' and since they admire the oppressors, they strive for *assimilation* to the supposedly 'superior' subculture of the oppressors. Admiration and imitation go together: the oppressed want to be like the oppressors. For many, this entails migration from the countryside to the city, adopting the language of the oppressors, their religion and their customs.

Those oppressed who reject assimilation may nonetheless address certain injustices as imperfections in an otherwise 'good' society. For example, a landowner neglects a plantation worker's need for medical care, despite the tradition of providing this. Something novel may occur when the newly assimilated oppressed encounter discrimination in the workplace, in schools or in law courts that are administered by oppressors. When the promise of assimilation has not been kept, naive consciousness may develop into fanaticised consciousness. The predominance of oppressed persons at the naive stage is an answer to the initial question about why the oppressed so seldom rebel against their oppressors.

Second stage: fanaticised consciousness

The oppressed now reverse their identification within the bi-polar pair of complexes, but remain one sided in a new way. This reversal may occur suddenly when moral outrage is their response to humiliation at the hands of oppressors. The ego of the oppressed now aligns with paternalism; they encounter inferiority and dependence in projection onto the oppressors. Believing that they are superior, they experience *psychic inflation*. The oppressed rebel and try to dominate the oppressors. If they succeed, the system of oppression will remain unchanged, only the oppressors and oppressed will have traded places.

This stage involves a fanatical one-sided identification with the subculture of the oppressed. When the oppressed praise their own ethnicity in exaggerated terms as superior to that of the oppressors, it is natural that the oppressed will try to impose their own subculture on the 'other'. Furthermore, the fanatical nature of this identification can be understood as a result of the *repression of any doubt* concerning their own superiority (Alschuler, 2009). The inner voice expressing that doubt is repressed because it is inconsistent with their new self-image as superior. The unconscious doubts are projected along with other complexes onto those who express opposition to the oppressed. The oppressors and their 'voices', heard or imagined, must be silenced or convinced of their error. To be silenced may require violent *rebellion* against the oppressors. Those oppressors who are convinced or silenced serve to confirm the supposed superiority of the oppressed, resulting in even greater one-sidedness.

Third stage: liberated consciousness

I consider liberated consciousness to be the stage in which the oppressed succeed in overcoming one-sidedness by *holding a tension of opposites*, where the opposites are the images of the two ethnic groups (subcultures) in conflict. By integrating the split bi-polar pair of complexes, they reduce their identification with dependence (or paternalism in the fanaticised stage) and also withdraw many of their projections onto the oppressors. Instead of perceiving them through a 'veil of illusion', the bi-polar pair of complexes, the oppressed perceive themselves and their oppressors as they truly are (Perry, 1970, pp. 4, 6). They recognise both the strengths and weaknesses in themselves and in the oppressors. They even perceive the humanity in their oppressors. Rather than attempting to dominate the oppressors, they seek the *transformation, with or without violence, of an oppressive society* into one where both former oppressors and former oppressed can resolve conflicts through negotiation. This would not be a utopian society free of conflict, rather one in which injustices are addressed through legitimate institutions of governance.

The development of political consciousness of the oppressed: the experience of present-day Native people

My concern for the plight of Native people led me to examine their oppression in the present day. I gained access to their experience through the *published testimonies* that Native persons made to anthropologists. A Kwakiutl man, James Sewid (Spradley, 1972), and a Coastal Salish woman, Lee Maracle (Maracle, 1990), from British Columbia, Canada provided two testimonies. In Guatemala, a Quiché Mayan man, Atanasio (Vigor, 1993), and woman, Rigoberta Menchù (Burgos-Debray, 1984), completed the set of four autobiographies on which I would test my ideas about the conditions for the development of political consciousness.

When I speak of oppression I am referring to unjust relationships between people in a society: the denial of human rights, state repression, economic exploitation and ethnic discrimination. In Guatemala, at the time of my case life histories, a 30-year civil war was still in progress (until the late 1980s). *Genocide by military repression* decimated over 200,000 Native people. Discrimination in the justice system served to deprive Native people of their land and subsistence. Working for low wages on plantations was to be a remedy; however, at desperation wages and under the harshest working conditions.

In Canada, in contrast, oppression took the form of *cultural genocide* through forced assimilation. Over the centuries since the colonial conquest, when Native people ceased to serve as allies of the French or English settlers, strenuous efforts by the Canadian state aimed to assimilate Native people. Forced resettlement of Native children in residential schools broke up families and destroyed their ties to indigenous culture. Ethnic discrimination in urban areas violated their human rights, while the appropriation of Native land reinforced their impoverishment.

In these two national contexts of oppression, what would explain the passivity of some Native people and the active resistance of others? My answer lies in their lesser or greater political consciousness. The crucial question then becomes: what might be the conditions promoting or hindering the development of political consciousness as I define the term? My research revealed two key conditions: *ego strength*, achieved through the successful resolution of a maturation crisis, and *rootedness in the ancestral soul*, a concept borrowed from Roberto Gambini (1997, pp. 70–1). Rootedness is the opposite of assimilation and refers to a vital connection with one's Native traditions, language, spirituality, songs, history, healing practices, legends and relationship to the land. This is equivalent to a connected ego–Self axis as described by Erich Neumann (1966, p. 85) and Edward Edinger (1973, pp. 48–52, 69, 97).

What did I find in my four cases of Native persons? First, they all achieved liberated consciousness. This is a remarkable accomplishment, considering that none benefited from completed secondary education. Furthermore, they all passed through the prior stages of political consciousness. When they had neither ego strength nor rootedness in the ancestral soul, they remained in the *naive* stage and usually sought *assimilation* to the oppressors' subculture. It is perhaps natural that the oppression they suffered at the hands of the oppressors would seem 'justified' by the oppressed's supposed inferiority. This corresponds to the notion of blaming the victim. Since they may lack pride in their Native culture or even remain ignorant of it, belonging to the dominant subculture would be an appealing alternative. Without ego strength the oppressed would be vulnerable to the ideology of oppressors expressed through schools, mass media, certain churches and government propaganda.

Native persons who become rooted in the ancestral soul but still lack ego strength enter the stage of *fanaticised* consciousness and begin to *rebel* against the oppressors. Unless counterbalanced by ego strength, knowledge of the Native culture in its full manifestations (language, history, customs, legends) leads to psychic inflation in the form of ethnocentrism. Being overwhelmed by ethnic pride results in a fanatical state of mind according to which the oppressors are all judged as unworthy to govern, to lead the economy or to determine cultural standards. The evaluations of the social roles are reversed: what was deemed inferior (the Native) becomes superior; what was deemed superior (the dominant class) becomes inferior. A natural consequence of fanaticised consciousness is open resistance to the oppressors.

When their ego was sufficiently strong to counterbalance their rootedness, the Native persons in my study overcame their fanatical one-sidedness and attained *liberated* consciousness. The Natives' rootedness in the ancestral soul, understood in Jungian terms as a connected ego–Self axis, empowered them to promote their own culture in the face of the oppressors' cultural arrogance and denigration of the Native culture. A strong ego enabled Native persons to resist being overwhelmed by their cultural pride (psychic inflation) and to being fanatical in the pursuit of their own aims.

Conclusion: from analysis to activism

In this chapter I have presented the highlights of my book, *The Psychopolitics of Liberation.* I began with the engaging question: why do the oppressed so seldom revolt against their oppressors? I formulated answers in terms of their political consciousness. Before doing my study I wondered whether analytical psychology could contribute to our understanding of one of the most important social issues of our time, human oppression. I can now say, *yes, it can!*

My psychopolitical *analysis* has revealed the kinds of *activism* typical at each stage of political consciousness. At the naive stage the oppressed sustain oppression especially through assimilation. At the fanaticised stage the oppressed attempt to take the place of the oppressors without altering the oppressive system. Those at the stage of liberated consciousness seek to transform their oppressive society through the establishment of universal political rights and civil liberties. My book ends with proposals for *activism* of the general public in the Americas. The public can avoid colluding with discrimination against Native people and support politicians who pursue public policies that would promote the development of liberated consciousness of Native people. Examples of the latter, in harmony with my analysis, are the protection of Native land rights and the promotion of Native languages and customs in Native schools.

References

Alschuler, L. (1992) 'Oppression and liberation: A psycho-political analysis according to Freire and Jung.' *Journal of Humanistic Psychology*, 32(2): 8–31.

Alschuler, L. (2007) *The Psychopolitics of Liberation: Political Consciousness from a Jungian Perspective.* New York: Palgrave Macmillan.

Alschuler, L. (2009) 'Fanaticism: A psychopolitical analysis.' *Spring: A Journal of Archetype and Culture*, 81: 59–83.

Burgos-Debray, E. (ed.) (1984) *I, Rigoberta Menchú: An Indian Woman in Guatemala.* London: Verso.

Edinger, E. (1973) *Ego and Archetype: Individuation and the Religious Function of the Psyche.* New York: Penguin.

Freire, P. (1972) *Pedagogy of the Oppressed.* New York: Herder and Herder.

Gambini, R. (1997) 'The soul of underdevelopment: The case of Brazil.' In *Zurich 95: Open Questions in Analytical Psychology*, edited by M. A. Matoon. Einseideln: Daimon Verlag, pp. 139–48.

Maracle, L. (1990) *Bobbi Lee, Indian Rebel.* Toronto: Women's Press.

Neumann, E. (1966) 'Narcissism, normal self-formation, and the primary relation to the mother.' *Spring*, 81–106.

Perry, J. W. (1970) 'Emotions and Object Relations.' *Journal of Analytical Psychology*, 15(1): 1–12.

Singer, T. (2004) 'The cultural complex and archetypal defences of the group spirit; Baby Zeus, Elian Gonzalez, Constantine's Sword, and other holy wars (with special attention to the "Axis of Evil").' In *The Cultural Complex: Contemporary Jungian Perspectives on Psyche and Society*, edited by T. Singer and S. Kimbles. New York: Brunner Routledge, pp. 13–34.

Singer, T. and Kimbles, S. (2004) 'Introduction.' In *The Cultural Complex: Contemporary Jungian Perspectives on Psyche and Society*, edited by T. Singer and S. Kimbles. New York: Brunner Routledge, pp. 1–9.

Spradley, J. P. (1972) *Guests Never Leave Hungry: The Autobiography of James Sewid, A Kwakiutl Indian.* Montreal and Kingston: McGill-Queen's University Press.

Vigor, C. (ed. and trans.) (1993) *Atanasio: Parole d'Indien du Guatemala.* Paris: L'Harmattan.

9

PIECING THE STORY TOGETHER

The political and psychological aspects of oral history interviewing the Chinese/Vietnamese diaspora

Kevin Lu

Introduction

Oral history, a method of research that '[records] the speech of people' and 'then [analyses] their memories of the past' (Abrams, 2010, p. 1), has its roots in understanding the social and cultural experiences of individuals in times of political strife (Perks and Thomson, 2006). This approach to the past, according to Thompson (1978), gives voice to those who have none amidst more traditional, source-based histories that can myopically forward economically elitist narratives. It is not to say that oral history cannot be used to supplement top-down approaches, but it has largely been a method promoting empowerment – a history for the people by the people. Accordingly, it is a highly politicised form of history.

Not only can oral history provide a more complete picture of the past by documenting the lives of people from different walks of life, it simultaneously records the emotions invested in pivotal moments, both individual and collective. It is in this association to the realm of feeling and psyche, as well as the self-reflection stimulated by the interviews, that we find a connection to depth psychology: it provides a framework within which we may comprehend the nature of these feelings and emotions.

In this chapter, I explore how the use of this technique captures the complex ways in which individuals construct their identity, particularly members of the Chinese/Vietnamese diaspora in London, who have experienced both political and cultural upheaval. Depth psychological ideas, especially Jungian ones, have helped me to understand a) the nature of the relationship between interviewer and interviewee and b) the psychological dynamics at play in the identity formation of participants who have matured in a climate of political unrest (experienced at the level of society, family and the individual) and who are faced with the (alarming) prospect of cultural fluidity and multiplicity. I argue, via a critical assessment of interviews conducted with a sibling pair, that a Jungian way of working provides insights to oral historians that enrich their work which is, at core, politically charged.

Methodological and ethical issues

I had reservations about interviewing siblings. Choosing siblings means that the data collected is not a random sampling of a given population. It further increases the loss of anonymity, which leads to an ethical issue. Although both R. (the elder sister) and J. (the younger brother) signed consent forms, this did not prevent the occurrence of ethically challenging situations. For example, R. was interviewed first and J. second, on a separate day. At the end of our conversation J. asked how long his sister's interview lasted. The length of the interview became for him a standard by which the 'better' interviewee could be established, a point to which I will return below.

I decided to proceed with the interviews for several reasons. First, there has been a growing realisation within sociology, social psychology and the academic study of social policy that more work needs to be done on horizontal family relationships to balance what has been a concentration on vertical ones (Edwards et al., 2006; Mauthner, 2002; Ryan-Flood, 2015; Sanders, 2004). Second, there is an existing literature on siblings from psychoanalytic and psychosocial perspectives (Abend, 1984; Coles, 2003, 2006; Lucey, 2011; Mitchell, 2003). Third, Jung did not shy away from studying families, including siblings. He applied the association test to 24 families, which consisted of 100 participants who produced 22,000 associations (1909/1973).[1] Finally, the researcher needs to be realistic about what the data provides and how he/she treats it. The interviews from which I draw are neither an indicative nor a representative sample of the Chinese/Vietnamese diaspora community in London. This does not mean, however, that single cases cannot be a source of insight (Hinshelwood, 2013). So long as one is realistic about what can be done with the data, the potential pitfalls are manageable.

Interview with R.

R., who is 23 years of age, was born and raised in Croydon and has completed a university degree. She displayed a complex understanding of her identity, one situated between opposites and evidencing the potential flexibility of her loyalties:

> I feel like I get the best of both worlds. At home, I get the Chinese . . . I even went to Chinese school, so I had that side of me, and then when I went back to normal school, I was the English R., so I had two sides.
>
> (Interview with R. 16/9/14)

R. establishes that there are two sides to her identity, embracing both her Chinese ethnicity and the influence of British culture. She describes how her brother struggled at Chinese school and how she helped him get by. In some instances, she completed his homework so that punishment was avoided. Her brother dropped out of Chinese school after one year. R. persisted and eventually achieved an A-level credit for Chinese. This accomplishment supports the belief (held by J.) that R. (more so than him) embraces her background. Such a judgement is buttressed by R.'s hobbies and interests, which are deemed typically Chinese, like watching Chinese serial dramas. Her sibling's indifference to Chinese entertainment explains, for R., his lack of interest in Chinese culture and his lower level of fluency.

For R., the ability to speak Chinese fluently becomes the barometer by which one's cultural competency is measured. She provides a sociologically nuanced account of why this might be. Her brother has befriended a diverse group of friends from different ethnicities, which explains why he is not as 'Chinese'. Yet a moment of tension arises when, upon reflection, she realises that the same could be said of her. It is only since entering university that the number of her Chinese friends has increased. This, she reasons, elucidates the 'two sides' within herself, although she understands why she is perceived as being more Chinese. Yet she is adamant that her 'Britishness' is what defines her:

> Just because I can speak Chinese and my friends are Chinese, doesn't mean I'm not influenced by British culture. Simple things like the music I listen to, the way I speak, it's British . . . Do you ever ask yourself, what language you hear in your mind? . . . My first language and everything I think in my head is English. So, I would say I'm more British.
>
> (Ibid.)

I now turn to J.'s interview before assessing the ways in which depth psychological ideas inform my understanding of these narratives and the nature of this sibling relationship.

Interview with J.

J. is 21 and has completed a university degree. What surprised me about this interview was the consistent emphasis placed on family and friends, especially the former. His social network comprises a variety of racial backgrounds, but he has very few Caucasian and Chinese friends. J.'s minimal interaction with other Chinese, however, does not curtail how close he feels to his heritage. The key to this sense of connection is the notion of family, as opposed to R.'s emphasis on language. Perhaps it is because J. is aware that his sister's fluency is stronger that he chooses to focus on a core value rather than a tangible illustration of ability (i.e. mastery of a language). Regardless, J. asserts the centrality of family; it is fundamental to, and the essence of, being Chinese:

> I've always got along with my mum and dad. My dad's always been at work, so he hasn't really looked after us. But he's been there . . . My mum . . . was like study, do this, do that, but she's always been there to help us as well . . . I don't argue with her . . . I . . . try to make her happy . . . At the end of the day you just can't hold a grudge.
>
> (Interview with J. 2/10/14)

J. then reflects on how his relationship to his parents is different from those of his friends. While others may treat their parents as 'mates', J. could never accept this type of interaction. His emphasis on the uniqueness and peculiarity of being Chinese is maintained throughout the interview:

> I wouldn't say I'm Vietnamese. I would say I'm Chinese. But if they asked me where I was born, I would say I was born here [in the UK]. I grew up here, but I'm Chinese. I'll never say I'm Vietnamese even though my parents are born in Vietnam. I never speak Vietnamese; all we do is eat Vietnamese food. But our culture is Chinese, isn't it?
>
> (Ibid.)[2]

Those who would base their understanding of J.'s connection to his culture on linguistic aptitude alone are mistaken:

> I don't look English, do I? Even though I'm British, I'm Chinese. I'm proud . . . When my mum used to call me on a bus packed with people, I wouldn't speak Chinese, I'd just speak English to my mum. When you're a little kid growing up, maybe you're a little bit embarrassed. But now I'm proud . . . I'd speak Chinese on purpose now.
>
> (Ibid.)

His resolve to speak the language, even though he is less confident than his sister, is a marker of his commitment to being Chinese. He is quick to add that his inability to speak fluently does not diminish his devotion to his ethnicity: 'No, I think if I spoke better Chinese, I'll just be speaking differently . . . But I'll be the same person' (ibid.).

A sibling transference

What fascinated me about both interviews was the constant reference to siblings when each reflects on their respective identities. It seems that one's sibling is crucial in the formation and articulation of one's identity. This might be a consequence of interviewing siblings, where interviewees know that one's brother/sister would also be questioned. There is a possibility that their responses anticipate what the other *might* say. These fantasies of the other sibling are related to what Coles (2003) terms a *sibling transference*, although I use the term slightly differently here. While she refers to a sibling transference between the analyst and analysand, I am specifying what is being projected onto one's sibling.

An initial observation is that the 'other' of one's hybrid identity – a *shadow* specific to this diaspora group – has been split off and projected onto the other sibling. Stated another way, a projection of alterity or shadow has taken place, based on a fantasy of the other sibling's perceived identity. The projection 'sticks' because the sibling's respective actions provide suitable hooks onto which those projections may be attached. So, J. is perceived to be more British because of his disregard for Chinese school and his racially diverse social network. Based on these experiences, R. forms a particular image of her brother's connection to their heritage.

R. is perceived as closer to her culture because she possesses excellent language skills and enjoys Chinese dramas. Based on this, J. perceives her strong connection to their ancestry as a defining characteristic of her identity. Yet in fantasising that the sibling manifests the 'other' of one's hybrid identity, one is blinded by shadow, which denies the possibility of seeing the other sibling's identity for all its complexities. An understanding of one's sibling becomes simplified: R. *is* Chinese and J. *is* British. In actuality, the opposite is the case.[3]

I propose that we take seriously the prospect of being blinded by shadow – a blindness that may lead to over-simplification – and apply it to how we analyse these interviews from the lens of depth psychology. By appreciating the multiplicity of possible interpretations, we avoid doing violence to the phenomenon under scrutiny; it becomes one way of being ethical.

The elephant/Canuck in the room

Are the participant responses informed by an image of their sibling as 'other' or are they responding to me – the interviewer – as 'other'? I may be like them, a product of the same diaspora, but I am Canadian, not British.[4] Could R.'s response – that she is British – be a reaction to the differences in identity I represent, and not necessarily what her brother personifies for her? Upon reflection, I gave her opportunities to ascertain this. When discussing her education, I sought the Canadian equivalent to GSCEs and A-levels, so as to establish in my own mind her developmental trajectory.

J., alternatively, stressed his identity with me as members of the same diaspora. As cited above, he referred at one point to '*our* culture' (Interview with J., 2/10/14, emphasis added). When he said 'our', he was not simply referring to his sister, family or even British-born Chinese (BBC). He was indicating *us*, building a rapport with me by emphasising ethnic similarity rather than the difference betrayed by my accent.[5]

Unconscious competition

I noted J.'s interest in how 'well' his sister did at her interview. There was evidence that sibling rivalry existed, although not in a destructive form. Friendly rivalries, for instance, endure in sports and propel protagonists to achieve their best. Yet J.'s inquisitiveness did compel me to consider the extent to which their respective responses may be expressions of unconscious competition (Adler, 1927/2010). R.'s insistence that she is British may be a defiant response to what she perceives as her brother's belief that she is Chinese. J.'s reply may be his answer to the pedestal on which he and his family have placed his sister (as the ideal of what it means to be Chinese), i.e. she may speak better Chinese, but that does not make him any less Chinese. Each sibling is perhaps attempting to outduel the other and who is triumphant is decided by the interviewer, hence J.'s curiosity about R.'s interview. Based on my impression of their relationship specifically and the family rapport more generally, I suggest that in this case, an explanation based on 'unconscious competition' to understand the psychological dynamics of identity formation at play in this sibling pair does not do justice to the genuine feeling expressed by both throughout the interviews.

A sibling connection

R. and J. share a relatively close and loving relationship, but maintain a respectful distance where their personal affairs are concerned (perhaps reflecting J.'s description of a 'Chinese' way of relating). The strength of their bond, I propose, was partly forged through a consistent paternal absence during their formative years. It is not the case that love was withheld, but because both parents were working tirelessly to run a takeaway, the children were left to fend for themselves and care for each other.[6] The formulation of their respective identities in the interviews – vis-à-vis the other sibling – may be read as an attempt to identify with, and reiterate the bond between, siblings; in essence, a sibling *coniunctio*. Where J. is adamant that he is Chinese, the following message may be implicit: 'If you, my sister, are Chinese, then I will become closer to what I perceive you to be.' Similarly, R.'s insistence that she is British may be an attempt to communicate the following to her brother: 'If you, as I perceive you to be, are British, then I will try to be more British too, as we are in this together.' One issue that arises, if this interpretation is appropriate, is that the attempt at identification is built on a fantasy of the other sibling, namely, the shadow projection held by the brother or sister. The need to recognise shadow brings us back to one of the aims of this chapter and will serve as a springboard to my concluding point.

In therapy, some work might be dedicated to the withdrawal of these projections or sibling transferences. An oral history interview, although similar to what a moment in analysis may resemble, is ultimately not analysis (Figlio, 1988; Roper, 2003). Depth psychology certainly provides tools that enrich our interpretation of interview material and frame our self-reflexivity as researchers. It cannot, however, serve as the sole lens utilised by oral historians. Despite these differences and difficulties, an emerging middle ground bridging the two disciplines may be the mutual concern for the political: the intrinsically political agenda of oral history and our deepening awareness of the political potential and impact of analytical psychology.

Notes

1 To my knowledge, Brodersen (2012) and Abramovitch (2014) are the only post-Jungians currently researching the topic of siblings.
2 On the animosity between the Chinese and Vietnamese, see Lawrence (2008).
3 Similarly, when faced with the numerous ways in which their respective identities could be discerned, both ultimately made clear-cut choices. The retreat into a definitive response is intriguing, but beyond the scope of this chapter.
4 Different diaspora experiences mean different narratives that have been transmitted down the family line. There are similarities, but they are not the same. See Chan (2011).
5 The dynamic experienced can also be understood from the perspective of gender roles and relations of power (Foucault, 1978/1990).
6 This sibling relationship can be understood as a *simulacrum* and repetition of the parental one. I have noticed that many of the first generation in this community were, or still are, involved in running takeaways or restaurants. An archetypal theme may be emerging amongst the second generation, mainly, that of parental absence. This has led to strong relationships – both positive and negative – being cultivated between siblings. This familial configuration may be a distinguishing feature of the Chinese/Vietnamese diaspora in London, which in turn shapes the psychological dynamics underpinning relationships between first, second and even third generations.

References

Abend, S. (1984) 'Sibling love and object choice.' *Psychoanalytic Quarterly*, 53: 425–30.
Abramovitch, H. (2014) *Brothers and Sisters*. College Station: Texas A&M University Press.
Abrams, L. (2010) *Oral History Theory*. London: Routledge.
Adler, A. (1927/2010) *Understanding Human Nature*. Mansfield Centre, CT: Martino Publishing.
Brodersen, E. (2012). 'In the nature of twins.' *International Journal of Jungian Studies*, 4(2): 133–49.
Chan, Yuk Wah (2011) *The Chinese/Vietnamese Diaspora*. London: Routledge.
Coles, P. (2003) *The Importance of Sibling Relationships in Psychoanalysis*. London: Karnac.
Coles, P. (ed.) (2006) *Sibling Relationships*. London: Karnac Books.
Edwards, R. et al. (eds) (2006) *Sibling Identity and Relationships*. London: Routledge.
Figlio, K. (1988) 'Oral history and the unconscious.' *History Workshop Journal*, 26(1): 120–32.
Foucault, M. (1978/1990) *The History of Sexuality, Volume 1*. New York: Vintage Books.
Hinshelwood, R. (2013) *Research on the Couch*. London: Routledge.
Jung, C. G. (1909/1973) 'The family constellation.' In H. Read et al. (eds), *The Collected Works of C. G. Jung, volume 2: Experimental Researches*. London: Routledge & Kegan Paul, pp. 466–79.
Lawrence, M. (2008) *The Vietnam War*. Oxford: Oxford University Press.
Lucey, H. (2011) 'Sibling ghosts in the machine.' *Journal of Psycho-Social Studies*, 5(2): 217–28.
Mauthner, M. (2002) *Sistering*. Basingstoke: Palgrave Macmillan.
Mitchell, J. (2003) *Siblings*. Cambridge: Polity Press.
Perks, R. and Thomson, A. (2006) *The Oral History Reader, 2nd Edition*. London: Routledge.
Roper, M. (2003) 'Analysing the analysed.' *Oral History*, 31(2): 20–33.
Ryan-Flood, R. (2015) 'Staying connected.' In L. Connolly (ed.), *The 'Irish' Family*. London: Routledge.
Sanders, R. (2004) *Sibling Relationships*. Basingstoke: Palgrave Macmillan.
Thompson, P. (1978) *The Voices of the Past*. Oxford: Oxford University Press.

10

FOUNDING A DISTINCTIVE JUNGIAN POLITICAL PSYCHOLOGY WHILE WE FORM OURSELVES INTO A NEW TYPE OF PSYCHOLOGICAL PRACTITIONER

Peter T. Dunlap

I live in Northern California. I earn my keep as a clinical psychologist in private practice; however, I also work in my political practice doing volunteer work with community groups and research at the interface between psychology and politics. In my political practice I work with progressive and liberal community leaders. I base this work on an integration of Jung's analytical psychology, group theory and practice, developmental psychology, and research that is emerging at the edge of several social sciences regarding the function of emotion in individual development and group transformation.

In this chapter I'm going to address the importance of founding a distinctive Jungian political psychology that could, for example, be used to help the political Left meet the rhetoric and aggression of the political Right. While there is something of value on both the Right and the Left, I don't think the Left has sufficient insight into its own political development, and as a result, as a species, we teeter dangerously to the Right and ignore a range of human crises including global warming, the increasing divide between the rich and poor, and, in the United States, an increasing abuse of money in our political system (Pye, 1966; Chilton, 1988; Samuels, 1993).

Unfortunately, the political Left is hobbled by its hyper-rationality and one-sidedly *public* focus on changing social systems. Until the political Left approaches its public work with a more balanced consciousness, one that is not simply rational but also emotionally intelligent, it will not develop politically.

I'm not saying anything new. This is a rather straightforward theme developed by several substantial social scientists including Drew Westen (2008) and George Lakoff (2008). But this is where it gets interesting. I trace the problems of the political Left to a problematic focused on the 'public' sphere of human experience. What politicos on the Left identify as our problems, what shapes the language they speak and the way they imagine solutions, is largely based on what is happening in our *public* institutions. As a result, they problematically participate in and perpetuate a divide in Western consciousness between our 'public' and 'private' life experience. This divide has been referred to by many social scientists, including Berkeley professor Robert Bellah and Harvard professor Michael Sandel, as a primary cause of the deterioration of democracy (Bellah et al., 1985; Sandel, 1996).

I have come to think of the public/private divide as a 'cultural complex', within which the *political Left* is a fragment of a larger liberal consciousness that includes many psychological *liberals*. Drawing from the work of Thomas Singer (2004) and Sam Kimbles (2004), I define cultural complex as a pattern of individual and collective thought, feeling, behaviour, communication and world-view that restricts the kind of transformation that would allow the emergence of new consciousness. While the political Left problematically focuses on changing social systems, psychological liberals can myopically focus on the 'private' life of the individual (Dunlap, 2008).

This public/private cultural complex originates in the failures of the Enlightenment to bring about a new humanitarian age. The result of this failure was a retreat from the concept of individualism as a public idea focused on citizenship (initiated by John Locke and others). What they now began to pursue was a more private individualism focused on the development of a person's interiority, often related to nature or spirituality, seldom if ever to the Commons.

In psychology we institutionalise this divide when we make the individual our subject matter, privileging it and deprecating the group. As San Francisco Jungian Arthur Colman writes: 'in the Jungian world the individual psyche is "sacred" and the group psyche is "profane"' (Colman, 1995, p. 45).

The divide between our public and private experience is culturally dissociative, which appears symptomatically in the gap between politics and psychology. In order to provide treatment for this condition, we can found *a distinctive Jungian political psychology* and cultivate a new type of psychological practitioner who takes responsibility for studying and 'treating' this condition. Such work would begin with ourselves, within our own psychological organisations, and then move into our communities. I imagine that this type of practitioner will earn their living, in part, facilitating the political development of the leaders, activists, therapists and organisations in their community.

How do we get from here to there? How do we work from our current Jungian identities and from our current organisations to support the development of a distinctive Jungian political psychology and a new type of psychological practitioner? One answer is that we need to start practising in public a certain type of openness, a making ourselves visible to one another, that we could think of, following Joseph Henderson, as taking a 'psychological attitude' into the public sphere (Henderson, 1984). This is one of the more important places to place the lever to move the world.

We cultivate a psychological attitude in ourselves and with our clients in our private practices. However, what works in such private settings is difficult to bring into our public and professional relationships. I know. I've tried! We are more inclined to follow the utilitarian fashion about what works and doesn't work in public, restricting what we show of ourselves, restraining our emotional intelligence and imagination, and especially our bodily response to situations. As a result, we rely too heavily on being narrowly rational in public, such as when we gather together at academic conferences and read our papers. This does not represent using a psychological attitude in public.

Through the use of a psychological attitude in public we can work out our differences without any overdependence on, or misuse of, rational debate. Not that we won't agree or disagree on the finer points of theory and practice; rather, we need to see how debates about theory and practice reflect power struggles that need psychological attention. This is our strength; we need to use it to learn to work psychologically with our public relationships with one another.

Rational debate alone reduces us to strategies effective in other sciences. In other disciplines it is appropriate to argue over interpretations of the results of observations. While we have similar goals, scholarship and good science, we have the added benefit and limitation of our psychological relations with one another as a resource. To grossly over-simplify it: they can base their work on facts; we need to base our work on relationships with each other. To do so we need to extend Carol Gilligan's 'ethic of care', in part, by modelling the use of a psychological attitude in public (1982).

Why is it that in public we do not use our most significant strength? Is it that being psychological is still relatively new and we've only had 100+ years of practice? If we turn, even a little, in this direction we will need to make ourselves more visible to one another because this is a central psychological challenge of our time.

A new type of psychological practitioner will risk this public openness. She will show how she connects her private life with what she sees taking place in public. This will not simply be vulgar confession. I am not advocating vulnerability simply because I subscribe to some naive fantasy that people are essentially good. Instead, we need a new type of practitioner to model how to bring the public and private sides of our personhood together, our psychology together with the politics of our communities. Jung understood something about this when he wrote:

> When a problem which is at bottom personal, and therefore apparently subjective, coincides with external events that contain the same psychological elements as the personal conflict, it is suddenly transformed into a general question embracing the whole of society. In this way a personal problem acquires a dignity it lacked hitherto . . .
>
> (Jung, 1921/1971, para 119)

We need to follow Jung here and we need to go further. We need to find the troubled histories that maintain the separation between our public and private selves.

Andrew Samuels is working on this through his 'political clinics' where he invites participants to tell the stories of their political histories, responding to questions like, *what did you learn about politics from being in your family?* And, *what is your first political memory?* (Samuels, 2001, p. 161).

When I use this practice in workshops participants express with excitement how they are able to feel a new connection to their own and their community's history, which helps them to connect to one another, through a new, shared history. One young woman reported with great relief that despite familial and peer attitudes, she realised she was 'political', which eased her shame and frustration. Is such an intervention something that could alleviate our cultural dissociation? Is this practice one remedy to our public/private cultural complex? Could it activate more grassroots political energy, which could be utilised by the political Left to aid its fight against the moneyed Right?

Could we learn to tell a story that binds us to one another and helps form the type of organisation needed to bring Jung and politics more effectively together? Practitioners trained in this and other techniques will be able to support activists and leaders in their communities to deepen community engagement. Let us turn this into a practice right now. I'll show you something about how it works.

Transparency will help us bind our stories together

I will tell you my own story to show you how I move through my subjective experience towards an objective political psychology, work which Jung thought of as 'subjective confession' (Shamdasani, 2003 p. 75). However, by moving towards storytelling, I am not leaving scholarship behind. I am willing to subject any assertion I make to scholarly and scientific scrutiny. But we simply must make ourselves visible to one another in order to show the way to bring our subjectivity together with objective science, our private side together with our public side, and our psychology together with our politics. Because of this, my job is not to make an argument to convince you of anything, but, rather, *to show myself to you*, show my subjective confession as one example of how to bring the public/private pieces of a cultural complex together.

I was born in the Napa Valley in California into a family with multiple privileges (Figure 10.1). Not only were we White, but we were part of the first wave of White settlers to occupy the Napa Valley. My great-great-grandfather Nathan Coombs (Figure 10.2) founded the town of Napa in 1848 and was the first of four generations to represent the Valley in the state Senate, ending with my father John Dunlap (Figure 10.3).

My dad, who recently celebrated his 92nd birthday (Figure 10.4), broke the mould of conservative Republicans and in the 1960s and seventies was a liberal Democrat. He helped pass legislation protecting the environment, endangered species (Figure 10.5), supporting education, and advocating for civil rights, including writing legislation in 1975 giving Cesar Chavez and the California farmworkers the right to unionise, and, in the late seventies requiring the California University

FIGURE 10.1 The Dunlap family

FIGURE 10.2 Nathan Coombs, who founded the town of Napa

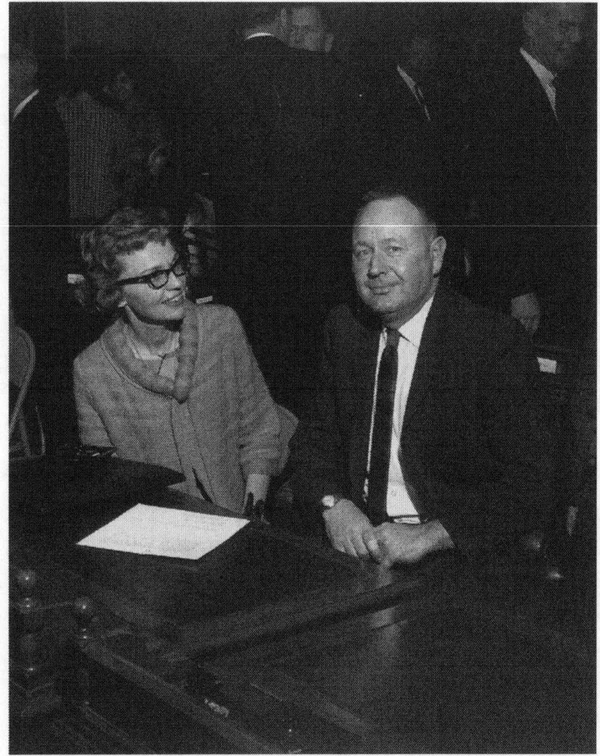

FIGURE 10.3 State Senator John Dunlap

pension system to divest all of its investments from any corporation doing business with apartheid South Africa.

Between the ages of nine and 21 I worked in my father's political campaigns. I remember how nervous he was when he stood up at a rally in downtown, conservative Napa and spoke out against the Vietnam War. In all, I grew up with the experience of believing that my family could make a difference; I was born into political energy. However, failure is an essential part of our political histories, as in 1978 when my dad lost his re-election campaign to the State Senate to a pesticide salesman. I remember the suffering of that evening's gathering, including when my dad took the family aside to apologise for letting us down. Needless to say politics is in my bones.

Unfortunately, my father's liberal identity was one-sided, focusing too intently on our public lives while neglecting our private lives. Nevertheless, I had hoped to be the fifth-generation political leader from my family; and I was on my way. I was elected president of my junior high school in 1972, at which time I started a George McGovern for President club (Figure 10.6). As a young adult I continued to work as an activist. However, I quickly learned that this extroverted practice

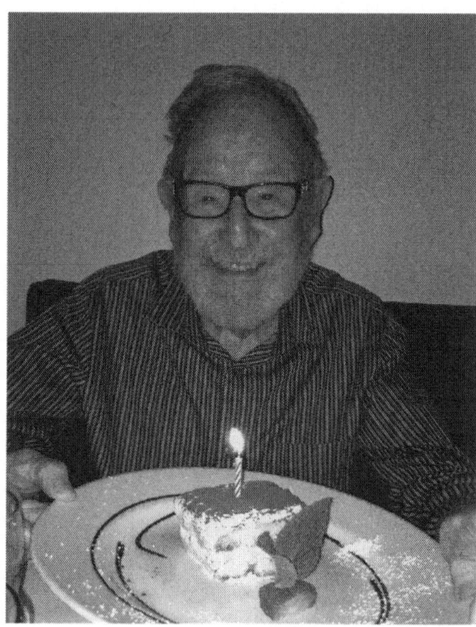

FIGURE 10.4 My father celebrating his 92nd birthday

FIGURE 10.5 John Dunlap campaigning for endangered species

FIGURE 10.6
President of my junior high school, 1972

was too difficult for me outside the context of my family. It fit who I was as John Dunlap's son, but it did not fit who Peter Dunlap needed to become.

Instead of following in my father's lineage, at 20 I collapsed and started limping down the trail into my own shadow work. Fortunately, my mother had already blazed this trail. While my father was the first political liberal in our family, my mother was the first psychological liberal (Figure 10.7). Her depressive and creative responses to the excesses, crises and freedoms of the 1960s led her to innovative forms of psychotherapy and to stock the refrigerator with health foods such as wheatgerm, one of the many sources of suffering in my childhood.

Unfortunately, the divide between my father's political identity and my mother's psychological one found *no* immediate unification. That has turned out to be my life's work. The divide between political and psychological liberalism has become the pivot point in my identity, where I turn *my* story, *my* subjectivity, into an objective political psychology. Armed with my mother's copy of the *Portable Jung*, I set out to explore the public/private cultural complex, including how it became instituted in the divide between psychology and politics, restricting any deeper healing in my family.

As I worked the gap between psychology and politics I returned to my tribe, but not as an activist. Instead I came back as a fledgling political psychologist. I began doing research with liberal/progressive leaders, which I've written about in my book *Awakening our Faith in the Future: The Advent of Psychological Liberalism* (Dunlap, 2008). I've also found others interested in bridging the public–private

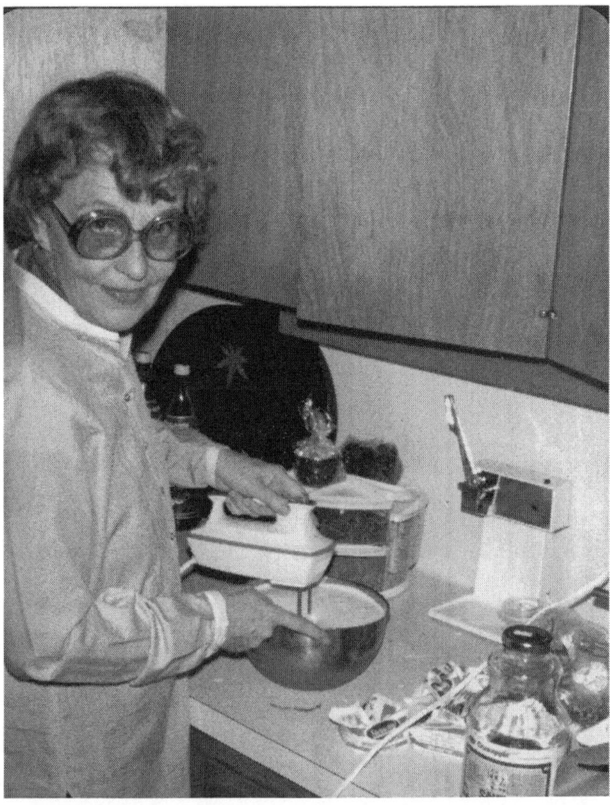

FIGURE 10.7 My mother, the psychological liberal

divide by bringing psychology and politics together. There is a growing recognition on the part of many of Jung's followers that we need to step out of the safety of our private practices and classrooms to try to do something about the politics in our communities. And there are doors that have opened for us on the other side, such as when politico Arianna Huffington writes, 'we need less policy analysis and more psychology . . . specifically, we need to hear from that under-appreciated political pundit Carl Jung' (Huffington, 2010).

This postcard advertisement (Figure 10.8) offers one idea of how a new type of psychological practitioner could earn their living supporting the political development of their community. Last month I started a community group focused on the development of a 'public emotional intelligence'. In this group, I support the emotional intelligence of community leaders, inviting the intimacy needed to transform their overly rational public personalities. I do not privilege the participant's private life; that was the necessary and problematic work of twentieth-century psychotherapy. Instead, I focus on each person's public and private suffering, using the small group as an incubator for community leadership. This is my subjective

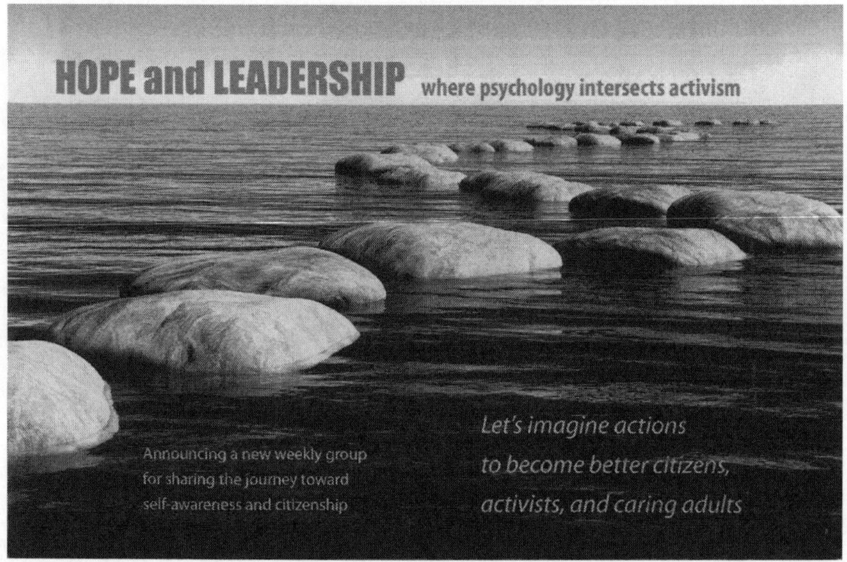

FIGURE 10.8 Advertisement for a new type of psychological practice

confession; this is my objective psychology. This bridges the unfinished work of my mother and my father; make of this what you will, how could it be any other way?

The time is right to look at the nineteenth- and twentieth-century retreat from the public sphere as a cultural complex that psychology has accidentally perpetuated and now has the responsibility for learning how to treat and transform. Jung's and our privileging of individual experience and scapegoating of group consciousness is a symptom of this complex (Dunlap, in press). We will become the people called for by our time as we turn our individuating paths back towards one another, sacrifice our idiosyncrasies, get off our hobby-horses and allow ourselves to be woven into a greater whole. We need to get something done. I recommend that this include founding a distinctive Jungian political psychology and a new type of psychological practitioner whose attention is on their communities. Our paths of individuation must return to a shared centre; that is, to the Commons.

Until we take up this challenge we will struggle to contribute to the remediation of the social, political and moral ills of our time. And supporting grassroots community organisations is only one use of a Jungian political psychology. We also can contribute analysis and technology to address and treat the current gaps in political leadership nationally and internationally. Cultivating such a psychology and shaping ourselves into this new type of practitioner will enhance our own organisational functioning, including increasing the enjoyment we have when we gather together with one another.

References

Bellah, R. et al. (1985) *Habits of the Heart*. Berkeley, CA: University of California Press.

Chilton, S. (1988) *Defining Political Development*. Boulder, CO: Lynne Rienner Publishers.

Colman, A. (1995) *Up from Scapegoating: Awakening Consciousness in Groups*. Evanston, IL: Chiron.

Dunlap, P. T. (2008) *Awakening our Faith in the Future: The Advent of Psychological Liberalism*. London: Routledge Press.

Dunlap, P. T. (in press) 'Renewing our faith in groups: A moral imperative for our community.' *Journal for the International Association of Jungian Studies*.

Gillian, C. (1982) *In a Different Voice*. Cambridge, MA: Harvard University Press.

Henderson, J. (1984) *Cultural Attitudes in Psychological Perspective*. Toronto: Inner City Books.

Huffington, A. (2010) 'Sarah Palin, "mama grizzlies," Carl Jung, and the power of archetypes.' Huffington Post. Retrieved from http://www.huffingtonpost.com/arianna-huffington/sarah-palin-mama-grizzlie_b_666642.html (accessed on 17 December 2015).

Jung, C. G. (1921/1971) 'Psychological types.' *CW6*.

Kimbles, S. (2004) *The Cultural Complex*. New York: Brunner Routledge.

Lakoff, G. (2008) *The Political Mind*. New York: Viking.

Pye, L. (1966) *Aspects of Political Development*. Boston/Toronto: Little, Brown & Co.

Samuels, A. (1993) *The Political Psyche*. London: Routledge.

Samuels, A. (2001) *Politics on the Couch*. London: Profile Books.

Sandel, M. (1996) *Democracy's Discontent*. Cambridge, MA: Harvard University Press.

Shamdasani, S. (2003) *Jung and the Making of Modern Psychology*. Cambridge: Cambridge University Press.

Singer, T. (2004) *The Cultural Complex*. New York: Brunner Routledge.

Westen, D. (2008) *The Political Brain*. New York: Public Affairs.

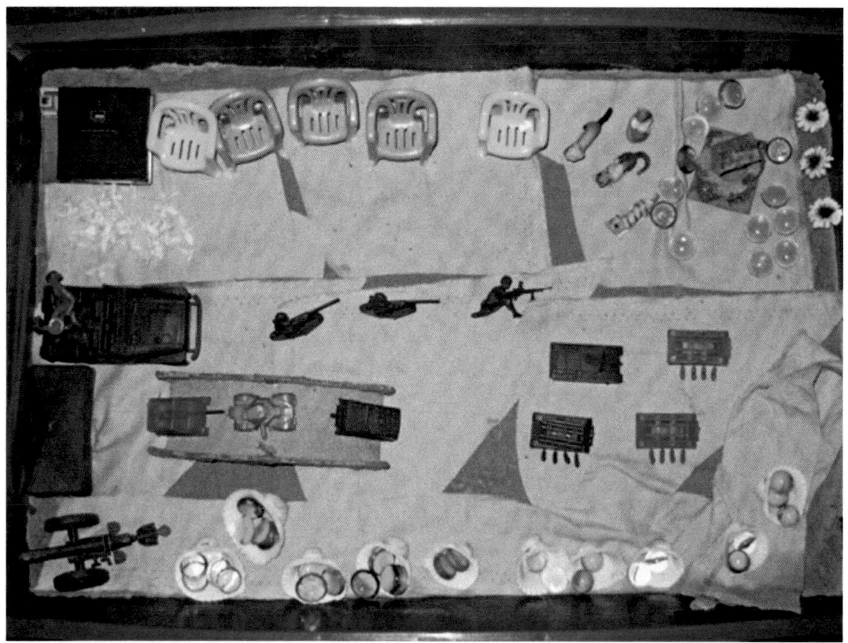

Plate 1 The horrors of war

Plate 2 Harmonious togetherness and shared meals

Plate 3 Archaeological site with remains of slaves who died shortly after arriving in Brazil

Plate 4 Chester Arnold: *Thy Kingdom Come II*, size 72" × 94" painted 1999

In the collection of the DiRosa Preserve, Napa. (Courtesy of the artist)

Plate 5 Beijing Opera mask

Plate 6 Smog masks

Plate 7 Sanxingdui god mask

Plate 8 Confucius' home in Qufu

Plate 9 Coming Home to the Mainland of China

Plate 10 A scene from the end of *Coming Home to the Mainland of China*

Plate 11 Aerial view of Earl's Court 2013

London Borough of Hammersmith & Fulham planning department

11

OUR FUTURE LIES HIDDEN IN OUR ROOTS

Roberto Gambini

My analysis of the deep crisis of contemporary humanity focuses on the alarming loss of essential values, as well as the psychological disconnection with the archetype of *coniunctio* of opposites – nature and technology, for instance. When studying societies such as the Brazilian one, or, for that matter, any modern society built upon an ancient aboriginal foundation later submitted to colonialism, I have called this complex array of lost spiritual, ethical, mythological, religious, aesthetic, ecological, cultural and social values our *ancestral soul*. If we do field research and study, as I have done since 1976, the growing disintegration and destruction of all that was created – a true *patrimony of sensibility* – through a historical process of soul-making that started very probably 30,000 years ago, and imagine/appreciate what life has meant and how it was lived, as compared to our present ways, we can detect human experiences – our roots – that point the way to meaningful solutions to the maladies of the modern spirit and their dangerous effects for life.

This 'future' of my chapter title is of course a fantasy, a mental representation of something that does not exist. But it is also a formidable screen for the projection of all our collective hopes and fears. What image of the future does each one of us hold? That would certainly be a good topic for research. There is no novelty in considering that humanity has lost a sense of orientation and a whole set of fundamental values. If one asks oneself what is the best future that can be imagined, one might be influenced by collective views, or what one dreamed in childhood, or what one chose to follow after long years of study digesting the teachings of eminent thinkers. One might then come to envisage some ideal future based on the proposals of utopic socialism, for example, or inspired by the fundamental values and aims formulated by all those who fought for a more humanitarian society, an improved democracy or a more balanced economic matrix.

To my mind, all this is fine. But I think that in all these endeavours we can notice that a living, inspiring imaginative connection with the archetype of a possible conjunction of opposites *as a mental procedure to weave a fantasy of future* is not activated. So our fantasies are one sided. And yet, opposites have certainly coexisted in other times, in other cultures, definitely shaping forms of existence that have disappeared. So I say: this impoverished capacity to fantasise is a serious problem – and this is the dimension in which I can *fantasise* an embryo of Jungian political activism.

With just one polarity to play with, imagination (or thought) gets stuck and sterile. In those circumstances, how can we conceive a historical alchemy that does not get aborted? Historians might laugh about all these ethereal concerns of ours, but has it not become a commonplace to say that politics is the art of the possible? Or, more philosophically, it has been said that 'possibilities are a temptation that reality might one day accept'. Alchemical imagination is political in the sense that it continually subverts the dominance of just one force and its predictable developments. But if a proposal for action is to be achieved, it is necessary that in the vessel of our mind certain established values be confronted with exactly those that have fallen out of this big container of collective consciousness. And this is what I believe Jung proposed: in order to be politically active, defending ideas that might hopefully lead to a desired social change, one has to align with contemporary symbols that emerge from the collective unconscious – symbols, images or thoughts that might bring back a whole set of lost, but irreplaceable values. This alignment with the unconscious, as Jung postulated, would in due time re-establish a creative sort of polarity.

If we think, naively or not, that Jungians – understood as a community of people sharing some basic ideas – may do something together in the world other than treating patients, doing research, teaching, writing, publishing and lecturing, maybe it is because we all, to some degree, share and cherish the alchemical metaphor that Jung was so apt to describe and explain. I am not proposing a new professional inflation, nor suggesting that we Jungians are the elected ones to inaugurate an enlightened form of psychological or political activism – we have already had enough of that! We have certainly paid quite an expensive price for entertaining an alleged kind of outdated and unscientific mysticism. What I am saying is, plainly, that since one central element in Jung's legacy is the use of alchemical thinking as a way of unveiling underground laws that regulate both unconscious and historical processes of change and renewal, we might as well resolutely apply the tools we have at hand to set fire to the retort of political imagination.

That means to say that it is possible and desirable to counterbalance current realities, such as the predominance of technological values, with the now practically lost wisdom created throughout the ages by the ancestral soul of mankind. Needless to say that my limitation in so doing is that I am conditioned by the fact that I live and breathe the historical oxygen of Brazilian society that was shaped in the matrix of colonisation, a historical process that implies the subjugation of one type of collective consciousness (the pre-Columbian one, as is the case for Latin America as a whole) by another, the European one from the sixteenth century onwards.

Let us say that our problem is that we have been trying our hand at an incomplete, and therefore short-term, political alchemy that has put enough sulphur in the retort to activate the raw matter (current facts reported by the media, for instance), but regretfully we have forgotten that without salt and mercury the process is doomed to abort. In my personal case, the sulphur I started with was my training and passion for the extraverted social sciences (sociology, anthropology, history, economics, political science and law). These disciplines caught my attention from 1963 (when I was 18) to 1974, when I started a Jungian analysis in São Paulo, which eventually led me to the Jung Institute in Zurich in 1978. The much more introverted flavour of Jungian psychology was the equivalent of adding much-needed salt and mercury to instil a spark of transformation in my received knowledge and habitual way of thinking. I longed to expand my concepts and my views. I needed a more reliable *Weltanschauung*, to use a classical term, that I trusted would enable me, one day, to face an audience and dare to present a political proposal, a way of thinking that would bring together the social sciences and Jungian psychology. For that to happen, I had to keep a low fire burning under my retort and wait in silence for fourteen years, until, in 1995, I presented a lecture called 'The soul of underdevelopment' at the 1995 IAAP Congress in Zurich (Gambini, 1995). In order to work alchemically with the opposites in my mind, I had to criticise and complement the narrative woven by official history, bringing to the fore the silenced voice of our indigenous ancestry and the end product of thirty centuries of soul-making that were, and still are, kept out of the mental image we make of ourselves. I hope you might agree that a broken mirror is not a sound basis for reflection, even less for political action.

I want now to give you a few simplified examples of what the values of the ancestral soul might be. If we look at a classical set of pairs of opposites from a historical perspective, trying to detect what has been their prevailing pattern of interaction, we might with no great effort come to agree that 'progress' and 'civilisation' have meant the predominance of one opposite over its counterpart, in some cases resulting in its dissolution or even effacement. What I have in mind is the understanding we have, in order to diagnose the structure of different cultural configurations, of the dialectics that take place between contrasting archetypal forces such as logos/mythos, nature/technology, masculine/feminine, consciousness/the unconscious, eros/power, inner/outer world, psyche/soma, and so on.

Some of us, perhaps not only we Jungians, use categories such as these to help us organise our overall vision of this illusive phenomenon we call 'reality', and come to some sort of understanding that seems to make sense. We then announce to the public, with varying degrees of conviction, that, for instance, patriarchal values have predominantly shaped the Judeo-Christian civilisation, to the detriment of all that thrives under the influence of the subdued feminine principle. This is, in short, one of the keys we use to understand symbols and stories created by the Western collective unconscious. According to Jung, this also explains what alchemy was all about: the other side of the story, suppressed by religious dogma, in which matter, the body and the feminine were not deprived of spirit.

So alchemy would be a way of restoring a more complete understanding of reality by bringing back what was cast away and rejected. And this is our problem here, in my view: what is missing, or has been lost, in our political imagination when we try to envisage what kind of future it is worthwhile fighting for.

Brazil was not 'discovered', as held by official historiography, but invaded and occupied by Portuguese explorers from 1500 (Mexico in 1516 and Peru in 1532 by Spanish conquistadores). The meeting of two worlds could have been a phenomenal alchemical achievement, with far-reaching consequences for the evolution of collective consciousness, something that only visionaries could imagine as a possibility. Two opposite modalities of consciousness met, but never mingled: a rational matrix with all its attributes, with a freshly structured agent called 'ego', freed from dogmatic impositions and endowed with a highly charged phallic energy, that is to say, a capacity to penetrate the obscurities of the unknown, from virgin forests to strange psychologies. The Aboriginal matrix, on the other hand, forged throughout the centuries another style of consciousness, based not on rationality and linear time, but on intuition and myth as viable sources of knowledge and meaning. It is not too difficult to notice that *colonisation and alchemy are opposites.* When power and domination prevail, not only conquered peoples are subjugated, but all their psychic attributes are devalued and not taken as useful contributions for the creation of a synthetic new civilisation – the only exception being culinary practices and technical and stylistic innovations, besides procreation with native females. But this is merely a physical, and not spiritual, alchemy.

In the case of Brazil, Jesuit missionaries, since 1549 helping Portuguese settlers to submit the Indians through Catholic catechisation, asked Church theologians, in their letters to Ignatius Loyola, if such people were human and had a soul, since perhaps they were just half animals who needed to be baptised to acquire a soul and be saved. That was the first attack on the ancestral soul and all the values it contained. On the Indian side, their question was to find out if the newcomers were spirits, or deities. There were probably ten million Indians in the sixteenth century, spread around most of what today corresponds to the Brazilian territory, organised in more or less one thousand different cultural groups, each with their own language and mythological system. According to Indian mythology, a mediating deity created the Indians alongside other people, who would then, through social interaction, make the Indians expand their consciousness, in other words, would stimulate their process of becoming. In this abbreviated example one can clearly see the different epistemological perspectives of the two sides, and how deep and complex was an ancient collective mental achievement that was ignored and dismantled by the conquerors. We could therefore say that there was not even a first step towards a historical alchemy of opposites, simply because the Indian psychological polarity was soon destroyed. As mentioned above, only the female body was retained and used to create a new, mixed breed, whereas male bodies were used for forced work.

In the beginning, our Latin American peoples had a White father and an Indian mother. Of course no maternal values were placed into the retort, and that would comprise spirituality, ethics, feelings, knowledge, interpretation of nature, mythology, aesthetics, meanings attributed to life and death – and this is obviously just a sketchy, compact list. Only artefacts were culturally absorbed: hammocks, threads, baskets, clay pots, bows and arrows, feather adornments, along with edible roots, herbs, fruits and recipes.

I present these brief comments, concerning matters that are probably known to many, in order to emphasise what is central in this brief chain of ideas: *our early tragedy was the destruction of soul in the place of alchemy*. Our millenary, but despised, patrimony of sensibility, wisdom and spirituality is what I have already described as *ancestral soul* (the subject of my thesis for the Zurich Jung Institute, later published as *Indian Mirror: The Making of the Brazilian Soul* (Gambini, 2000)). In this short chapter I could simply call it *roots* – and here the odd title of my discussion might acquire some meaning.

It is precisely these roots that are badly needed to fuel possible political fantasies of desirable futures. So here suddenly appears, implicitly, an image of evolving time: a mythic tree of my invention, whose roots, as an arrow, point to the times to come. A future time that will take over, and elaborate anew, values, ideas and choices that were present in the beginning, and now are brought back to interact alchemically with all the other qualities that make the present what it is.

What could these 'root values' be like? For the sake of clarifying our title, even at the risk of over-simplification, here is another sketch: (1) a relationship with nature conceived as sacred, endowed with meaning and perceived as a self-sustainable source of life; (2) life can be simple, and yet deeply meaningful; (3) work and leisure must not necessarily be separated; Eros can be present in all forms of endeavours; the same body that toils can also dance; (4) collaboration can prevail over competition; (5) aggressiveness can be culturally contained and organised; (6) altered states of consciousness can be experienced in group rituals; (6) consumption of goods can be limited to their utility; (7) sacredness can be present in everyday life.

Maybe this list sounds too fantastical. But political fantasy is my point. In the absence of values such as the above suggested, or perhaps even better ones that one might conceive and bring to light, imagination becomes too weak, deceptively uninspiring, and unable to release the necessary energies in order to break through the dreadful inertia of our poor hopes.

References

Gambini, R. (1995) 'The soul of underdevelopment.' In *Open Questions in Analytical Psychology*, edited by M. A. Matton. Einsiedeln: Daimon Verlag.

Gambini, R. (2000) *Indian Mirror: The Making of the Brazilian Soul.* São Paulo: Axis Mundi/Terceiro Nome.

SECTION 4

Culture and identity

12

RACISM

An unwelcome guest in Brazilian cultural identity

Walter Boechat

Latin America is the only really new culture in history created by human beings. Asia is a continuation of old Asia, with the addition of technology but without a radical change. Africa has not assumed a sense of modernity because it could not overcome completely the trauma of colonialism. Europe is a continuation of itself, and North America a continuation of Europe, with a hypertechnological dress. Only Latin America represents a new complexity (Zoja, 2006).

The building up of Brazilian identity

The new complexity of Latin America defined by Zoja applies especially to Brazil, which has a very unique history. The melting pot of Brazil, which began life with its discovery by the Portuguese in 1500, still experiences constant immigration, with diverse people from more than 60 different countries. A very special feature present in the colonisation of Brazil is the 'crossbreeding' of different races. Unlike the United States of America, which was initially colonised by traditional Protestant families with strict laws, the Portuguese navigators were single men, some of them outcasts from society, or *degredados* (Bueno, 1998). An intermingling with Indians was a central theme from the earliest colonial times. The first mother of all Brazilians is truly an Indian, a Great Mother Indian.

At the outset of the colonial period, this was reflected even in the language spoken in the green paradise of forests and rivers. At the time of the discovery of Brazil, there were 1,300 different indigenous languages in Brazil. This diversity of languages developed into two generic languages: the Tupi-Guarani of the Indians, and the Portuguese spoken in the cities. An amalgam of these two produced the singular dialect, a general language spoken by all, Indians and Whites, called *nheengatu*. Strangely enough this *nheengatu* remained an official language in Brazil till the end of the eighteenth century! Most people could understand it, but did not understand Portuguese. A strong unbiased admixture of races was therefore showing itself even in speech (Ribeiro, 1995, p. 122).

Crossbreeding happened early on between White Portuguese and Indians. Together with the Indians, those first mestizos were useful in the expansion of Portuguese domains from coastal areas to inland Brazil, where new riches of gold, precious stones and natural resources were discovered. During this initial period of colonisation, a virtual genocide of the Indian population came about due to epidemics of various diseases brought by the White men.

The slavery period

It proved very difficult to enslave the Indians to undertake the arduous work of colonisation. They did not adapt to the heavy work, either dying, or fleeing to the Amazon forests. Then started the traffic of human beings from various countries of Africa to work as slaves on sugar plantations and in the gold mines of central Brazil. Systematic traffic from Africa started at the end of the sixteenth century and only finished in 1895. In fact, slavery was abolished by decree only in 1888. Brazil was the last country in the civilised Western world to abolish slavery. Africans were, at that point, so unprepared to live as free men that many returned after liberation to work on large farms as before.

The Brazilian anthropologist Darcy Ribeiro brings this long period of slavery to the present time with a challenging psychological interpretation that, in Jungian terms, reveals an important cultural complex in Brazil:

> No people that go through this [the slavery period] as a daily routine through the centuries would get out of it without having been imprinted indelibly. All of us, Brazilians, we are the flesh of those tortured blacks and Indians. All of us Brazilians are, equally, the enslaving hand that tortured them. The tenderest sweetness and the most atrocious cruelty conjugated themselves here to make us the suffered and sorrowful people that we are and the insensible and brutal people that we also are. Descendants of slaves and masters of slaves, we will always display the malignancy that has been distilled and instilled in us . . . The most terrible aspect of our heritage is to carry always with us the scar of the torturer imprinted on our souls ready to explode into classic racist brutality.
>
> (Ribeiro, 1995, p. 120, author's translation)

This is a psychological interpretation of the permanence of the slavery period in the cultural unconscious of Brazil after almost 300 years of slavery. Working with sociological and anthropological concepts, Ribeiro is suggesting a psychological image. The conjoined image of the sadistic master and the suffering slave represents an important cultural complex of the Brazilian psyche.

Cultural trauma and cultural complex

Here we come face to face with the deeply intertwined relationship of cultural complex and cultural trauma. Luigi Zoja touches on this theme in his sensitive essay on the arrival of the Spanish navigator Cortés amidst the Aztecs in Mexico. Zoja compares cultural trauma to personal trauma, drawing on the ideas developed by Donald Kalsched. He quotes Kalsched, who reminds us that in severe trauma the ego's defences are unable to cope with the dangers that threaten the whole psychic system, so that the archetypal defences are set to work in order to protect the self (Zoja, 2004, pp. 78ff.).

The cultural complex constellated in Brazil by slavery has therefore created archetypal defences against the trauma in the cultural unconscious. Zoja suspects that the whole Mexican culture was traumatised and that this trauma had an indelible effect, even on future generations. In a similar way, Brazilian culture was also traumatised. No doubt the prolonged relationship between the slave and his master is a stereotypical image that continues to exist in the cultural unconscious, affecting the psyche of all Brazilians. The cultural complex continues to influence society in various ways. One of them is the sadistic class system, with its low salaries and lack of opportunities.

Cordial racism and social class structure

I believe we can relate this cultural complex, so strongly constellated in Brazilian history, to the building up of very stratified social classes in Brazilian society. In fact, one of the central problems in Brazilian society is the concentration of wealth. And a strong prejudice against the lowest classes goes hand in hand with the ethnic prejudice, since the Blacks and Indians predominate in the lowest classes and have tremendous difficulties in ascending to higher social classes.

Sociologist Gilberto Freyre wrote the most important research about the coexistence of races in Brazil. His book *The Masters and the Slaves* [*Casa Grande e Senzala*] (Freyre, 2009) describes how the cohabitation of masters and slaves contributed to the formation of the patriarchal colonial family in rural Brazil during the colonisation period. This book became his masterpiece and was translated into many languages. The peculiar way in which multiple people of different origins have comprised Brazil's social structure since colonial times led Freyre to state that a *racial democracy* exists in Brazil. This assertion has been challenged through time by many anthropologists and scholars who demonstrated that racial democracy does not, in fact, exist in Brazil. Rather there is strong evidence of the existence of a peculiar kind of racial prejudice, quite different from Anglo-Saxon racism. This last has a more defined character, based on separation of races and places. The word *apartheid*, as we know, means separation. In the USA Martin Luther King confronted segregation by challenging the separation of Whites and Blacks in buses and public spaces. But in Brazil strong racial prejudice is hidden, which led Freyre to reach his wrong conclusion of a racial democracy.

The prevalent crossbreeding in Brazilian history is a major factor in its social makeup. According to Brazilian historian Laurentino Gomes, 90% of Brazil's population in 1882 – the year of independence – was made up of Black slaves, recently liberated slaves and mestizos. Only a minority of Whites, a true elite, had a proper education and was literate. The relationship of social class structure and skin colour may be observed already at the very beginning of Brazil as an independent country (Gomes, 2010, pp. 70ff.).

The strong crossbreeding in Brazilian history favours a racial prejudice that continues to exist in disguise, hand in hand with social prejudice. This consequently causes racism to be a central element in Brazil's collective shadow. I named this peculiar kind of racism present in Brazilian society *cordial racism*. This name is based on the notion of *the cordial man* introduced by the sociologist Sérgio Buarque de Holanda. According to Holanda: 'Brazil's contribution to civilisation will be *cordiality*. We will give out to the world the *cordial man*. The affability in dealing with other people, hospitality, generosity, virtues so praised by foreigners who visit us represent, in effect, a defined feature of the Brazilian character, to the extent, at least, that patterns of human sociability formed within the rural and patriarchal milieu continue to exist' (Buarque de Holanda, 1936/1999, p. 146).

Holanda reminds us that it would be a mistake to understand cordiality as merely good manners or civility. The word cordial should be understood in its precise etymological sense (the word cordial derives from Latin: *Cor*, *cordis*, heart.) This cordiality, foreign to formalism and social convention, includes not only positive feelings. On the contrary, hostility can be as cordial as friendship, since both are born in the heart (cf. Buarque de Holanda, 1936/1999, p. 205, n. 6).

The author gives us a vivid description of the *archetype of the persona* as it expresses itself in the collective psyche of present-day Brazilian society. Holanda introduces us to the implications and contradistinctions contained in the word 'cordial', which can function as disguise for violence, rejection, a superior attitude and, most important, closed doors to equality in jobs and education for Blacks, mulattos, mestizos and Indians in Brazil. The cordial man has difficulties in showing negative feelings of racial prejudice openly. After five centuries of crossbreeding, the integration of the non-White population did not occur and good jobs and salaries are still the prerogative of a social elite of the White population.

Social class and perception of colour

It is most difficult for a Black person to acquire a higher standard of living in Brazil. When it does happen, the Black becomes White, or, to express it more clearly, he even perceives himself as being White. . . he is considered White. There is a strong connection between skin colour and social class in Brazil, or between racial prejudice and class prejudice.

Brazil's multiracial society includes all shades of colours between the White European and the Afro-Brazilian. Skin colour, hair texture and other physical signs determine to a great extent an individual's capacity to rise in the social scale. This happens because in a subtle way the Black population still has limited access to proper education and health. The mulattos or mestizos, being lighter, are generally considered as White. As the cynical Brazilian saying goes: 'money turns things White.' As a person acquires money and he or she is able to go up the social scale, his or her skin, as if by a miracle, becomes more White.

In Brazil, in fact, it is very surprising, even dazzling, to discover the extent to which social class interferes with the perception of skin colour. In this context, listen to what the well-known soccer player Ronaldo Nazario had to say when asked about racial incidents in football matches in Europe and South America. Ronaldo responded that he was quite sad about the incidents, but, in his words, 'as [he was] a White man', he was not directly subjected to these racists attacks, although he could quite understand his friends' suffering (*Veja*, 2005). In fact, Ronaldo is a light-skinned mulatto. But as Ronaldo has risen in class, the perception of his skin colour has changed. Surely Ronaldo Nazario would have admitted to being a mulatto when he was a very poor boy in Rio de Janeiro's Bento Ribeiro district. But after representing Brazil during the 1994 World Cup in the United States, he became a world champion at the age of eighteen. Since then, he has become a multi-millionaire through playing in professional teams in Italy and Spain. Ronaldo is no longer a mulatto. People don't identify him as a mulatto and he seems to agree with them.

Another interesting example of this mixture of social class and perception of skin colour was reported by the anthropologist Darcy Ribeiro, demonstrating that this is a very old attitude. Ribeiro tells the story of Henry Koster, an Englishman travelling in Brazil during the nineteenth century, who was surprised to see a mulatto occupying the high rank of Chief-Captain. He then heard the following explanation: 'Yes, he was originally a Mestizo, but now as Chief-Captain, he has clearly become a White man' (Ribeiro, 1995, p. 225).

The Whitening of the race

The unique style of racial prejudice in Brazil involves a powerful fantasy about the Whitening of the race. According to the American Brazilianist Thomas Skidmore, facilitating White immigration from Europe at the end of the nineteenth century was not just an economic decision. At that time, the Brazilian intellectual elite was strongly influenced by European racist ideas and wanted a Whitening of the race (Skidmore, 1989, p. 225). The *Whitening* thesis maintained that White genes were stronger than Black ones and that, through repeated crossbreeding, White genes would prevail over Black or Indian genes. The theory held that, in time, a White population would predominate after various generations of mestizos through the penetrating power of the White gene. Brazil would reach ethnic purity through miscegenation! These racist ideas are more comprehensible in the context of knowing that Brazil's intellectual elite looked to the prevailing ideas originating among Europeans and North Americans at the time.

This ideal led to the fantasy, among parts of the Brazilian elite in the years between 1889 to 1930, that Whitening the race would occur not by separation or exclusion, but, surprisingly enough, by crossbreeding. The first ethnologist to present this theory was João Batista de Lacerda during the first Universal Congress of Races in London, 1911. It was often presented as a scientific formula, but it was never adopted elsewhere (Skidmore, 1989 pp. 81ff.). This theory has been unique to Brazil and deserves to be discussed in its symbolic aspects.

The almost alchemical idea of Whitening of the race was opposed by another sociological movement started in Brazil in the 1930s: the cultural anthropology and cultural syncretism movement led by Gilberto Freyre, among others. Freyre strongly attacked the Whitening-of-the-race idea, since cultural anthropology argued that environment and culture were the main issues and 'races' in themselves were less important for sociology. From 1930 onward, with the rise of Nazism and fascism in Europe and its fanatic overvaluation of the 'race' factor, Freyre's emphasis on the environment proved to be correct.

The old ideas of race disappeared in Brazil and theories of scientific racism became an anachronism in South America. But the idea of the inferiority of non-White groups still remains in the cultural unconscious, under the potent influence of the cultural complex of racism. This complex has led to the odd idea that Blacks may come to a position of social prominence only through sports or music, but not through other professional avenues.

The Memorial of the New Blacks: efforts to recover memory and face the cultural complex

The Memorial of the New Blacks (see Plate 3) is part of the Institute of Research and New Black Memory – IPN [*Instituto de Pesquisa e Memória dos Pretos Novos*] – which aims to reflect on slavery in Brazil, as well as on the development of educational and research projects to preserve the memory of the 'New Blacks'. This was the name given to newcomers taken captive in Africa and deposited in Rio de Janeiro in the mid-eighteenth century in an area of the city known at the time by the name of Little Africa. In this place, today the port area of Gamboa, the selling market of captive Blacks was situated.

The memorial is located at the archaeological site of the Cemetery of New Blacks. It pays homage to Blacks who were buried at the site, between the years 1769 and 1830. It is conceived of as an act of reverence and respect to thousands of newcomers to the colony, who died because of maltreatment during the crossing of the Atlantic. It is estimated that the bodies of 20–30,000 Blacks have been deposited in mass graves, although these numbers are not contained in official records. With the prohibition of the slave trade, the cemetery was closed and the memory of their existence buried because of successive landfills in the area. This constitutes a deletion of the history of slavery in the city of Rio de Janeiro.

The Memorial of the New Blacks is one of many necessary social phenomena happening now in Brazil that are connected to the recovery of African roots and memory. This has to do with memory, and memory is a central issue by which a country might rediscover its own identity. Brazil has a strong challenge to face nowadays. Like a traumatised patient in psychotherapy who is called to face the repressed emotional complexes that are hidden in his or her shadow, the country is called to face the cultural complex that occupies an important place in its history: the long slavery period of the nineteenth century. This non-integrated cultural complex continues to affect Brazilian society, underpinning the concentration of wealth and the perpetuation of massive inequalities.

References

Buarque de Holanda, S. (1936/1999) *Raízes do Brasil, 26th edition.* São Paulo: Companhia das Letras.

Bueno, E. (1998) *Náufragos, Traficantes e Degredados* [Navigators, Traffickers and Outcasts]. Rio de Janeiro: Objetiva.

Freyre, G. (2009) *Casa Grande e Senzala, 26th edition.* Preface by F. H. Cardoso. São Paulo: Global. American edition: *The Masters and the Slaves.* New York: Random House, 2000.

Gomes, L. (2010) *1822.* Rio de Janeiro: Nova Fronteira.

Ribeiro, D. (1995) *O povo brasileiro.* São Paulo: Companhia das Letras.

Skidmore, T. (1989) *Preto no branco.* Rio de Janeiro: Paz e Terra, 2nd printing. American edition: *Black into White: Race and Nationality in Brazilian Thought.* Oxford: Oxford University Press, 1974.

Veja (2005) Quotation by Ronaldo about racism in European football teams. *Veja on-line,* 1 June 2005. Available at: http://veja.abril.com.br/010605/vejaessa.html (accessed 21 April 2014).

Zoja, L. (2004) 'Trauma and abuse: the development of a cultural complex in the history of Latin America.' In T. Singer and S. Kimbles (eds), *The Cultural Complex.* New York and London: Brunner Routledge, pp. 78–89.

Zoja, L. (2006) 'The Latin American psyche.' Interview with Gustavos Barcellos in *Cadernos Junguianos,* 2: 48–60.

13

JUNG FOR/WITH FEMINISM? THE GENDERED IMAGINATION AND JUNG'S INFAMOUS QUOTE

Susan Rowland

Who is speaking?

> The anima has an erotic, emotional character, the animus a rationalising one. Hence most of what men say about feminine eroticism, and particularly about the emotional life of women, is derived from their own anima projections and distorted accordingly. On the other hand, the astonishing assumptions and fantasies that women make about men come from the activity of the animus, who produces an inexhaustible supply of illogical arguments and false explanations.
>
> (Jung, 1925/1954, para 338).

C. G. Jung was not a feminist, if by that we mean a straightforward supporter of gender equity. Yet the above quotation is a delightful example of just how non-straightforward his writing can be. Indeed, as I shall argue in this chapter, his writing provides material for a rich development of the complexities surrounding the term 'feminism', 'marginalisation' and even 'activism'. Jung's writing is tricky. These Trickster words are both wounding and productive in challenging what is, and is not, 'feminism'. For example, here these three sentences take different gendered positions. From the lofty ungendered (because disembodied) pronouncing of unassailable concepts that the anima is erotic and the animus rationalising, the second sentence takes the perspective of a man looking at women. The anima, as inner feminine unconscious other of a man, distorts the male view of women. So far so feminist.

And then, who is speaking? Who spouts the ludicrously unbalanced and unsubstantiated claim about women's annoying babbling? By the logic of Jung's own words, it is not the noble male ego but rather his anima who is speaking. So what is the internal relation of this author's inner creatures? Does the anima momentarily push rationalising ego aside or does the Trickster calmly decide to play a trick on the reader in order to *show* what anima distortion actually looks like? Is the irrational anima rationally deployed to demonstrate the argument that the anima messes with the sober male authorial voice? We cannot know what Jung 'intended' the reader to understand, which brings us to the problem of legitimacy in interpretation.

For a moment I want to leave the matter of indeterminacy in writing, which *matters*, for the related topic of legitimacy of speaking for, or about feminism. As a White, middle-class and relatively privileged woman, I have received all the benefits of a century of feminist activism while having contributed little. I am also not an analyst, while being asked to speak on Jung and feminism to a conference named Analysis and Activism. As a teacher of adults taking degrees, I find little liveliness in the term 'feminism' in my students. Yet women, often but not always women of colour, are still systematically disadvantaged all over the planet. What has happened to a feminism that has lost its collective bite, and who can speak for it?

One of the essential aspects of Jungian ideas is his (sometimes reluctant) commitment to the margins, whether these are the liminal margins of consciousness or the social margins where despised shadow and *feminine* qualities reside. As neither analyst nor activist, perhaps I am directed by Jung to the margins of my own role as a teacher of women and men? Where I do not teach but am rather taught? Where I listen to voices who want to be heard in such marginal, undocumented, even secret fashion?

For it is in these margins of what is not 'official' educational practice that women and a very few men have come to talk to me over the years about rape. Rape happens more than is recorded by crime statistics and the operations of the law courts. Often, students I did not actually teach wanted me to *hear* their stories and accept them. Even today, working with older students, it is a surprise, and yet not a surprise, how many women are rape survivors.

Feminism 'comes up' in the classroom in the teaching of literature and of Jungian psychology. Because I wrote *Jung: A Feminist Revision* (2002), I am frequently asked, usually with a sense of incredulity: 'Susan, why are you a *feminist*?' What really needs addressing is that gap between feminism's ideals and the student's tone, suggesting that it is a character flaw to be still obsessed with such distant history. So I say, 'I am a feminist because two women a week in my country are killed by their domestic partners, usually men.' At this moment, the men in the room look surprised and the women look interested.

Of course men beating up women is a criminal issue, just as rape is. What is a *feminist* issue is that unspoken social and gender assumptions permit the ubiquity of both crimes and the difficulty of prosecuting them. Perhaps feminism's still vital role is to investigate those margins where the unarticulated beliefs about masculinity built on dominance, and the unspeakable desires for power through sex remain. I suggest that Jung's uncanny ability to break apart the so-called rational voice of psyche-logic, psychological theory, to hear an irrationality deemed feminine, might have contemporary resonance. Could Jung aid a feminist desire for justice and healing, in hearing what is not, even cannot, be spoken?

In addressing a conference of analysts and activists, I decided to speak *from* my experience of listening to sexual suffering; women raped and/or beaten. I am speaking from the role of being spoken *to*. Of the three sentences in the initial quote from Jung in this chapter, I chose to talk from the second sentence position: of a gendered embodied being with an 'other' in the unconscious. The first sentence is the conventional scholarly ungendered voice of psyche-logos. It gestures to transcendence in its evocation of concepts as universally applicable: anima for men, animus for women. The third anima-irrational voice, Jung can supply himself.

> No matter how friendly and obliging a woman's Eros may be, no logic on earth can shake her if she is ridden by the animus. Often the man has the feeling – and he is not altogether wrong – that only seduction or a beating or rape would have the necessary power of persuasion.
>
> (Jung, 1959, para 29)

Speaking as a woman addressing a conference of women and men, I said that we women had a different relationship to the city streets outside the well-lit room. As we all left the building, women would adopt our half-conscious awareness of potential danger. Early-learnt safety strategies would kick in: stick to well-populated streets, walk fast and look straight ahead, never go where the street's lamps do not . . . Every time a woman goes out alone, particularly after dark, she is afraid in a way a man is not, even if statistics tell another story that men are more *likely* to be attacked. And yet women's fear has a double inevitability: we dread rape as well as other forms of physical harm.

What I did not say in this role of a woman for whom, in Jung's terms at least, 'man' is other, is that men are not immune from domestic violence, even from women partners. I considered including this unbiased statement, but I felt, I *felt* impelled to speak as one-who-has listened-as-a-woman to mostly women speaking in the margins because they *felt* they would not be believed or accepted if they publically acknowledged their suffering. After I presented this talk, a man spoke privately and said that as gay, he too suffered the fear of incipient violence on the streets. He thanked me for describing this half-conscious, almost never discussed, *different* embodied relation to *outside* and said he felt included by my words – which was remarkable and even joyful.

Women and men are, perhaps crucially, less a binary division through sexuality. Women (and gay men) fear violence, including rape, *outside*, and are disproportionately subject to violence, including rape, *inside*. What I would testify to, and a legal connotation here is deliberate, is the brutal and lasting violation of the psyche – imagined as another *inside* – from rape and/or physical attack by a partner. Spoken *to*, I witnessed suffering that did not necessarily diminish with time. Encouraging these victims to get what therapy they could find or afford, did not seem to be a passive act. For who can ask for help if they feel too shamed to deserve it? How difficult is it to hold oneself worth fighting for, if the sense of self is destroyed, leaving only contamination?

To return to Jung's writing that 'often the man has the feeling – and he is not altogether wrong – that only seduction or a beating or rape would have the necessary power of persuasion', I am deliberately putting it in the context of my role as the one spoken *to*, of rape and domestic violence and of the gendered embodied second 'position' of the first quotation in this chapter. It may appear perverse that I am not placing this utterance in the context of Jung, the man with a well-documented history of anxieties about women, beginning with his mother (Jung, 1963/1983).

I am also not placing these words in the context of 'what did Jung really mean' by them? The notion that writing should be interpreted according to the biography or the intention of the author is a fine one. It feels natural. Like many 'natural' activities, it proves to be profoundly cultural. Treating the author as the source of meaning is, in effect, to promote him or her to the position of deity. The author becomes the god of the text: the source of all its meaning and being. Not only is this to strip away centuries of 'reading differently', for example, according to genre, tradition, etymology, divine inspiration or performativity, but it is also a highly dubious practice for Jungian psychology.

Putting Jung's comment about seduction, beating or rape into the context of his own relations with women to be 'explained', or explained away, easily coalesces into second guessing 'what did Jung *really* mean?' Such a strategy imports an ego as a superior rational will into the text. Reading for rational ego is surely contrary to the direction of Jungian psychology's prioritisation of 'other' qualities in the psyche (Rowland, 2005). Such a deification of the presumed rationality of intention reveals the notion of author as sole god of the text's being to be the last-ditch stand of a monotheistic culture. Here we have monotheism's most patriarchal moment, God as Father eclipsing all 'others' as textual coherence is manufactured from the supposed rational will embodied by the divine author.

What I am suggesting is that Jungian psychology can be regarded as support for a mode of reading that relieves a piece of writing from the demand that it be coherent, that it produce *one* or a *whole* meaning. Jungian psychology allows a shift from monotheistic to polytheistic reading, which dissolves patriarchy's insistence on masculinising meaning, for it no longer has to be *one*. So the three positions formulated by the initial Jungian quote here: transcendent making of concepts, gendered in a dualistic and embodied sense, and finally the anima voice, can all remain at liberty. Put another way, in my approach to Jung's more infamous suggestions about seduction, beating and rape, taking the gendered and embodied perspective is only a prelude to offering more than one interpretation for what is going on.

I propose that Jung's sentence beginning 'often the man has the feeling – and he is not altogether wrong', be considered in at least three ways: as in itself unreadable, as saying the unspeakable and as offering the unthinkable. This final reading is of the sentence as sublime in the sense of putting forward that which cannot directly, or completely, or literally, or rationally, be represented (Shaw, 2006).

Jung's infamous quote is unreadable because it is impossible to follow the interpretative options. Reading here demands great effort to maintain a rational perspective in the face of extreme feelings invoked by these words. The writing is incendiary. 'Seduction, beating or rape' ignites the gendered imagination whatever the gender of the particular reader. For I am not arguing that only women may read such lines as condoning rape or sexual violence. All of us of any gender and/or sexual diversity do find it hard to stop and *examine* these words.

However, the quotation does not in fact necessarily condone any of the actions indicated. First of all, the subject here is 'a man', not Jung. Secondly 'he' has a 'feeling' rather than a well-thought-out evaluation of the situation. Thirdly he is 'not altogether wrong', which could mean not morally wrong *or* not factually wrong. Is the quotation saying that violence is a morally justifiable option when the woman's animus is dominant, or that such brutality is merely efficacious without being right?

And yet, ambiguity in these sentences surely does not exonerate Jung from appearing to countenance such behaviour. After all, Jung is 'a man'. So we cannot be sure that 'a man' does not refer generically to all men rather than some males who get 'a feeling' when confronted by the animus of their female partners. In the animus, the man faces the irrational unconscious masculinity of a woman. It is striking that the quotation makes no mention of the mirroring it implies between uncontrolled aggression in the psyche of a woman and the violent desires of the man. While 'a feeling' in these circumstances is also connected to the irrational other in us all and not presented as a guide for behaviour, the Jungian emphasis in valuing the unconscious other tends to legitimise such emotional responses.

On the one hand, Jung is culpable for offering such an ambivalent analysis of gender conflict that it can be read as condoning violence. On the other hand, what if these unreadable words are so because they touch unspeakable truths? What is this 'feeling' when faced by a partner possessed by their own gender other? Put another way, if a judicious editor removed this passage from Jung's work to make it more reasonable or rational, what, if anything, would be lost? Seduction or beating or rape are three modes of tyranny, two explicitly sexual with 'beating' lacking a gender while emphasising bodily strength.

The prevalence of rape and domestic violence is far greater than the law punishes. But perhaps the *desire* to forcibly control a partner is greater still? Jung's writing definitely depicts women as beset by unstoppable inner aggression, while a man 'might feel' that only sex as tool of power or actual imposition of superior strength would enable him to regain control. Here in the mirror of two extreme drives for dominance are the darker powers of the psyche in women and men, portrayed differently, because of Jung's essentialist assumptions that a male body means simply a masculine ego wholly different from a female body connoting a feminine ego. Before challenging that essentialism, I want to point again to the incendiary impossibility of reading these words *straight* and suggest a value in how they force recognition of the potential for violence in everyone.

Jung's essentialism is hard on men for depicting the 'feeling' for actual bodily and psychic harm while the woman is simply possessed by animus aggravation. In fact, in the mirroring effect of dismembering rage between the man and the woman, we see how far Jungian essentialism breaks down because of his commitment to a gender-fluid and compensatory psyche. The mirroring occurs because ego gender is not stable and essentialist but rather subjected to the other as the other gender. Jung's unreadable writing is also inscribing the unspeakable as recognition of the potential for violence and the lust for power in sexual relationships.

I want to end with a further sublime possibility in interpreting the infamous quote by turning to the ultimate disaster in relationships: murder. To me murder is inferred in these lines not just because rapists sometimes kill and beatings can end in death. Rather murder is connoted, because of the extreme emotions generated when lovers reach the point of needing to utterly control or entirely quench the other. The endgame of irrational aggression is the destruction of the spirit opposing it.

So if the unspeakable here is the violence in all of us, does that include murder? With this possibility comes the sublime: here the unrepresentable notion that we might all be capable of murder if anima or animus pushed us too far. Given that murder is not, fortunately, acted out in most relationships, what is offered by sublime murder by Jung's words?

The possibility of murder is not overtly present in these sentences by Jung. It is, I suggest, sublimely and terribly present because of the overwhelming impulse to kill the spirit of the other. As in the mirroring aggression, it is matched by the alternative of suicide. Murder occurs when one of the partners *has to die*. Only in the escape from the literal can a third option be figured. If 'I' cannot go on living until 'you' are dead, then either 'I' has to die or 'I' has to die in the sense of transformation, becoming someone completely different, reborn.

While not pretending that Jung's infamous quote is a straightforward boon to feminism, I do propose it to be astonishingly oracular and fertile in its unreadability, in saying the unsayable about violence and in being the sublime prompt to transformation.

And so, I ended my talk gazing at the women and men analysts, those who can nurture the soul's transformation. 'Now,' I said, 'it's over to you.'

References

Jung, C. G. (1925/1954) 'Marriage as a psychological relationship.' *CW*17.

Jung, C. G. (1959) *Aion. CW*9ii.

Jung, C. G. (1963/1983) *Memories, Dreams, Reflections*, recorded and edited by Aniela Jaffe. London: Fontana.

Rowland, S. (2002) *Jung: A Feminist Revision*. Cambridge: Polity.

Rowland, S. (2005) *Jung as a Writer*. New York and London: Routledge.

Shaw, P. (2006) *The Sublime: The New Critical Idiom*. Oxon and New York: Routledge.

14

DEFENCES OF THE SELF

Cultural complexes and models for nonviolent conflict resolution

Joerg Rasche

On the first night of the Second European Conference of the IAAP in St Petersburg in 2011 (with the theme of 'Border*land*'), I had a dream. I was in a group. We wanted to walk on a melting glacier in the mountains. We and our guide were approaching the cliffs of the glacier. Somehow I knew that it would be possible and not dangerous to walk on the melting ice if one set one's feet carefully. But before we reached the edge of the ice, we came to a torrent of melting water, flowing out from under the glacier. The rushing water washed out a deep bed and took stones and bushes and even trees with it. I saw a tree falling down into the torrent and realised that I should not try to intervene. Otherwise I could myself fall into the wild water.

A social dream

It was a social dream. The melting glacier was in my mind during the days of the conference. Melting emotions were triggered in most of the presentations by colleagues from so many different countries on the background of decades of mutual violations, frozen projections and reactivated cultural complexes and identities, but also of a new freedom and creativity. It was helpful to walk slowly and to set the feet carefully. The term 'Border*land*' was introduced by Jerome S. Bernstein to describe a world 'between darkness and light' in the face of trauma and helped to keep many experiences and emotions together (Bernstein, 2005). Another triggering term was 'the replacement child'. Kristina Schellinski (Schellinski, 2011) spoke about 'Dreams and existential questions of clients whose family members have died or disappeared'. This was a fate in reality that was familiar to many of the participants of the conference, and, as it came out, somehow all of us were revealed to be children born with legacies, carriers of shadows and hopes of former generations.

Remarks on the cultural Self

In the two decades after the collapse of the eastern bloc, many old and new 'nations' appeared in Europe. The bloc fell apart and showed what was hidden under the surface of the totalitarian system. Some of the new-old nations behaved in a relatively harmless manner; others reactivated long-forgotten strong nationalistic or neo-religious nightmares. It was as if the melting glacier expelled and excreted rudiments of former living structures, like the melting permafrost in Siberia sometimes gives birth to the fossils of a mammoth, and some scientists even try to breed and to raise them again. The only point is that these twice-born monsters would not find their original habitat of a million years ago. They would become psychotic.

The situation is not so different in a way from what is going on in Europe. For a better understanding we have to go back in history. The first period of the 'Birth of Nations' was when the European peoples fought against Napoleon's troops 200 years ago. 'Nation' in the modern sense is a phenomenon of the era after the Enlightenment, say the eighteenth century, a period of early industrialisation and longing for a secure market (Renan, 1882). But there were also intrinsic needs for a psychological container, after the collapse of the old world of ancient monarchies and the union of altar and throne, of spiritual and political power (Rasche, 2013).

The shift from God to the Earth archetype

My dream referred also to an ecological theme: the warming up of the atmosphere and the growing awareness of ecologic conditions of our existence on the globe. Erich Neumann (1953) wrote about the shift from the hegemony of the God archetype to the Earth archetype after the Renaissance, which opened new and unforeseen possibilities for the expanding modern mind. C. G. Jung in *Aion* (1951) amplified the remarkable synchronicity with astrological pattern, the turning point of the Fish Aion and the reappearance of the Antichrist around 1789. What was previously projected into the God archetype as representative of the collective Self was, step by step, rediscovered in the earth, the world, nature, in the family, in the people and finally in the 'Nation' as an imagined community on a special spot on the earth's surface. With the Earth archetype, the repressed feminine came back. The paradigm shift in the sixteenth century evoked panic reactions of the patristic Church and led to numerous witch trials. Today the earth, its limited space and resources appear as the limiting ultimate reality – as absolute as the God archetype had been until 500 years ago. We project our Self onto the blue globe, a symbol of the Round, of Totality and Wholeness. It has a religious dimension, because symbols of the Self and symbols of God are – empirically – the same. If we destroy the earth, the blue planet, we destroy our Selves and God.

Cultural complexes bind the psyche together. They are tools of the collective psyche, and they are neither good nor bad. We need them, as we need our culture, but they like to behave like autonomous complexes and can be abused in times of crisis for the collective Self. This may be the hour of demagogues, and the cultural complexes can become very dangerous. I think that the psychology of Islamist terrorists follows this pattern. We remember what Jung said in *Wotan* (1936) – having in mind that the demagogue himself was passively possessed by and actively pushing forward the collective paranoia.

Today in the age of globalisation, with mass migration and the loss of cultural identity, the idea of a nation may seem to be superseded by the longing for rudiments of identities, or at least artificial surrogates. What is needed is something to make one feel at home even in the homeless state of exile. It is a kind of collective Self, or a projection screen for what a collective Self could be. Nationalistic self-surrogates seem easily to be triggered around the world – or artificial religious phantasms like the 'Islamised Islam' of Salafists (Bauer, 2011; Rasche, 2015). The cruel behaviour of its protagonists and 'warriors' reminds of the paranoid crisis of Christian Europe in the sixteenth century. It is about what Singer called 'Archetypal defences of the group spirit' (Singer, 2002). Sometimes even an artificial or synthetic group spirit will be created and defended, to protect the individual and the collective from the abyss of paranoid nothingness.

To come back to my dream: global warming, ignored by most politicians for decades, now becomes a real danger for the industrialised nations and economies as well as for the poor countries who are suffering from aridity and unforeseeable rains and storms. Mother Earth has become incalculable, or even dangerous.

About nonviolent conflict resolution

The highly loaded complexes seduce to projections and aggressive acting out. Our world today is again shaken and shuddered by war, horrifying massacres, mass flights and traumata. The environmental movement has sometimes deployed violent actions in the service of protecting nature. It is not easy to find a consistent rhythm in what is being done. What, generally speaking, are the conditions for a nonviolent solution?

The first condition is that both parties agree not to act with violence. It is a paradox – but without a ceasefire no dialogue will be possible. This is common sense for all who are engaged in this field. Early historical attempts we see in the pipe-smoking convents of the natives in America, or in today's armistice arrangements even in Ukraine, or sometimes in the history of Israel and Palestine. Donald Winnicott once called the Berlin Wall an example for a wise regulation to end the hot war and to give both sides time to reflect on their positions (Winnicott, 1969). This worked in the magnetic field of the Cold War, with the threat of 'overkill', and because both sides were able to create a functioning economy. If you simply kill your enemy, you kill the enemy in yourself, as Erich Neumann would say in his *Depth Psychology and a New Ethic* (1949). The first condition for this statement is ceasefire. Sometimes it takes many years, but a dialogue about violent history will be possible.

Talking about history

I want to describe two experiences I had in the last years with conflict resolution in today's mostly peaceful central Europe. One was at a small conference on 'Talking about History' that I arranged more than ten years ago at the German–Polish border. We were a small group of Polish, German and British colleagues, and one colleague whose family was originally from Russia. The idea was that we could not enter into dialogue with each other before we knew more about the real history of our families. We discovered how closely connected the biographies of our ancestors were, and that we were a true European 'family' much more than members of different nations. During the process many of us came to 'hate our own history' because it felt so humiliating to realise what our parents did to each other. (The experience of humiliation is, by the way, one reason for the self-hatred of Islamite terrorists; their knowledge of the bloody history of mutual killing in the last 100 years.) Ten years later, I was honoured by the President of Poland with the Golden Cross of Merit for having arranged the conference and seminars in subsequent years. This shows how much my little contribution was valued!

Conflict resolution in Stuttgart

Two years ago I was invited to a public hearing in Stuttgart, an industrial capital in southern Germany with a great cultural history (Friedrich Schiller, Hegel, Hölderlin. . .). The railway company, the city and the state arranged this meeting in the Stuttgart city hall, and 20,000 people were online and wrote emails during the session. We were four 'experts': three represented the trees in a park nearby and one (me) stood for the psychological aspects of the matter. The meeting was about the railway station. The company, affiliated with the state, had decided to destroy most of the protected historical station building of the 1920s, to build a new station for hundreds of millions of euros, sacrificing for the new tracks a huge part of an old park. The wonderful trees there were up to 300 years old; they had provided shelter for the citizens when Stuttgart was bombed and burned during World War Two. The situation was highly loaded. The state had arranged a public vote, and the majority was in favour of the new station. The tricky point was that the government had consulted not only the afflicted citizens of Stuttgart, but the entire country. The Stuttgart citizens felt cheated and the park was occupied by demonstrators, who lived in tents as well as high up in the trees ('Robin Wood' activists). After two weeks, the police wanted to clear the park, and shot an old man in the eyes with a water cannon, so that he lost his sight. I visited the people in their tents, and some said that they would not leave the place alive if the police cut down the trees. Their arguments ranged widely, and many Buddhist emblems were fixed to the trunks, as well as photos of the Brazilian rainforest.

I was deeply concerned about the suicidal attitude of the young people, and I felt deep sorrow for the wonderful huge trees. I was alarmed by the pending violence and readiness for martyrdom, which reminded me of the escalation of Baader-

Meinhof terrorism in the 1970s in Germany. I wanted to address the emotions being engendered.

In the public and online meeting I spoke a lot about the psychological meaning of trees: trees as living symbols of the cycles of nature, of growing and individuality, of identity and so on. I wanted to open minds for the deep symbolic dimension of what was going on. I also mentioned that new religions often cut down the trees of the former traditions, and that the Schlosspark in Stuttgart was something like a little Brazilian rainforest, an icon for the environmental movement. In fact the park close by the station was the green lung of the big city, and its destruction would have a deep impact on the environmental situation. During the hearing, a question came via the Internet: What would the Dalai Lama say? This was a difficult question! I had to answer, and said: 'I think the Dalai Lama would say: "Take care of the trees in yourself, and care for the democracy in your country! You had the vote, and now you have to realise what the majority voted for – even if you feel cheated by the government. Take care of your democracy – I (the Dalai Lama from Tibet, living in exile) know what I say."'

Of course my statement was not welcomed by everybody. Nevertheless, the removal of the people living in the park two weeks later was carried out without killing or martyrdom. I was told that my statement had a clarifying and calming effect, and in this respect it was a successful intervention.

In those days, I often thought about what C. G. Jung did in 1933, giving his Berlin seminar (Jung, 1933a) and the Weizsaecker Interview (Jung, 1933b) a few months after the election of Hitler as Reichskanzler. Jung did not speak directly in a political manner, but he tried to open the eyes and ears of his audience for an ongoing symbolic process. What he did was group therapy. I don't know if he was right to do so. He was obviously not aware that Hitler had already suspended all democratic safety and order. In Stuttgart I tried to create consciousness instead of emphasising the emotions, in order to support democratic processes. It was a dilemma. The centre of Stuttgart today is devastated and the building of the new railway station becomes more and more of a financial and ecological nightmare. Was I wrong?

When I was writing this chapter it came to my mind that in posing our question to the Dalai Lama, my fabricating an answer put some projection of the spiritual leader upon me. It is what Jung called the *mana personality*, the unquestionable wisdom of the archetype of the Old Wise Man. When Jung gave his seminar in Berlin in 1933, he carried the *mana* projection of many German psychoanalysts and psychotherapists who were suffering from the terror, not knowing how to behave in the totalitarian system. Some in Jung's audience, for example James Kirsch, had already arranged their emigration in flight from the Nazis. Jung was regarded as a leader, and in this position his utterances (what he said and what he did not say) had a greater weight than he was aware of. He wanted to be a 'healer', as Barbara Hannah and Jolande Jacobi said later (Rasche, 2012). In those years, too, to act in an openly political manner was taboo for psychoanalysts, and Jung followed this general line. When he took over the presidency of Allgemeine Ärztliche

Gesellschaft für Psychotherapie, the General Medical Society for Psychotherapy, to aid the survival of psychotherapy in Germany, he acted politically, put his foot in it and stepped into a sea of traps, projections, identifications and hostile criticism. We can therefore learn that if someone takes over political responsibility, he should be aware of different dimensions: the therapeutic one, and the possibly projected spiritual meaning, with the danger of inflation.

Conclusion

What is needed for the development of the Self, be it an individual or collective Self, and be it a psychological Self or the *anima mundi*, is space for play and, in critical times, protection by a responsible ego complex. Western European nations, after two disastrous world wars, have learned that war and violence can't be a solution for any disagreement. Nevertheless, in Kosovo we witnessed the worst genocide since the Holocaust, and today Russia and Ukraine are in an open military conflict. Expanding NATO is part of the same game. European states produce and sell weapons worldwide, and not only for the use of democratic states. It is for control of oil supplies and for shareholders' profit that states and big business still today work closely together with dictators and betray the ideals Europe once stood for. But we will see that economic and military power will not be the last word.

But what were these ideals? Symmetric patterns tend to either–or solutions. Following Johan Galtung, a renowned scholar for peace studies, a creative discourse will be possible only if common and shared interests can be found. Then the exclamation mark (!) can be replaced by the question mark (?) and a playful dialogue about similarities and differences commence (Galtung, 2007). Paradoxically, older cultural patterns that were not obsessed by the fear of ambiguities could be examples for us – see the history of old Islam before its falsification by the Salafists (Bauer, 2011). The collective Self behaves and has the same needs as the individual Self. It wants to play, to enjoy its life. It hates rigidity. Psychologically speaking, what is needed is something like Winnicott's transitional space, or Dora Kalff's 'free and protected space' of sandplay therapy (Kalff, 1979), or the free experimental and emotional field of psychoanalysis. Well understood, analysis is not a technique applied by an emotionally detached technical expert, but rather a process of mutual discovery and development. To defend the Self means to defend life, diversity and the rights of the other.

References

Bauer, T. (2011) *Die Kultur der Ambiguität. Eine andere Geschichte des Islams*. Berlin: Verlag der Weltreligionen, Insel.

Bernstein, J. (2005) *Living in the Borderland: The Evolution of Consciousness and the Challenge of Healing Trauma*. London: Routledge.

Galtung, J. (2007) *Konflikte und Konfliktlösungen, Die Transcend-Methode und ihre Anwendung*. Berlin: Kai Homilius Verlag.

Jung, C. G. (1933a) *Das Berliner Seminar*, typescript.

Jung, C. G. (1933b) 'Interview with A. Weizsäcker', *Berliner Funkstunde*, 26 Juni 1933. In M. von der Tann/A. Erlenmeyer (eds) *C. G. Jung und der Nationalsozialismus*. Berlin: DGAP, 1991, pp. 7–11.

Jung, C. G. (1936) *Wotan*. *CW*10.

Jung, C. G. (1951) *Aion*. *CW*9.

Kalff, D. (1979) *Sandspiel. Seine therapeutische Wirkung auf die Psyche*. Zurich: Rentsch Erlenbach.

Neumann, E. (1949) *Tiefenpsychologie und Neue Ethik*. Zürich: Rascher (*Depth Psychology and a New Ethic*. Boulder, CO: Shambhala, 1990).

Neumann, E. (1953) 'Die Bedeutung des Erdarchetyps für die Neuzeit.' *Eranos Jahrbuch*, 11–56 ('The meaning of the Earth Archetype for modern times', *Harvest: International Journal for Jungian Studies*, 27, 1980).

Rasche, J. (2012) 'C. G. Jung in the 1930s: Not to idealize, neither to diminish.' *Jung Journal, Culture and Psyche*, 6(4): 54–74.

Rasche, J. (2013) 'European cultural complexes.' In E. Kiehl (ed.), *Proceedings of the IAAP conference Copenhagen*. Einsiedeln: Daimon, 2014.

Rasche, J. (2015) 'Europe and Islam: A paradigm of activated cultural complexes.' In J. Rasche and T. Singer (eds), *Europe's Many Souls: Exploring Cultural Complexes and Identities*. San Francisco, CA: Spring Books.

Renan, E. (1882) 'What is a nation?' In M. Flacke (ed.), *Mythen der Nationen. Ein europäisches Panorama*. Berlin: Köhler & Amelang, 1998.

Schellinski, K. (2011) 'The ghosts of two world wars: Is the replacement child part of a cultural complex in the European psyche?' In J. Rasche and T. Singer, *Europe's Many Souls: Exploring Cultural Complexes and Identities*. San Francisco, CA: Spring Books (2015).

Singer, T. (2002) 'Archetypal defences of the group spirit.' *Jung Journal*, Spring.

Winnicott, D. (1969) 'Berlin Walls.' In *Der Anfang ist unsere Heimat*. Stuttgart: Klett, 1990, pp. 247–54 (*Home is Where We Start from*, London: Norton, 1986).

15

SNAPSHOTS OF THE OBAMACARE CULTURAL COMPLEX

Thomas Singer

The collective psyche and cultural complex

The notion of complexes forming sub-personalities as a central part of the way in which Jung thought about the psyche and its structure is familiar to many. The extension of Jung's complex theory into our tradition's thinking about social and political realities makes use of this idea of sub-personalities or splinter parts of the psyche as having an autonomous life of their own in the collective psyche of groups as well as the psyches of its individual members. Cultural complexes are actually made up of bits and pieces of psyche from all the individuals who are drawn by the numinous power and energy of political, social, economic and spiritual forces that can engulf those who share a specific time, space and unique historical moment. *The Rumour*, by the German artist A. Paul Weber in 1944 (Figure 15.1), illustrates how a sinister collective beast can be formed by the psyches of individuals who are sucked into the orbit of a cultural complex – becoming its eyes, its ears, its thoughts, its emotions. I use images throughout this chapter as a way to imagine how these phenomena live in the collective psyche, which, at its deeper levels, is far less about differentiated thought and much more about affect, image and instinct.

The splinter personalities that come to embody the conflicts of a culture start to look and feel in the media as if they are actual personalities in their own right. Obamacare has become just such a character and player in the American political psyche. The issue of how best to deliver healthcare has been on the national agenda in one form or another for almost 100 years. I became actively involved in the discussion during Senator Bill Bradley's 2000 run for the Democratic Presidential nomination. I served in a very minor role on Bradley's healthcare team, but in the process, I became more familiar with the crisis of medical care delivery. At that time, approximately 40 million Americans had no form of healthcare insurance whatsoever. By the time Barack Obama was elected President in 2008, this national scandal had grown to close to 50 million uninsured.

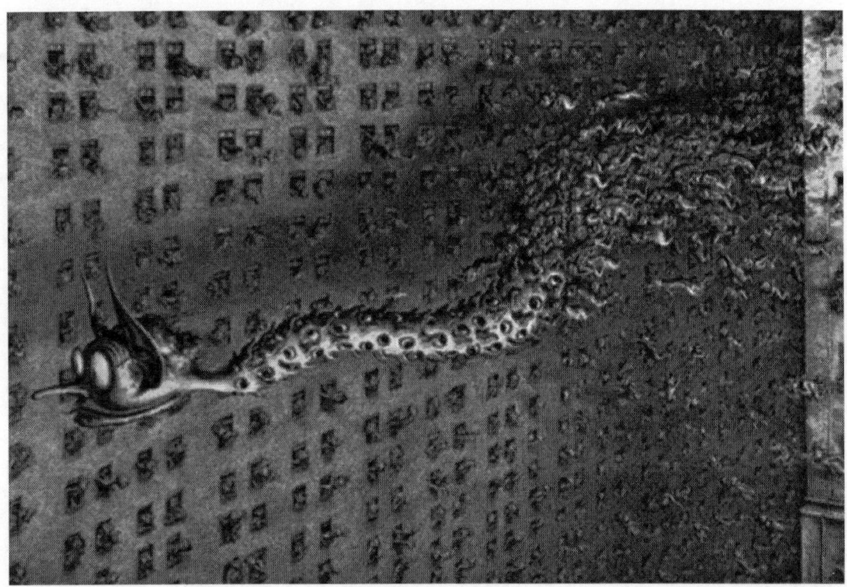

FIGURE 15.1 A. Paul Weber, *The Rumour*

Obama promised – as had his predecessors without success – to deliver healthcare reform, and his Affordable Care Act was signed into law in March 2010. With an uncanny ability to change a law into a psychological cultural complex, the Republican opposition quickly renamed the Affordable Care Act, calling it *Obamacare*, and, with their own political genius, created Obamacare as the Fourth Stooge poster child (Figure 15.2). In doing so, it attracted all the loathing, frustration, fear and distrust that lurks in the American cultural unconscious, dividing and paralysing the national will in its ability to address the healthcare delivery crisis in a straightforward and realistic way.

You may wonder why I started with a 1944 image from Germany, but a recent quote from a Republican official brings the visual association closer to home in terms of how Obamacare is perceived by many Americans – perhaps even a majority. The official said, 'Democrats bragging about the number of mandatory sign ups for Obamacare is like Germans bragging about the number of mandatory sign ups for "train rides" for Jews in the 40s' (Terkel, 2014). It is the emotional inflammation of the national psyche around Obamacare that makes this a subject worthy of psychological exploration. If we were to create a contemporary word association test of cultural complex trigger words in America, *Obamacare* would be at the top of the list. It activates the cultural unconscious of Americans in the same way that the word *father* might have activated Schreber in the early days of psychoanalysis if he had taken Jung's word association test.

I suggest going to the Internet link (Taibi, 2014) to view and hear the not atypical exchange about Obamacare to get a feel for what I am writing about. You don't

FIGURE 15.2 Obama as the Fourth Stooge

have to pay attention to the specific arguments or so-called facts, because they are not the point. The point is what happens to a discussion of complex issues when they get caught in a complex and its highly charged field of emotional reactivity.

Some facts about Obamacare

The number of medically uninsured Americans in 2010 was 49.9 million or 16.3 percent of the total population. In 2014, after Obamacare's shaky start, that number has decreased to about 41 million or 13.1 percent of the population. Democrats consider this a major achievement; Obamacare's critics portray it as the beginning of the end of the United States; and others of us view it as a small but significant improvement in an ongoing national disgrace. As Richard Wilkinson and many others have been telling us, the increasing discrepancy between the rich and the poor results in all sorts of social problems, including a decrease in the health of the population as a whole (Wilkinson and Pickett, 2009, p. 20).

This amazing graph (Figure 15.3) shows the relationship between income inequality and 'ill health' – the United States is almost off the charts among the industrialised nations of the world as having the poorest health as correlated with income inequality.

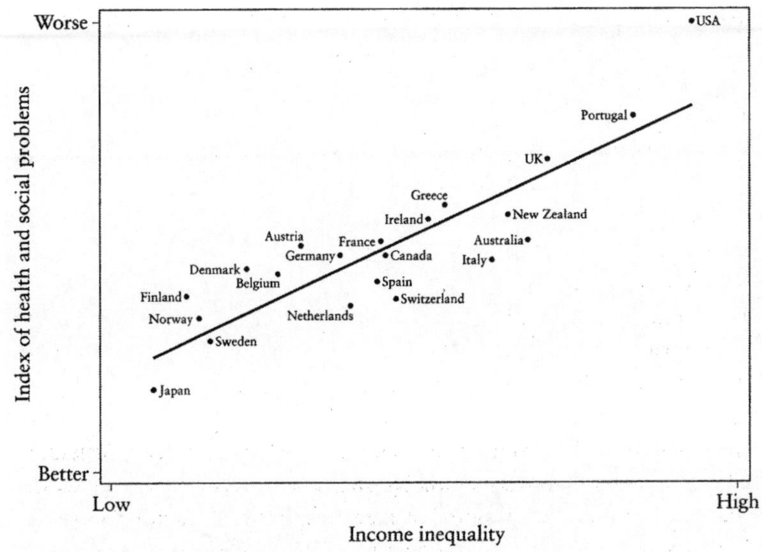

FIGURE 15.3 The relationship between income inequality and 'ill health'

Obamacare as a cultural complex

The problem of healthcare delivery has become exponentially more difficult to address because it has been hijacked and polluted by the potent affects and ideologies of the cultural unconscious in the form of a cultural complex.

As in the painting by Chester Arnold (Plate 4), the Obamacare complex draws to itself every bit of flotsam and jetsam in the American psyche, preventing anything but the most primitive ideation and affect, dividing the country into Us vs Them polarities across which no bridges can be built. It is a Sisyphean ball that includes the American flag, the kitchen sink and everything in between. It rolls over the population in a mind-numbing and dumbing-down assault on every reasonable human faculty. Rational dialogue is non-existent; the emotional charge on the issue is extreme; the collective memory of various competing groups carefully selects its own stories and facts by which to tell the story, rendering the discussions on the issue endlessly repetitive and appealing to the most basic, ongoing conflicted themes in American history. I have created a simple diagram to illustrate these ongoing conflicted themes in the American collective psyche and history, which have become the central ingredients in the Obamacare cultural complex (see Figure 15.4).

The Obamacare complex is a lightning rod that ignites just about every divisive issue in the American psyche. The following core issues are the fuel rods of the complex. There is a profound divide about the role of the individual and the role of the community in looking after the health and welfare of the citizens. This

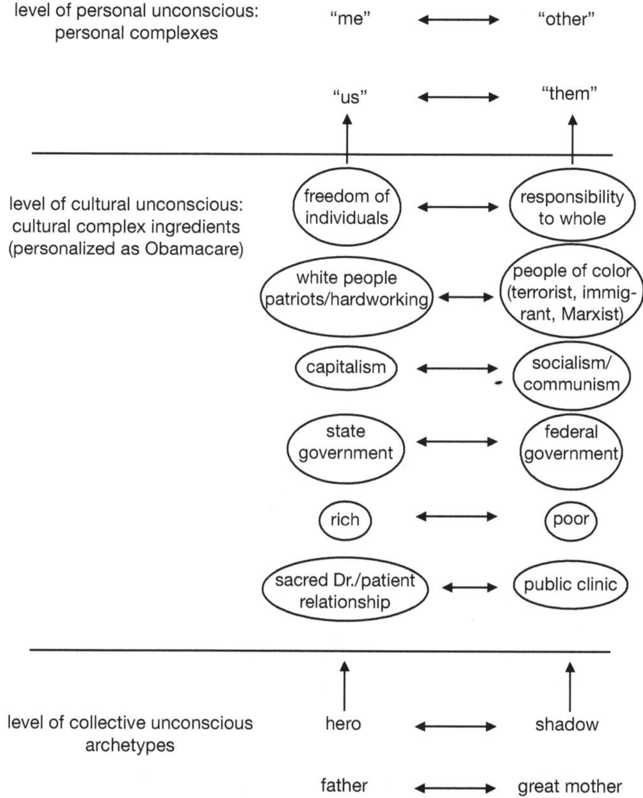

FIGURE 15.4 Diagram of the Obamacare cultural complex by Thomas Singer, MD

sometimes gets characterised as the tension between capitalism and socialism or communism. There is a profound divide about what it means to be free and what it means to be responsible as a citizen – those advocating freedom often championing the notion that every citizen should look after themselves and even act as laws unto themselves by carrying guns, with few responsibilities to the whole community. This gets characterised as the rights of the individual being impinged upon by the demands of the government, which is further projected at a group level onto the fight between the states and the federal government. There is a profound divide between the rich and the poor, with the poor being scorned as failures in their ability to provide for themselves. There is a profound racial divide between White people and people of colour. There is a profound divide along regional differences, between the coasts and the 'heartland of the country' and between the North and the South. All of this swirls around in the cultural unconscious and fuels the Obamacare complex. At the archetypal level, each side on the divide sees itself as being the 'hero' of the culture, wanting to save and protect what is of greatest value in the country. And each side sees its opposition as carrying everything shadowy and destructive in the country's history, acting as a curse on the nation's past, present and future.

The telos of the Obamacare cultural complex

Jungian theory has it that there is an archetype at the core of every complex. It further posits that something of potentially positive value is locked up in the neurotic-seeming complex that has accrued around the nidus of the archetypal issue. This Aristotelian telos of a cultural complex, however, is often impossible to see, much less realise, in the fog of confusion and conflict that swirls around a culture's way of acting out one of its complexes. That is why the Chester Arnold painting is so true to the felt reality of a cultural complex – it collects more and more garbage that tends to roll over, dumb down and numb all but the most fiercely persistent on either side of the conflict generated by the complex. Seeing through to the purposeful goal of the archetypal core of the Obamacare cultural complex is no easy task as the issues accruing around the core are all ferociously loaded with intense political energy, including rights of the individual, responsibility to the whole, the role of government, the divide between rich and poor, racial differences, the sanctity of doctor–patient relationships, the right to die, just to name a few. In this regard, John Beebe, who called my attention to the need to focus on the telos of the Obamacare cultural complex, reminded me that we might think of many of these themes as circulating around the controversial theory of Social Darwinism that Obama himself has cited as a core difference between Republicans and Democrats. For instance, in responding to a Republican budget proposal in 2012, Obama said the following:

> It's nothing but thinly veiled Social Darwinism. It's antithetical to our entire history as a land of opportunity and upward mobility for everyone who's willing to work for it, a place where prosperity doesn't trickle down from the top, but grows outward from the heart of the middle class.
>
> (Parnes, 2012)

Social Darwinism emerged in the late nineteenth century as an offshoot of Darwin's theory of evolution from which the concepts of natural selection and survival of the fittest were adopted by various groups as a scientific justification for their political, sociological and economic philosophies. Those adopting Social Darwinism as their foundational value believe that 'the strong should see their wealth and power increase while the weak should see their wealth and power decrease'

(Social Darwinism, 2015). To those who embrace one form or another of Social Darwinism – whether they call it that or not or even know of the theory – the tenets of natural selection and survival of the fittest are embraced as if they are inviolable laws that govern the healthy development of societies as much as they govern the process of biological evolution. Of course, different movements make different claims as to which groups actually constitute the strong and the weak. Those who are economic Social Darwinists make the distinction about weak and poor based on economic success or failure. Those Social Darwinists who make the distinction between strong and weak on the basis of race, ethnicity or gender will work covertly or overtly to ensure that the identified weaker group remains weak or gets even weaker – whether the group is Black, Jewish, Palestinian, female, gay, White, Islamic, Christian or whomever has been identified as weak.

The Social Darwinist vision of the human condition and destiny is tough and deterministic. That a threat to its thinking might be the 'telos' at the archetypal core of the Obamacare debate is not what is clear to most, and certainly not what one hears about in the day-to-day struggle over Obamacare's efficacy or value, and the almost comedic way it is equated with the end of democracy. As John Beebe has written to me:

> The telos of the Obamacare complex is to force us to *look at* Social Darwinism in action, so as to make us see how inadequate that or any other theory might be when summoned to prevent a more deeply soul affirming inquiry into the issues that surround a matter as serious as how a society proposes to care for those of its citizens who fall ill.
>
> (Beebe, 2015)

Nobody says outrightly, 'Why should the strong, those who can afford healthcare in one way or another, bother about those who are poor and can find no way to afford healthcare coverage?' The fact is that the fundamental issue underlying the Obamacare debate, the way culture itself reacts to the Social Darwinist assumption, is what is at stake. The Tricksterish telos of the complex, paradoxically, is to reveal the complex's fundamental absurdity. But this is not grasped by a nation whose energies are fully engaged in an unconscious debate about Social Darwinism. Instead, what we witness is the absurd lengths to which the unconscious devotees of Social Darwinism are willing to go to stop Obamacare. They display a level of *reductio ad absurdum* within the complex itself. Tragically, neither side on the debate can see that the cultural complex itself might be urging us, like in a dream in which we behave absurdly, to take a more critical look at our cultural thinking. And so the issues fester and are taken far more seriously than they deserve; all sides accumulate grievances, collect their respective memories and make their same polarising arguments over and over again. The archetypal pressure fuelling the debate, our culture's deep wish to think and feel more consciously about what we do and do not owe each other, without a theory to pre-empt such an effort, is simply not made conscious. The telos of the complex, which is finally nothing other than cultural consciousness, rarely surfaces and even more rarely enters the discussion of the issues, which remain stalemated. Beebe puts it this way:

> The Obamacare debate should move our culture to see the degree to which, in the Economic Myth, we have managed to assume a Social Darwinist baseline as the given for how culture solves its most fundamental problems . . . to see that, and to force us to realise, given the absurdity of some of the resulting debate, how narrow a base that really is.
>
> (Ibid.)

This does not mean that we don't have the psychological, political and human responsibility to make these unconscious dynamics of the cultural complex as conscious as possible. As the Obamacare example may suggest, our goal as Jungians might be to help reveal, with a healing irony, the telos of such cultural complexes and to look beneath their overt content with a psychological attitude at the purposive process of the complex itself. Let me put it another way: imagine what the discussion of Obamacare might be like if we substituted the African concept of Ubuntu, of the 'interconnectedness of all human beings' for the Social Darwinist core of the cultural complex. Of course, the *reductio ad absurdum* vicious cycle would come full circle when those advocating a more Social Darwinist position about Obamacare might challenge my substituting the Ubuntu vision of human connectedness and say simply that I am caught in a cultural complex and refuse to look at the economic realities of delivering healthcare.

The coelacanth and the primitive filtering system of the collective psyche

Cultural complexes are both highly specific to unique historical situations and, as structures of the group psyche, ubiquitous in human society. We have been exploring this theme of specificity and general applicability in recent volumes on Australia, *Placing Psyche*, and on Latin America, *Listening to Latin America*, with another book on European Cultural Complexes in the works. I sometimes think of how the collective psyche – both as it lives in the world and as it inhabits each individual – as being that part of the psyche/brain that filters what is happening in the world in a way that is analogous to the primitive kidneys that enabled the first amphibians such as the coelacanth (Figure 15.5) to survive out of the water. Their kidneys allowed these creatures to maintain an inland sea, even as they walked out of the ocean. The kidney filters out what is toxic and retains what is essential for the survival of the organism. The evolution of the kidney, as opposed to the Social Darwinist derivative of evolutionary theory, allowed human beings to develop from our amphibian ancestors by allowing us to survive on land while maintaining our individual inland sea. Today, humans also swim in the sea of our collective human psyche, and we can think of cultural complexes as the distillates of the collective psyche's rather crude filtering function. I am quite certain that

FIGURE 15.5 A coelacanth closely resembles the ancestral fish that first emerged from the water to walk on land some 400 million years ago.

one day, something akin to what we call cultural complexes will, when stimulated by cultural complex trigger words such as *Obamacare*, light up in neuroimaging studies those parts of the brain that link affect, memory, ideation, image and behaviour.

References

Beebe, J. (2015) Personal communication.

Parnes, A. (2012) 'Obama: Paul Ryan's budget "nothing but thinly veiled social Darwinism."' *The Hill*, 3 April. Available at http://thehill.com/video/administration/219731-obama-paul-ryans-budget-nothing-but-thinly-veiled-social-darwinism (accessed 4 March 2015).

Social Darwinism (2015) *Social Darwinism*. Wikipedia. Available at http://en.wikipedia.org/wiki/Social_Darwinism (accessed 4 March 2015).

Taibi, C. (2014) 'Anti-Obamacare guest has meltdown on live TV.' *Huffington Post*, 27 March. Available at http://www.huffingtonpost.com/2014/03/27/chris-hayes_0_n_5042261.html (accessed 4 March 2015).

Terkel, A. (2014) 'Tennessee GOP State Senator likens Obamacare sign-ups to Nazi death trains.' *Huffington Post*, 5 May. Available at http://www.huffingtonpost.com/2014/05/05/obamacare-holocaust_n_5267120.html (accessed 4 March 2015).

Wilkinson R. and Pickett K. (2009) *The Spirit Level: Why More Equal Societies Almost Always Do Better*. London: Allen Lane.

SECTION 5

Cultural phantoms

16

'AND DEATH SHALL HAVE NO DOMINION'

Attending to the silence

Gottfried M. Heuer

In 2006, Dr Elya Steinberg, a bodypsychotherapy colleague, invited me to co-lead an ongoing psychotherapy group for post-Shoah generations of victims, perpetrators and bystanders. We envisioned a group where descendants of survivors could meet with descendants of German/Austrian perpetrators and bystanders as well as those of the former Allied and other nations who, at the time, had stood by in passive silence. We based this perspective on the 1938 Evian/France conference, to which Roosevelt invited representatives of 33 countries to limit immigration of Jewish refugees from Germany. The Nazis took this as tacit acceptance of their subsequent genocide. Although initially expressed in a different context, in the continuing collective silence Jung's words appear to address the dilemma of a thus wounded history: 'The repressed problems and the suffering . . . fraudulently avoided secrete an insidious poison which seeps into the soul . . . through the thickest wall of silence and through the whited sepulchres of deceit, complacency, and evasion' (Jung, 1954, para 154).

Trans-historically understanding history as a current event, and considering victims, perpetrators and bystanders, however different their roles, as being caught up 'in the same malignant cultural complex' (Beebe, 2006), we intended the group to approach the past in terms of individual and collective traumas to understand and help heal one of the sources of the present Israeli/Palestinian conflict, one of the major issues currently dividing our world.

Our project was inspired by Dan Bar-On's work, who, some 30 years ago, initiated groups where descendants of Nazi perpetrators and Jewish survivors met to share their individually differing historical and political truths in the hope of creating a common one. Bar-On had also facilitated similar groups of Israelis and Palestinians.

Correspondingly, Vamik Volkan convened a group of German and Jewish psychotherapists in Germany in 1997/8 (Volkan et al., 2002). There,

> the struggle to establish . . . contact . . . reactivated *malignant but previously hidden German-Jewish interactions* . . .Contact . . . could induce a 'time collapse' . . . where perceptions, feelings, deeds and defences . . . would be condensed with current events.
>
> (Halasz, 2006, p. 107)

Towering in the background as collective effort and moving example was the mid-1990s' South African *Truth and Reconciliation Commission*: nationwide, thousands of victims and perpetrators took the opportunity to publicly engage with the possibility of reconciliation by speaking their truths.

Following these examples, our group would hopefully enable participants to work in-depth towards redemption. We were also invoking a spiritual dimension, essential for healing to occur.

With this flyer, we introduced our project:

> The Post-Holocaust Generations: Attending to the Silence
>
> Although well over half a century ago, the trauma of the Shoah continues to affect our daily lives and our relationships – . . . personal as well as collective. **The wounds have not been able to heal**, the terrors still too fresh for us to have been able to attend to them. Deep inside, we are still paralysed . . . shocked into silence . . . This seems to be true for *all* sides – victims as much as perpetrators, *and* bystanders – as well as their descendants . . . We understand this silence as a protective reaction to that which is **beyond comprehension**. Yet, *this* kind of silence prevents healing. Building bridges together with hope for truth and reconciliation . . . we want to attend to the silence to further the capacity for pleasure and joy, happiness and love, in the words of the prophet, to *'restore the years that the locust hath eaten'* (Joel 2:25).
>
> We are inviting all those with whom these thoughts resonate to an ongoing group.

This flyer was distributed to bookshops and therapeutic organisations all over London and was also put on several websites of the latter, as well as sent out electronically via their lists. Holocaust organisations and Jewish schools, community centres and cultural institutions were informed, as well as German/Austrian embassies (a single nation under Nazi rule) and their respective cultural and trade organisations, the Goethe-Institut, the Austrian Cultural Forum, the German-British Chamber of Industry & Commerce, and some two dozen German-language churches, schools, banks and companies. The text also went out on the discussion lists of the *International Association for Jungian Studies* (IAJS). The editor of the PCSR newsletter (Psychotherapists and Counsellors for Social Responsibility) published the text, and we put paid adverts into *The Jewish Chronicle* and *Green-Events*.

The predominant response to our call for *Attending to the Silence* was – *silence*, yet again, and yet more of it. Some Orthodox Jewish institutions refused to display our leaflet. Most noticeable was the near-total silence from the German side. A German male acquaintance explained, 'For Germans the Holocaust is no longer an issue. We are looking *forward*, not backwards to the past!', whilst noting as an aside – and literally in the same breath – that anti-Semitic crimes in Germany had risen by 26 per cent compared to the previous year!

Total silence from therapeutic colleagues and academics – with barely a handful of exceptions, all female – as well as from all firms, companies and institutions. Only the German Embassy responded: regretfully, they saw themselves unable to support our project because it pursued 'commercial' besides therapeutic interests. They kindly suggested that we turn to the Israeli Embassy and Jewish organisations. I emailed back that we were in an awkward position, as we were indeed unable to offer our group free of charge because we had no financial backing from anybody, and it was hard to get financial support because we did not offer the group for free. As to the suggestion to turn for support to the Israeli Embassy and Jewish organisations, I wrote that it reminded me of a certain previous German government, which forced the Jewish community to pay reparations for damages caused by the so-called *Kristallnacht*, the euphemistic-sadistic Nazi term for the nationwide 1938 pogrom in Germany/Austria, four months after the Evian conference.

The single exception from the resounding silence was the IAJS: in their online discussion group our leaflet caused a considerable stir and ignited an almost month-long discussion. There was a considerable gender difference: women generally tended to respond from a perspective of empathy, whilst men were more intellectualising and attacking.

As in this context, cultural/racial affiliations are obviously important, the following definitions are how the respondents identified themselves: a Jewish academic voiced strong criticism, stating that declaring the Holocaust 'beyond comprehension' was the standard way of absolving Germans of responsibility. He found comparison of the shock endured by victims with that endured by perpetrators and bystanders shameful, and thought charging 'a hefty fee' disgraceful. He felt it insulting to bring together the kin of Jews and Germans to share their pain, asking, 'Are you saying that if Jews and Nazis had gathered for coffee and Danish, they could have come to feel each other's pain?' (I responded that I indeed believed that.) He declined my invitation to join, writing that he did 'not plan to come to London to hold hands with the progeny of Nazis' (Segal, 2006). (We did meet in a different context 18 months later, and *did* shake hands.)

Susan Rowland, then IAJS Chair, appealed to the list members to discuss 'what is most sublimely terrible in a way that cares for this present, and for our future' (2006). A half-Jewish male academic considered it 'a bit creepy' for a German to take part in this project for payment. 'Germans . . . can only really validly apologize for what took place, and, . . . contribute their scientific expertise to understanding what shouldn't be too incomprehensible' (Gaist, 2006a). The money issue raised considerable concern, focusing on my being German – ignoring the fact that my co-therapist was Jewish. A Jewish woman spoke of the flourishing 'Holocaust-Industry', which was like 'dancing on the graves of the victims'; prompting Andrew Samuels to ask, 'What's the Holocaust-Industry, please?' (Samuels, 2006a). It was suggested we work for free or just ask for donations. (Although this certainly is problematic, where am I to draw the line? *Always*, history is in the consulting room. A White Northern-European male, should I not charge Black patients? Should I not charge women patients in view of millennia of male abuse? Should I, as a grown-up, treat children or should a straight therapist treat gays and lesbians for free for the same reason?)

Relativisations were frequent: 'Why the Jews? What about Blacks, the Armenians, the genocide of Amerindians, Chinese, Rwandans?' etc., etc., including lists comparing victim numbers. Samuels argued in our defence:

> I perceive an assumptive bias against political action and in favour of reflection, because political action merely makes those involved feel good, or political action involves taking sides which is in itself politically shallow . . . or that political action crowds out psychology (as it were). All of these points, though well taken, lack something in terms of morality and integrity . . . I want to say that, without the always ready availability of political action, things in our world might be MUCH worse and those who take a supercilious, pseudo-mature, disengaged, 'academic' sceptical line need to be challenged . . . This kind of 'seeing-through', this clever idealization of rupture and lack as the default positions, is itself extremely sentimental and self-congratulatory – and cruel, as well, when used as a cool way to 'smear' . . . creative work.
>
> (Samuels, 2006b)

Only women respondents, Jewish and non-Jewish, expressed feelings of grief and shock in terms of how they continued to be affected by the aftermath of the Shoah. It was rare for a man to write, 'spirituality and politics not being separate, this kind of work touches so much on the spiritual and the future of humanity' (Gaist, 2006b).

A mere handful of people signed up for the ongoing group – all women, mostly Israeli, one overseas Jewish woman, one German woman (who left after two meetings). Clinical experience with individual clients had led us to assume our project a burning issue: we had expected many more people. Disappointed, we came close to giving up. Where were the men, the Germans, the British Jews, the follow-up generations from the bystanding nations? A colleague commented, 'Of course it would have been nice if you'd got a male/female-balance, if you had equal proportions of descendants of victims, perpetrators and bystanders – but that's not the reality. The reality is what you've got. *That's* what you have to work with!' (Encke, 2006). And that we did. We decided to leave the group an open one until there were enough members to continue as a closed group, determined to continue regardless of the number of participants.

A problem emerging right at the start was the difficulty to acknowledge the suffering of those who survived, rather than seeing their survival in a heroic light only. We could only tentatively look at how surviving the Shoah might have influenced the present Israeli attitude towards the Palestinians. According to Bar-On, internalised aggressions found an outlet in the Israeli/Palestinian conflict (2004, pp. 87–8, 220). It seems extremely difficult to see the previous generations in the role of potential or certain perpetrators. This may well be one of the main reasons for the silence from the German side. I found this confirmed in several conversations outside the group with Germans whose fathers had taken part in the 1941 German assault on the Soviet Union: none of them was able to conceive of their fathers as perpetrators of atrocities, but only as victims.

Silence in reaction to the Shoah is not confined to the German/Austrian side of perpetrators. In a chapter 'Breaking the Silence', Bar-On writes about the 'taboo in society' that in a very similar way has had a hold on the Jewish side:

> For the Jewish-Israeli society it took at least 40 years to recognize the fact that Shoah-survivors were usually encouraged to keep silent about their experiences during the Holocaust . . . This silencing by society . . . applied also to countries where survivors had emigrated . . . Nevertheless the Jewish-Israeli society had special reasons to silence Shoah-survivors: they fared badly in comparison with the model of Israeli heroism, as 'they had not fought for their survival'.
>
> (Bar-On, 2004, p. 49)

Difficulty with engaging the perpetrators has also been acknowledged in the context of the Truth and Reconciliation Commission. With moving humbleness Tutu regretted, 'For me, our greatest failure was not to be able to engage White South Africans more enthusiastically' (Tutu, 2004, p. 3).

Reflection

How are we to understand the multi-faceted responses to our project – including silence? What does the gender difference mean? Why did mostly Israelis respond? Might our own initial impulse to give up in response to what felt like an overwhelming disinterest be understood from a countertransference perspective? Then, in part, it would point to a continuing frozenness in reaction to the trauma of the Shoah – a fear of re-approaching 'the black hole' (Clark, 1982) of both the individual and the collective psyche for fear of being sucked into it. This would mean resigning to 'death's indeed *having* a dominion' (paraphrasing Thomas). This would be colluding with the shadow. Nevertheless, in our work, resignation is always closely at hand. One group member saw us as 'dabbing at a tsunami with a single paper tissue' (Eitan, 2007).

Two kinds of silence need to be distinguished: a nourishing meditative one, and the toxic silence Jung speaks about (1954), a form of paralysis in which feelings need to be frozen and split off. Intellectualisation and the bias in favour of reflection as protection from trauma are not conducive to 'healing wounded history' (Parker, 2001). This kind of silence is like an unattended cancer poisoning our lives. The outright and, at times, offensive condemnations of our engagement similarly seem to originate from an ongoing depression in which there is no space to hope for change and healing; nothing but a cold-war-like continuation of the racist divisions in a repetition compulsion of the atrocious past – *and* present – into the future: continuing to follow the talion-law of 'an eye for an eye' would ultimately render everyone blind.

With regard to the attempted relativisations, where both Jewish as well as non-Jewish respondents had indignantly pointed to *other* genocidal catastrophes past and present: the industrialisation of mass murder, sustained over years, at times going to the extreme of even using the bodies of the victims as industrial raw material, make the Shoah a unique event – so far.

Why the predominance of female response and attendance of our group? Does this continue to reflect the traditional patriarchal gender imbalance, where important shared human qualities can be feminised and thus be rejected as 'other'? In this, feelings might be considered 'women's stuff', implying that *women* are supposed to deal with them, *not men*. Might men, because of their historical record, also be more likely perceived as perpetrators both by others and by themselves, and might that have made it harder for them to join the group?

Might the fact that the strongest positive responses came from Israeli women mean that there, where a whole country and its population are under threat for their existence, the shadow of the Shoah is most painfully felt – and hence the urge greatest to try and work on a solution via relating instead of the traditionally male way of cutting off from feelings and resorting to either silence or/and violence?

Planning and organising took us one year, and we ran the group for a further two. I left then, due to the difficulty of linking the past trauma of the Shoah to the current Israeli/Palestinian deadlock. The group continued, facilitated by Steinberg and a different male therapist from a German-speaking country. Ongoing, the group continues and welcomes new participants (http://www.gerhardpayrhuber.com/information.html).

Conclusion

I have presented a preliminary account of the attempt by Israeli/German psychotherapists to offer a therapy group for the post-Shoah generations. Although clearly one of the sources of the split in current global East/West relations is due to Israel's position, and the way this nation rose mostly from the ashes of the Shoah, the engagement to deal with this legacy in a way that links the past with the present, the personal with the collective, and politics with the sacred, almost exclusively attracted women, predominantly from Israel.

In the light of the poor response it would be easy to conclude that the idea for our project was wrong and that there is no need for the kind of work we envisioned. However paradoxical it may seem, for me the echo we did have nevertheless confirms that work towards a mutual understanding and respect between the different groups and generations is, after all, urgently needed, if there is to be any real hope for a restoration 'of the years that the locust hath eaten' (Joel, 2:25) in a peace where we may all learn to 'love our neighbours as we love ourselves' – the tenet that stands at the very heart of all three world religions that originated from the deserts of the Middle East.

I conclude by repeating some words of Jung's: 'The repressed problems and the suffering . . . fraudulently avoided secrete an insidious poison which seeps into the soul . . . through the thickest wall of silence and through the whited sepulchres of deceit, complacency, and evasion' (1954, para 154).

References

Bar-On, D. (2004) *Erzähl Dein Leben!* Hamburg: Körber. (*Tell Your Life Story: Creating Dialogue Among Jews and Germans, Israelis and Palestinians.* Budapest: European University, 2006.)

Beebe, J. (2006) Personal communication, 7 November.

Clark, G. (1982) 'A black hole in psyche.' *Harvest*, 29: 67–80.

Eitan, Y. (2007) Personal communication, 22 March.

Encke, J. (2006) Personal communication, 8 December.

Gaist, B. (2006a) Personal communication, 7 November.

Gaist, B. (2006b) Personal communication, 10 November.

Halasz, G. (2006) 'Is "new" anti-Semitism really "new"?' *Psychotherapy and Politics International*, 4(2): 101–9.

Jung, C. G. (1954) 'Analytical psychology and education.' *CW*17, para 154.

Parker, R. (2001) *Healing Wounded History.* Cleveland, OH: Pilgrim.

Rowland, S. (2006) Personal communication, November.

Samuels, A. (2006a) Personal communication, 7 November.

Samuels, A. (2006b) Personal communication, 9 November.

Segal, R. (2006) Personal communications, 6 and 11 November.

Thomas, D. (1933) http://www.poemhunter.com/poem/and-death-shall-have-no-dominion/ (accessed on 10 January 2016).

Tutu, D. (2004) 'Heaven can wait.' *Independent Review*, 26 January, 1–3.

Volkan, V. D., Ast, G. and Greer W. F. (2002) *The Third Reich in the Unconscious.* New York: Brunner Routledge.

17

PHANTOM NARRATIVES

A framework for cultural activism in the consulting room

Sam Kimbles

My chapter introduces a way to think about and to work with what I am calling cultural phantoms, the phantom narratives that become active presences in cultures and in our analytic work. My hope is this approach to narrative truth will begin to open up psychic spaces for thinking about and working with some of the most painful and intractable aspects of our psycho-cultural life. As the great African-American playwright August Wilson expressed it in a foreword to a play: 'the long line of forever stretches into the future and the last night of the universe is already suspect and falling' (Wilson, 1992, p. 11).

The topic of analysis and social activism brings together opposites in the way we typically conceive of our analytic field. There are obvious issues around the analytic frame of neutrality, the use of internal constructs and the transference/countertransference with their emphasis on the dyadic, witnessing vs. detachment, privileged, apartness vs. active participation or, as Peskin indicates, how therapeutic neutrality is to psychic reality as witnessing is to the recovery of social reality. I have found that wrestling with these issues, while sitting in my office at the crossroads where individuality and culture meet, can be a challenge to generating for my clients an intersubjective space that releases the potential for humanising the contact around differences, and for processing our mutual messiness when cultural complexes are activated and society enters the treatment room, filling the space with the hope for social change. Though we might put cultural issues of class, race, gender and ethnicity in the background, every word, gesture, indeed the very structure that we set up and participate in, exudes a cultural stance. We are always in the cultural unconscious. To paraphrase Bromberg, the really real are not just fantasies but real events that shape our psyches and their processes.

We become awake or conscious out of the cultural unconscious, from which we are born, through the contemplation of signs, signifiers, and symbols that antedate us. We become conscious of what life means to us, that is, in a world already ripe with meaning. Thus, dissociating the individual patient from that person's cultural background distances us from what our patient is struggling to construe. An analyst then risks becoming a voyeur or a bystander, masquerading as an objective observer. As Bodnar says, 'interpretations, enactments, and the relationship construction unconsciously replicate unexamined tenets of the analyst's cultural beliefs' (2004). Not to become aware of the interpenetration of psyche and cultural factors within the analytic context may turn the analysis into a scene for the enactment of cultural history where the intergenerational transmission of personal and cultural trauma will meet once again within a nuclear family, this time a dyadically configured unconscious shielding the pair who are actually repeating cultural history from the larger social world they would have otherwise wanted to transform. The ongoing difficulties of bridging some of the tensions of culture and psyche are made more complicated when these make their appearance simply as anxiety around differences and when they are expressed as acted-out cultural complexes.

A parable related by Slovenian social theorist and psychoanalyst Slavoj Žižek (2005), about the ignorance of a chicken, speaks to the inextricable bind we find ourselves in when we try to quickly rectify a culturally replicative clinical course by bringing culture and psyche, activism and analysis together. Žižek's story goes, a man finds himself admitted to a mental hospital because he believes himself to be a piece of grain. Working with his mental health team within the hospital, he comes to accept that he is not what he fears and seems to have conquered his delusion and is therefore released from the hospital. Shortly after his departure he comes running back to the hospital and reports to the staff that upon leaving the hospital he had come upon a chicken and had a panic attack.

The doctor reassures the patient that he has nothing to worry about, for he is not something to be eaten, so not to worry about the chicken. The patient responds that 'I know I am not a piece of grain, and you know I'm not a piece of grain, but I am not so sure that the chicken knows that I'm not a piece of grain.'

In responding to this story Prager (2011) makes the point that not only do benign objects get transformed into terrifying ones here, but 'the parable captures the limits of therapeutic cure' – the close system of the dyadic relationship (p. 426). The (analytic) pair can become its own closed system as bulwark against the world. I think we, in this volume, are trying to think about how to open up the pair and include the world with all its ambiguities and messiness.

On a larger scale, cultural themes in our globalised world inevitably express forms, figures and presences that carry the fears, hopes and identity needs derived from breakdown in traditions and disruptions in continuity of our life processes. I feel that a large part of the role of analytical psychology in cultural and political affairs is to help elaborate our understanding of, and relationship to, intersubjective forms that actually represent cultural complexes. It is these masquerading forms that I am calling cultural phantoms, and inviting my colleagues to observe how they play themselves out in psychological and cultural life. Cultural complexes and projective defences (often appearing as strikingly revenant images) are powerful players in the generation of phantom narratives that offer themselves, once again, as a counterpoint to received notions of progress in history and social policy. These narratives are the expressions of marginalised, invisible stories that surprisingly often haunt the analytic narrative. They express drives towards the need for recognition and urges against death and annihilation, and they are regularly expressed in social structures and policies that produce non-recognition. Among those are analysis and how analysis is taught.

In what is therefore a moral crisis for our analytic field, the question is how to transform collective processes when they enter the consulting room or the training institution. Toward this end we might want to understand our own group process in a way that facilitates greater consciousness. We can contribute to a training group's development when we learn to recognise and work with presences in the collective unconscious and of the unconscious in the collective that are unprocessed cultural phantoms. I suggest that behind cultural attitudes and expressions of cultural complexes, cultural phantoms often manifest the absences of marginalised history – the many collective histories from genocide, holocaust and slavery to the everyday presences of cultural background of analysts and patients that manifest the very same power disparities and racial hierarchies that are found in the culture.

Fortunately, racial and ethnic identity formation are not only shaped by internalised negative cultural attitudes towards a particular racial, ethnic, gender group, but also by the positive contribution that one's cultural group contributes to identity formation.

Shamdasani and Hillman, through their long conversation stimulated by Jung's *Red Book*, contained in the book *Lament of the Dead* (2013), constantly return to a theme that relates human cultural ancestry, the weight of human history, with the paradox that the dead 'present themselves as figures of a historic moment, or of a historic period at least, but they're not historic figures' (p. 3). This theme relates to my notion of cultural phantoms and their relationship to politics and social life. Just as the spirits of the dead are, as Jung says, 'voices of the Unanswered, Unresolved, and Unredeemed' (Jung, 1963, p. 191), cultural phantoms are expressions of our unevolved collective imaginary, 'haunted' by phantoms of specifically stuck historical events (traumas) that then get passed along to later generations and organised in politics, social forms, rituals and relationships that turn on inclusions/exclusions and repressive and dissociative power dynamics. Cultural phantoms are images (formations) of cultural complexes that link individual valence with group narrative.

To encounter such hungry ghosts in the background of analysis, the psycho-political terms we too often summon to explain them away must find a way to break with the comforting linear chronology of history we call 'progress' and look beneath the received history of developing consciousness towards another narrative that makes room for stuckness and repetition of unsolved cultural issues. I call the narrative we need to uncover in our work phantom narrative, one which calls into question the official narrative of the evolution of consciousness that many analysts live in and take for granted, because it authorises analysis to succeed without having to look at all it has been leaving out. To reflect on phantom narratives, and let in other perspectives than the accepted ones, brings competing interpretations into play, and opens questions, conflicts and wounds that cannot be so easily closed in the name of healing. For as Avery Gordon (2008) says, to write about these narratives brings out the invisibles, marginalised, the excluded is to write 'ghost stories', i.e. not love stories with happy endings. Phantom narratives call into question a future based upon taking care of past grievances, harms and traumas by transcending them; rather it bids that we open the mouths of the dead (as in Jung's *Red Book*), to see what still needs to be voiced. Cultural phantoms call into question the modern stories we tell ourselves about how things have become, which so often delude as to the way things really are. Descriptions of past historical events, escaping from the mouths of the dead, represent the persisting damage done, and haunt us with the memory of missed historical alternatives. These phantomatic presences richly conjure, describe, narrate and inform and thus they begin to explain to us the costs, the forfeits and the abusive powers that have also shaped us in the name of progress.

Nor are phantom narratives simply 'the return of the repressed' and therefore 'the past'. The future haunts us too, in the name of the present, in the spirit of being millennially 'with it'. Simultaneity, multiplicity, virtuality, new media, digital technology, are also spectres, ways of describing our world that attempt to transcend distinctions like inner/outer, subject/object, the immaterial/material only to bring forth new traumas, dilemmas and phantoms for future generations to struggle with. We, as it was for Jung a hundred years ago, when his worst private fears were confirmed in the history emerging around him, are at a theoretical crossroads. We are being born into a new myth of collective consciousness, and we are learning that this is still what Henderson was the first to call the cultural unconscious. These days, I think of the cultural unconscious as having a spectral quality. As Derrida puns, ontology and hauntology have flipped, and the spectral has taken precedence over the fantasy of cultural ontology. The familiar, with its past, has become the unfamiliar with its future: marginalisation, alienation, homelessness and existential anxiety at a level the existentialists never imagined. These have become the familiar context, not just for our being, but for our becoming, and form a spectre that haunts the future of individuation in our consulting rooms.

The phantom, as image, arose as an expression of historical memory, one that conveys a kind of living continuity between past and present. It has always, ontologically, been an internal, not external, history that brings 'something prior to history' (Corbin, 1978). This inner history, as Murray Stein states,

> is the story of meaning, in which time and eternity, consciousness and unconsciousness, specific historical and archetypal forces all together perform their roles and produce a particular configuration in time.
>
> (Stein, 2014, p. 111)

And I would add particular representations.

But it is now a protonarrative too, heralding the uncertainties of the future. Living, internal memories create a cultural symbolic space in which memories and events are held, elaborated, and come to signify the spirit of the group that will shape many things still to come. This living spirit becomes a rolling zeitgeist – the spirit of a particular historical time and place continually becoming incorporated as part of the group and individual's identity, not just now, but as its future as well. Jung's reflections on this shocking conservative level of the group psyche are present in his use of Lévy-Bruhl's term *participation mystique*, referring to that level of group functioning in which we conserve the nature of culture by acting and reacting, thinking and feeling like others in the group in a way that challenges any possibility of genuine individuation. This level of archaic identity can evolve into symbolic images that designate the ongoing 'presence of the absence' of a piece of transgenerational narrative. Through this, marginalised or dissociated psychic states can be represented as phantoms with a frightening future.

But I would point out that there is hope in knowing this. August Wilson said it best: 'There are always and only two trains running. There is life and there is death. Each of us rides them both. To live life with dignity, to celebrate and accept responsibility for your presence in the world is all that can be asked of anyone' (Wilson, 1992, p. 11).

References

Bodnar, S. (2004) 'Remember where you come from: Dissociative process in multicultural individuals.' *Psychoanalytic Dialogues*, 14(5): 581–603.

Corbin, H. (1978) Preface to D. Miller, *The New Polytheism*. Dallas, TX: Spring Publications.

Gordon, A. (2008) *Ghostly Matters*. Minneapolis, MN: New University Minnesota Press.

Jung. C. G. (1963) *Memories, Dreams, Reflections*. New York: Random House.

Peskin, H. (2012) 'Man is a wolf to man': Disorders of dehumanization in psychoanalysis.' *Psychoanalytic Dialogues*, 22(2): 190–205.

Prager, J. (2011) 'Danger and deformation: A social theory of trauma, part 1.' *American Imago*, 68(3), Fall: 425–48.

Shamdasani, S. and Hillman, J. (2013) *Lament of the Dead: Psychology after Jung's Red Book*. New York: Norton.

Stein, M. (2014) *Practicing Wholeness*. Asheville, NC: Chiron.

Wilson, A. (1992). Foreword to *Two Trains Running*. New York: Plume/Penguin.

Žižek, S. (2005) 'The ignorance of chicken.' Retrieved from http://www.youtube.com/watch?v=LBvASueefk4 (accessed on 4 November 2013).

18

JUNG'S RELATIONSHIP WITH JEWS AND JUDAISM

Thomas B. Kirsch

This chapter is about Jung and his relationship to Jews and Judaism. This topic has stuck to me like glue from childhood through the present, and I am now 80 years old. Basically I have had to defend Jung on too many occasions to remember, and at the same time my views on Jung's relationship to Jews has evolved over these many years.

My father was one of the first Jews to consult Jung after the breakup between Freud and Jung in 1913. James Kirsch, a psychiatrist practising in Berlin, came from an Orthodox and entirely materialistic Jewish family, and he was looking for something meaningful and spiritual to enrich his life. He also had personal neuroses that demanded attention. After two years of Freudian analysis and a Jungian analysis in Berlin, he sought out Jung in 1928. He began his analysis with Jung in May 1929 when he went to Zurich for two months. In 1930, he gave a lecture at the Jung club in Zurich on the dream symbols of his Jewish patients (Lammers, 2016). Many of his patients already had dream images of Nazi thugs. His lecture was so popular that it was given twice, and both Jung and his wife Emma attended. My father decided to leave Germany in 1933, advising his family and all his Jewish patients to leave, because he believed what Hitler had written in *Mein Kampf* (2013),[1] which was that he wanted to kill all German Jews. He emigrated to Tel Aviv, where he was living when he read 'The State of Psychotherapy Today', in which Jung outlined the differences between Jewish psychology and Aryan psychology (Jung, 1934). Jung's description of Jews needing a 'host culture' to thrive was similar to Nazi propaganda about the Jews being parasitic and needing a 'host culture'. These statements by Jung gave credence to what Freud had already written in 1914 in *The History of the Psychoanalytic Movement* – that Jung had temporarily given up his anti-Semitic prejudices to join the psychoanalysis movement, but that he had reverted to his anti-Semitic feelings after leaving it. Ever since, Jung has been labelled 'anti-Semitic' by many critics (e.g. Kuriloff, 2013). This has especially been true in America, where Jung has been defiled in psychoanalytic institutes. A psychoanalytic friend reports that in her training she was taught to consider Jung's name as poison, and until we became friends and colleagues she, like so many other psychoanalysts, had never considered actually reading Jung. One of my colleagues arranged for her to meet with Joe Henderson, a leading Jungian analyst in the United States, and she found the meeting meaningful.

After my father's death in 1989, I discovered his extensive correspondence with Jung, in which my father questioned Jung's relationship to Jews and was aghast when he read what Jung had said about the Jews needing a 'host culture'. He also questioned Jung about his affiliation with the Nazis and asked whether he had become a Nazi. Jung answered him strongly to say that all those rumours were untrue, for in fact he was trying to save German psychotherapy from the Nazi regime and to ensure that Jews would be allowed to participate in the renamed 'International General Medical Psychotherapy Association' as individual members. I think the fact that Jung had even deigned to work with the Nazis during the 1930s was enough to label him a Nazi! Jung's stance was a very Swiss kind of action. The Swiss idea is to work with the enemy in order to find a compromise. It is why Switzerland has a reputation for neutrality and so many international meetings take place there. Jung answered my father fully to state that he was definitely not anti-Semitic, and that he got along well with the Jewish colleagues who had been drawn to him. This satisfied my father at the time, but upon reading Jung's answer today, it would not satisfy most people. Jung's answer would be seen as racist. He did go on to say that Jews were too sensitive, however, and that any personal criticism was too easily and quickly generalised as an anti-Jewish statement. Jung ended by saying,

> In general, you really ought to know me well enough not to attribute to me uncritically a non-individual stupidity like anti-Semitism. You know well enough to what extent I approach each person as a personality, whom I endeavour to lift out of the collective conditioning and make into an individual.
>
> (Lammers, 2011, p. 47)

At the end of the letter he becomes a little defensive, saying that if necessary he will provide letters from sworn witnesses who will attest to the truth of his statements.

My mother, who came from an assimilated professional Jewish family in Berlin and had not known much about her Jewish roots, began her analysis with Jung in 1935. For the rest of her life she often said that Jung had helped her to connect with her Jewish origins and to her Jewish soul.

My parents ended up in Los Angeles at the end of 1940 after their circuitous journey leaving Nazi Germany, with intermediate stops in Tel Aviv and London. They began the Jungian community in Los Angeles. In the 1940s, relations between the Freudians and Jungians were ice cold. When my father gave a talk in public at a well-known hospital, the Freudians in the audience left the room. My father had no love for the Freudians either, so my first experience of the Freud/Jung debate and Jung's anti-Semitism was seen through the eyes of my parents. I sided with them and shared their idealised view of Jung. For years, I continued to share their view of Jung and rejected completely the notion that Jung was anti-Semitic. Only later was I able to differentiate my thinking from theirs, but I continued to defend Jung because the attacks on him were often so fantastical and based on very little fact. I attempted to bring facts about Jung into the picture.

This idealisation of Jung continued through my college and medical school years and was reinforced by three meetings with Jung when I was in my early twenties. The first was in 1955 at his 80th birthday celebration when I was introduced to him and experienced the warmth of his handshake. For many years, I thought that my reaction to the handshake was pure transference, but then at *The Red Book* Conference at the Library of Congress in Washington, DC in 2010, I heard that one of Jung's grandsons had a similar reaction to a handshake with his grandfather. Yes, there was transference, but there was also something special about Jung's handshake. In 1956, after the death of Jung's wife Emma, my father and I went to his home in Küsnacht, where we sat in the garden to have tea. By then I had read *Two Essays on Analytical Psychology* (Jung, 1953a), and questioned him about some matters written in those pieces. In retrospect, I was sophomoric but he was non-defensive and straightforward. I asked him about his statement that 'all knowledge was relative', but I thought that was an absolute statement. I cannot remember how he answered me. What is interesting is that I have never been able to find that statement in *Two Essays*! He made a tremendously positive impression on me. Then in 1958 I had an individual hour with him, which was even more powerful. His opening remark to me was 'So you want to see the old man before he dies'! I was completely taken aback, but of course it was true. He was direct, personal and absolutely friendly. This encounter solidified my desire to become a Jungian analyst. I mention these encounters with Jung because they had a huge impact on me and eventually settled the issue for me to become a Jungian analyst. It was perhaps the most significant vocational experience of my life and so it has been difficult for me to hear some of the criticism that has been thrown about. It does not coincide with my own personal experience. I might add that I have had similar warm experiences with Jung's son and grandsons. His grandson Andreas and his wife, Vreni Jung, are exceptional people, and we have developed a real friendship.

Even though my own attitudes towards Jung remained positive, I heard persistent comments that Jung was a Nazi and an anti-Semite. I defended Jung by stating that my Jewish parents were in analysis with Jung during the time that Jung was supposedly most anti-Semitic, and they never felt a trace of it, and I knew many other Jewish patients of Jung who had similar feelings; this silenced some of his detractors but did not satisfy most.

The first person within the Jungian community to do research with regard to the anti-Semitic question was Andrew Samuels. He demonstrated Jung's shadowy relationship to the Nazis and found statements that could be read as anti-Semitic. Samuels (1993) has researched the history of writings on racial differences and has shown that Jung's writing style and phraseology is similar to some of the early racist writers in Germany (pp. 283–312). Whether these connections were conscious, or what we might today recognise as an implicit influence, is a question that cannot be answered at this moment. It is unlikely that this question will ever be answered definitely. The really important thing is that Samuels' research opened up the question of Jung's anti-Semitism to the larger Jungian community. It was no longer coming solely from the Freudian camp, but from within our own community. Jungians then began to research this question, and now we have many interpretations of Jung's behaviour from the 1930s. No one has found a 'smoking gun', so to speak, and it has become quite difficult to pinpoint Jung's position on this most sensitive subject, which has influenced his acceptance in many places, especially the United States, where in the last several years Jungian scholars and analysts have undertaken to enlarge upon this subject. For example, there is Jay Sherry, who in his book *Carl Gustav Jung: Avant-Garde Conservative* (2010) claims to have the definitive word on Jung's relationship to Jews! Sherry has much interesting new information about Jung, but in my opinion, it is in no way definitive. New material on the subject has come out since his book, which gives a different picture, including the Jung–James Kirsch correspondence and, more recently, the Jung–Neumann correspondence. The Italian scholar Giovanni Sorge's yet-unpublished thesis on Jung in the 1930s includes what Jung did to help individual Jews get out of Nazi Europe. Sorge's material is more up to date and shows a more sympathetic side of Jung's attitude towards Jews. In Sorge's doctoral thesis, he has cited many letters Jung wrote on behalf of individual Jews to aid their escape from Nazi threats in the 1930s; for instance, he wrote a letter of recommendation for my father, which enabled him to enter the United Kingdom and practise as a Jungian analyst.

Jung was fascinated by what was going on in Germany in the early 1930s. Initially, he had great hopes that Germany would recover from the awful economic inflation and social chaos that decimated German society after World War One. But, by 1935, Jung had definitely diagnosed Germany's collective psychosis. In Lecture V of the Tavistock Lectures, he speaks about the power of the collective unconscious to infect the psyche and how he himself, when he went to Germany, was similarly infected:

> It gets you below the belt and not in your mind, your brain counts for nothing, your sympathetic system is gripped. . . . And because it is an archetype, it has historical aspects, and we cannot understand the events without knowing history.
>
> (Jung, 1935, para 372)

He states that there is no way to reason with people gripped by this phenomenon. One just has to accept the collective explosion. In light of our greater awareness today of the destructive power of such collective phenomena, I disagree with Jung's conclusion. We cannot just accept the collective explosion.

In 1962 I began my psychiatric residency. I was immediately identified as a Jungian, and although I was personally respected and generally liked, my being a Jungian held me back from receiving recognition in my training programme. So often I have been asked how could I be Jewish and a Jungian – as if the two were incompatible. Jung is still generally not accepted in the psychiatric and psychological field, and Jung's statements about 'Jewish psychology' in the 1930s still play a large part in his non-acceptance. The professional stance towards Jung has gradually changed and become more positive as his views on the role of religious experience and spirituality have become more acceptable. At the same time Freud's influence has waned as the neuroscientific study of the brain has gained in prominence. I like Jung's approach to the psyche, and personally, he was most gracious to me. I know that there are many interpretations to Jung's behaviour in the 1930s, and I do believe that he made a grave mistake in writing about Jews needing a 'host culture'. He realised that after World War Two, and privately he apologised to his Jewish colleagues about his writings on Jewish psychology in the 1930s. He never made a public statement on the subject, which many of his Jewish followers wanted him to do. He thought that it would be seen as defensive. Instead, he let his Jewish students do the speaking for him. I also recognise that in 1934, when my father was living in Palestine and wrote about the changes he witnessed there, Jung wrote back optimistically about the opportunity for Jews to develop their own culture. So even in the 1930s Jung was open to Jewish psychology being grounded in new roots and removed from its 2000-year history in Europe.

Another place where Jung speaks about his relationship to Jews and Judaism is in an interview that he did with the psychoanalyst Kurt Eissler on 29 August 1953 (Jung, 1953b). Eissler wanted to know about Jung's relationship to Freud. He never had agreed before to speak about Freud, but at age 78, he was candid about Freud and also about Jewish psychology. One interesting observation was about Martha Bernays, Freud's wife, as having been 'extinguished, without an ego'. Both he and Emma, according to the interview, found that Martha Bernays had no idea what Freud was up to with the creation of psychoanalysis. Her role was attending to the children and the household. Jung thought this role was common for women in general, but especially for Jewish women of that era. In order to compensate for that lack of ego 'many of them are so loud, aren't they. . .but please do not think that this is anti-Semitism'! Eissler agrees with Jung that this is not anti-Semitism and adds 'the position of women in Judaism is very unique, and they really come up short'. Jung responds, 'I have treated a great many of them, very many Jewish women – in all these women there is a loss of individuality, either too much or too little. But the compensation is always for the lack. That is to say. . . not the right attitude.' Jung states that Jewish men have always been the brides of Yahweh, which means that the women are obsolete. Therefore, Freud was only occupied with the father. Jung never developed this line of thinking about Jews further, but it is an interesting and controversial statement about Jewish psychology. I am sure many people would see this as anti-Semitic, but Jung saw it as a clinical observation. As Jung said, he had many Jewish patients, including my mother and father, so this was not just a throwaway comment.

Jung's most profound experience of Judaism came in 1944 after he broke his foot and then had a heart attack. He lived between life and death for several weeks and had the following vision, which he describes in *Memories, Dreams, Reflections* (Jung, 1961). His nurse became an old Jewish woman who was preparing kosher dishes for him. Jung himself was in the *Pardes Rimmonium*, the garden of pomegranates, and the wedding of Tifereth and Malchuth was taking place. Jung was Rabbi Simon Ben Yochai whose wedding in the afterlife was being celebrated. It was the mystic marriage as it appears in the Cabbalistic tradition. Other marriages followed, including the Marriage of the Lamb and then the marriage of Zeus and Hera as described in *The Iliad*. Jung had a prolonged recovery from this illness and basically retired from his clinical practice. He did see old patients from time to time, but spent most of his final 15 years writing. In his writings, he now referred to Jewish mystical sources with great frequency as he had experienced the mystical tradition in his 1944 vision. So a profound change had occurred in Jung's psyche towards Judaism.

Note

1 The British edition of *Mein Kampf* was published in 1939.

References

Hitler, A. (2013) *Mein Kampf*. Translated by J. Murphy. Camarillo, CA: Elite Minds, Inc.

Jung, C. G. (1934) 'The state of psychotherapy today.' *CW*10.

Jung, C. G. (1935) 'The Tavistock Lectures.' *CW*18.

Jung, C. G. (1953a) 'Two essays on analytical psychology.' *CW*7.

Jung, C. G. (1953b) *Interview by Kurt Eissler with Jung on Freud, 29 August*. Washington, DC: Library of Congress.

Jung, C. G. (1961) *Memories, Dreams, Reflections*. New York: Random House.

Kuriloff, E. (2013) *Contemporary Psychoanalysis and the Legacy of the Third Reich*. New York: Routledge.

Lammers, A. C. (ed.) (2011) *The Jung–Kirsch Letters: The Correspondence of C. G. Jung and James Kirsch*. Translated by U. Egli and A. C. Lammers. East Sussex: Routledge.

Lammers, A. C. (ed.) (2016) *The Jung–Kirsch Letters: The Correspondence of C. G. Jung and James Kirsch, revised edition*. Translated by U. Egli and A. C. Lammers. London: Routledge.

Samuels, A. (1993) *The Political Psyche*. London: Routledge.

Sherry, J. (2010) *Carl Gustav Jung: Avant-Garde Conservative*. New York: Palgrave Macmillan.

19

BEHIND THE MASK OF CHINA

The continuing trauma of the Cultural Revolution

Heyong Shen

If I refer to 'the mask of China', most readers will think I am referring to the masks worn by performers at the Beijing Opera (see Plate 5). However, these artefacts are not referred to as 'masks' in Chinese but are called 'Lian Pu', the 'Face Book'. This theatrical convention is intended to mark the general nature of the role being played but there is also an invitation to the audience to enjoy some kind of affective identification. For instance, the red mask conveys the symbolic meaning of loyalty, honesty, courage and uprightness. The mask with black detailing suggests something serious, stern, reserved, keeping up a grave demeanour (this is usually the mask for the good guy in the plot). The white one speaks of deceit, betrayal and suspicion. One of the main functions of the 'Lian Pu' is to provide a nuanced range of expressions of good and evil, a bit more complex than stereotypes of good and evil.

Recently, we have seen newspaper accounts of people in China wearing masks because of the air pollution in Beijing and elsewhere. They even wore them to run the marathon in the city. But we don't call these 'masks' in Chinese, but rather refer to them as 'mouth covers' ('Kou Zhao'), in the sense, perhaps, of a surgical mask. Pollution, smog, fog and haze is almost everywhere in China, so people genuinely do have to put these on (see Plate 6). But then you cannot see the person's real face and any real feelings that might be displayed on an open face. It seems to me important that we make a psychological analysis of the depth symbolism of these face cover masks.

Behind this kind of mask lurk people's angry and unspeakable protests. In China today, it is virtually impossible for people to express their truth in the sense of their true thoughts and feelings. The mouth cover and the silence it engenders offers us a different kind of political speech or language. Even Confucius has to wear the mouth cover today, watching silently, but unable to speak.

Shown here is a contemporary image of a mask of god, derived from an original dating from the Bronze age Sanxingdui culture (see Plate 7). Originally, this mask represented language and knowledge. And, behind the mask, we sense heaven, nature and deities. But, if we lose our connection with them, then the mask shackles us with its coldness and callousness. It is important for healing and therapy processes that the links be rediscovered.

I am reminded of the old joke about national variations on the theme of neurotic symptoms: America is a country for depression, Japan is a country for autism and China is a country for obsessive compulsive disorders (OCD). (I would add that, sadly, China is also a country for autism and depression today.)

It is estimated that 3% of the general population of China suffer from OCD. Among therapy patients, OCD is present in about 16% of them. About 12 years ago, research was carried out on OCD in China, looking for significant patterns. The main symptoms of OCD in China include obsessively checking things such as locks or stoves, compulsively and repeatedly washing hands, and many specific rituals or repetitive behaviours. Behind these symptoms lie fear and anxiety and a deep sense of insecurity and lack of safety. We also see widespread fear of making a mistake coupled with this deep need for order and symmetry. Assuredly, there are biological factors inherent in OCD, but, for therapists and analysts, it is environmental, social and cultural issues that are more important.

As the research developed, we became interested in discovering what cultural complexes might lie behind OCD in China. In this context, examining clinical phenomena, the trauma of the Cultural Revolution (1966–76) suggested itself. To give one example, the Red Guards destroyed Confucius' home, temple and grave. The Chinese characters on the statue of Confucius read 'The Number One Big Bad Wolf'. In Qufu, where Confucius is buried, more than 1,000 stone tablets were destroyed, 100,000 books were burned, 5,000-year-old pine trees were felled, and more than 2,000 tombs were dug up, including Confucius' grave. Behind the Red Guards was Chairman Mao, who accompanied them on their mission to eradicate any traces of Confucius.

About twenty years ago, I dreamed that I walked to a tomb that was situated in withered grass, wizened trees, in a barren and uncultivated landscape. I realise this is Confucius' tomb (see Plate 8). I was so sad and sorrowful in the dream. I wanted to do something, but could not think what. Finally, I made a decision, I threw my living body onto the tomb, trying to use it to feed and nourish the desiccated grass and trees.

Since the experience of this dream, I have visited Confucius' home many times (and the nearby Spring City and Tai Mountain). I take with me my students of analytical psychology, as a ritual to mark the commencement of their training. Many international Jungian friends, who came China to support our work, have visited there too.

Returning to the research, we found, through research and clinical cases, as I mentioned, that the main symptoms of OCD in China included fear and anxiety, feelings of lack of safety, worries about dirt and contamination, a need for order, and persecution delusions related to cultural complexes, especially that of the trauma of the Cultural Revolution.

Recently, some famous Red Guards (for example, Song Binbin, who is the daughter of General Song Renqiong, and Chen Xiaolu, son of the supreme commander Chen Yi) tried to apologise openly for what they did as guards in the Cultural Revolution. Song Binbin, who put the Red Guard armband on Mao's arm during the Cultural Revolution, had participated in beating to death the principal (Bian Zhongyun) of her school. It seems that, without such a confession, they feel deeply insecure.

The seriousness of the problem is that most of the participants of the atrocities of the Cultural Revolution did not perceive themselves to be 'bad'. In a way, they had become ill and the cause of the illness was, broadly speaking, fear – the kind of emotions that fuelled what Hannah Arendt called the 'banality of evil'.

I have discussed these issues with Lu Yaogang, one of the most important writers in China today. As Chinese, we had been used to being organised, controlled, depressed, trodden under foot and frightened. We have gradually learnt to take this habit for granted. The natural has been turned into a logical train of thought, so then it is perfectly justified for some people to argue in favour of the habit of being abused and the habit of abusing others.

Ba Jin, one of the most famous writers in China, wrote in a truth-telling book (Ba Jin, 1988) of his personal sense of repentance over the collective trauma of the Cultural Revolution. He was the first to suggest that there should be a museum of the Cultural Revolution. This would serve a confessional purpose not only on the personal level but also for healing the wounds of the country and nation.

In 2006, travelling with Luigi Zoja, Eva Pattis and Gao Lanto to visit the first Museum of the Cultural Revolution in Chenghai in Southern China, I recounted an old dream.

In the dream, I was in a village with 36 followers. It felt like being in an Autonomous Region of the country. Two persons came towards us on a mountain road. I recognised one of them was Chairman Mao. Mao looked very tired, it seemed that he had walked a long way. Mao told me that he was hungry, and asked me for food. I tried to find the cook, but the cook was not there, I tried to open the kitchen but it was locked. Finally, I asked someone through the kitchen window to open the door, and I cooked noodles for Mao and his companion. After the meal, Mao looked quite satisfied, and asked me: 'What do you want?' It appeared that I could ask him for anything I wanted. 'May I ask a question?' I said. Mao said, 'Sure, you can ask if you want.' So I asked, 'Why did you start the Cultural Revolution?' He immediately looked angry and I woke up.

In China today, mental illness statistics are startling. According to the data announced in 2009 by the Mental Health Centre of China Centre for Disease Control and Prevention, there were more than 100 million people suffering from all kinds of mental illness, 16 million of whom were seriously ill (the number is still increasing). In the eyes of many commentators, mental illness is often rooted in the social system and lifestyle of the population. It is a reflection and a projection of social problems. Arthur Kleinman's book *The Social Origin of Misery and Disease in Modern China* (1988) was the first by a psychiatrist to try to explain how this works in the lives of people.

I agree with Lu Yaogang when he said to me in private conversation that 'the utmost humanistic spirit of literature lies in spreading humanitarianism. It has always been the intuition and duty of literature to restore the normal thinking of people; that is, to help them gain freedom from fear, alleviation of anxiety, extrication of depression, self-salvation and pursuit of the true, the good and the beautiful.'

Lu Yaogang and I have been instrumental in setting up a project called The Garden of the Heart and Soul; it is a form of self-salvation. In the past eight years, we have set up over 70 work stations at orphanages, and in earthquake zones such as Sichuan and Yushu. These provide psychological relief for orphans and victims alike. This project constitutes an important practice of the Jungian group working in China today.

Lu Yaogang continued: 'During the Modern Age, for over 160 years, and especially during the recent 60 years of communistic revolution, the Chinese have suffered serious psychological damage, and even to this day the wound is still festering and difficult to heal.' I replied that we have to face the trauma and its related shadow, or therapy and healing will not take place. The use of language here is important. For example, Qian Liqun (a Beijing University professor) summed up the national situation in China as living in the 'Mao Zedong Trap'. In my view, in terms of the ongoing shaping of the national spirit of the Chinese, the Jungian term 'shadow' is a more accurate term than 'trap'.

Although they officially denied that the Cultural Revolution took place, the Fourth Plenary Session of the Eleventh Congress of the Communist Party of China (September 9–28, 1979) also prohibited study of it. Perhaps as a result of this contradiction, there came the reviving of the radical Maoist Left in the 1990s, and the rising Chongqing Model and Bo Xilaism within the twenty-first-century Communist Party.

Analysis based on limited materials shows that the personality of Bo Xilai is characterised by a sort of cultural archetype. Bo Yibo, his father, was prosecuted, insulted and put into the Qincheng prison during the Cultural Revolution; Hu Ming, his mother, was persecuted to death; brothers and sisters from the Bo family were also persecuted or discriminated against during this period. So, the Bo Xilai phenomenon can be viewed as one of the traumatic consequences of the Cultural Revolution. However, Bo Xilai stood for a Maoist Leftist ideology in his struggle for power, and gained great support from both the top of the Party and from the grassroots. This is truly profound, and the meaning of it, notwithstanding Bo Xilai's fall, requires extensive further study.

Relatively recently (2014) there was a film called *Coming Home to the Mainland of China*, based on the book *Criminal Lu Yanshi* by Yan Geling (see Plate 9). The film, like the book, is about the Cultural Revolution, the miserable sufferings of and the trauma to the generation who now are grandparents, and to their sons and daughters, to their grandchildren, and the intergenerational transmission of the trauma. After the end of the Cultural Revolution, Lu Yanshi came home (from prison) only to find his family broken, his wife suffering amnesia caused by shock following a sexual assault on the part of an official. This chimes with our national amnesia and speaks of a deep wound to the feminine elements in Chinese culture and society. The anima, in all her senses, is lost to us and the national soul is thereby diminished.

Yanshi is both the title of Yan Geling's book and the name of the main character of the film. It literally means 'how to recognise', and came originally from Sushi's Song dynasty poem 'Ten Years – Dead and Living Dim and Draw Apart' (1075):

> Ten years, – dead and living dim and draw apart.
> I don't try to remember
> but forgetting is hard.
> Lonely grave a thousand miles off,
> cold thoughts, where can I talk them out?
> Even if we met, you wouldn't know me,
> dust on my face,
> Hair like frost –
>
> In a dream last night suddenly I was home.
> By the window of the little room
> you were combing your hair and making up.
> You turned and looked, not speaking,
> only lines of tears coursing down –
> year after year will it break my heart?
> The moonlit grave,
> Its stubby pines –
>
> (translated by Burton Watson, 1993)

The great Sinologist, Richard Wilhelm, who lived in China for over 20 years, wrote in the preface of his 1928 book *The Soul of China*: 'In the old and in the new there was, nevertheless, a common element: the soul of China in the course of evolution; that soul which had not lost its gentleness nor its calm, and will, I hope, never lose them' (Wilhelm, 1928, p. xxi).

In a manner that Wilhelm would surely have found familiar, given his words quoted above, the movie ended with Lu's wife waiting to receive her husband outside the railway station and Lu standing with her on a snowy day, pretending to be pedicab driver (see Plate 10). After seeing the film, I wrote a reflection on my Chinese Facebook page: 'Went to see the Return, deeply moved, for Lu Yanshi, for Feng Wanyu, for Lu Dandan (the daughter); for the lost memories, for the suffering of the youth, for the national amnesia, for the broken dreams; Lu Yanshi, when are you coming home? Every month and everyday, waiting for your return.'

We in China are still waiting for something crucial to return. I would call it courage, intuition, knowledge, rediscovery of nature and of the deities. When this return comes about, we will see transformations in the Chinese heart and soul, which have indeed not lost their gentleness nor their calm, and will, I hope, never lose them.

References

Ba Jin (1988) *Selected Works of Ba Jin* (trans. S. Shapiro and J. Hoe). Beijing: Foreign Language Press.

Kleinman, A. (1988) *The Social Origin of Misery and Disease in Modern China*. New Haven, CT: Yale University Press.

Wilhelm, R. (1928) *The Soul of China*. New York: Harcourt Brace & Co.

SECTION 6

Nature

Truth and reconciliation

20

HEALING OUR BROKEN CONNECTION TO NATURE

The Psyche-Left-Behind

Jerome S. Bernstein

> We see and hear what we are open to noticing.

I will shortly give an outline of my current research, which I offer as a thought/picture of the unique power of Jungian theory to address conundrums,[1] and pointedly the crisis of global warming, which threatens the very survival of our species. In 1929 Jung wrote the following:

> Western consciousness is by no means the only kind of consciousness there is; it is historically conditioned and geographically limited, and representative of only one part of mankind. The widening of consciousness ought not to proceed at the expense of the other kinds of consciousness.
>
> (Jung, 1929, para 84)

Thirty-one years later, in 1960, in one of his last essays, entitled 'Healing the Split', Jung made this clinical diagnosis of the Western psyche:

> Nothing is holy any longer . . . Through scientific understanding our world has become dehumanized . . . [Our] immediate communication with nature is gone for ever.
>
> (Jung, 1961, para 582)

> No wonder the western world feels uneasy, for it does not know how much . . . it has lost through the destruction of its numinosities . . . Its moral and spiritual tradition has collapsed and has left a *worldwide disorientation and dissociation*.
>
> (Jung, 1961, para 581, emphasis added)

Recently, a report from the Intergovernmental Panel on Climate Change issued its most dire warnings, reflecting that the scientific consensus is that 'we', humanity, have less than 100 years to reverse the process we are in. Some scientists in the group said that the point of no return is more likely 15–20 years. Michael Oppenheimer, a climate scientist at Princeton University and a principal author of the report, said that a continuation of the political paralysis on emissions would leave society depending largely on luck. To quote him, he said, 'So the need for a lot of luck looms larger and larger. Personally, I think it's a slim reed to lean on for the fate of the planet' (Gillis, 2014, p. A8). Whether Dr Oppenheimer knows it or not, he is directly addressing the dissociation of the Western psyche.

What I think Jung was getting at, and certainly what I believe, is that through the interaction of scientific thought which does not recognise the spiritual dimension of life and treats Nature as inanimate matter, we have been left with an over-inflated psyche that behaves as if its technologies are omnipotent and its thinking function is infallible. Jungian analysts are trained to recognise that a primary defence mechanism attendant to the pathological state of dissociation is the defence of denial. We also know that our complexes are put into service by the dissociative process to rationalise the split-off psychic states that we are in. The more unconscious the dissociation, the greater the rationalisation of the current state of being. This is no less true on the collective level than for the individual. As far as I am concerned, this is where we are with respect to the crisis of global warming.

Euro-America has long projected *mana*[2] onto the indigenous populations of the world, especially Native Americans, as if they had all the answers (Deloria, 1999). They don't. But they do have communication with nature and can speak nature's language. Theirs is a psyche that operates on laws and principles different from those of the Western psyche. I call this the Psyche-Left-Behind. It seems that what the Euro-American psyche is seeking is a reconnection and dialogue – a communion – with that psyche, and through *that*, a reparative relationship with nature in its natural sacralised, *spirit-filled* form.

My term 'the Psyche-Left-Behind' refers to the fact that in the beginning of the Genesis myth Adam and Eve *were* in an original state of at-one-ness with nature, prior to their sin and subsequent expulsion. We have forgotten that our species was connected to a psychic state of at-one-ness with nature before the expulsion. Adam and Eve were expelled. But that *pre*-expulsion psyche was not. And although the path out of the Garden of Eden has led to the kind of *Logos* left-brain dominant Western psyche that we know, another dimension of psyche was 'left behind' – and is still there, so to speak. I believe this is the basis for Jung's term 'dissociation' when referring to the 'Western world'. I believe that the Psyche-Left-Behind lives on in the surviving indigenous *tribes*, *communities* and *individuals* in the wake of Western culture's genocide towards indigenous peoples. Is it Euro-Americans' intuitive sense that Native Americans carry a lost part of their own psychic roots and that this results in their projection of *mana* onto Native Americans? I think so.

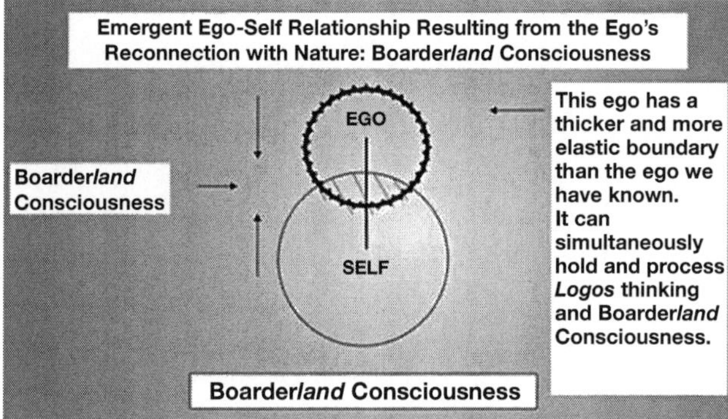
Emergent Ego-Self Relationship Resulting from the Ego's
Reconnection with Nature: Boarder*land* Consciousness
EGO
SELF
Boarder*land*
Consciousness
This ego has a
thicker and more
elastic boundary
than the ego we
have known.
It can
simultaneously
hold and process
Logos thinking
and Boarder*land*
Consciousness.
Boarder*land* Consciousness

FIGURE 20.1 Border*land* consciousness

It is my view that the collective unconscious, in a compensatory response to the crisis of global warming, appears to be pushing the Western psyche towards re-engagement with its psychic roots in Nature. But what does that mean and how can we participate in bringing that about? One of the things that results from this re-engagement is the emergence of what I call 'Border*land* consciousness' (Bernstein, 2000, 2005). It is the latter that is the link for a re-engaged dialogue between the Western psyche and the 'Psyche-Left-Behind'. In Figure 20.1 we see an ego that is being brought back into connection with the Self – in spite of itself. The two vertical arrows on the left, one ascending, one descending, depict a dynamic *that is in process* on a collective basis, not one that has happened and is complete. I wish to reiterate that this process is being forced onto the ego as an evolutionary compensatory response to the threat of annihilation of our species. The resultant new kind of consciousness is what I have called Border*land* consciousness (Bernstein, 2000, 2005).

Rather than try to describe Border*land* consciousness in words, I think it would be better to *see* what one form of it looks like when it is embodied. Readers are strongly encouraged to find a means of viewing the video, "The Animal Communicator", with Anna Breytenbach, in order to fully understand this paper. The video is 52 minutes long, and the clip that is integral to this chapter begins at minute 8:12 and runs through to minute 12:40.

What I want you to notice is what Border*land* consciousness actually looks like on the face and body of someone while they are functioning in that psychoidal dimension. Also, notice Anna's explanation of how she enters that realm and the scientist's explanation of his understanding of the Border*land* realm. The voice that you hear first is that of a professional environmental reporter who is narrating the film.

This video portrays Border*land* consciousness between humans and animals. Ultimately, the critical transformative test will be connection and dialogue between humans with all of Nature enabled through Border*land* consciousness.

The most important implication of Border*land* consciousness is the possibility of reconnection with Nature in *its* natural state, not the one that Western philosophy and science desacralised, coming out of the seventeenth-century Cartesian Enlightenment.

I have been emphasising that the structure and character of the Western psyche is fundamentally different from that of the Native American psyche. One difference is the structure of the language characteristic of each psychic form.

Western culture and its languages are *Logos* based, binary, based in reason, are linear and, importantly, *noun dominant* (Cajete, 1999; Whorf, 1964). As a result, these language structures tend to abstract experience and interpose abstract concepts and ideas in place of imaging and somatic understanding.

Oral Traditional Native American languages are metaphoric in structure, speak images, *are verb dominant* (Cajete, 1999); they are psychoidal in that they reflect and speak to archetypal dynamics, and reflect relationship with all of life. I argue that these characteristics of each psychic form are endemic to the languages themselves.

Gregory Cajete (1999), a Tewa Indian and Assistant Professor at the University of New Mexico's College of Education, in his book *Native Science*, speaking of the character of Native languages, writes the following:

> Language is more than a code; it is a way of participating with each other *and* the natural world. . . At the deeper psychological level, language is sensuous, evocative, filled with emotion, meaning and spirit. Meanings are not solely connected to intellectual definition but to the life of the body and spirit of the speaker. In its holistic and natural sense, language is animate and animating, it expresses our living spirit through sound and the emotion with which we speak. In the Native perspective, language exemplifies our communion with nature rather than our separation from it.
>
> (Cajete, 1999, p. 72)

So, what is this all about?

1 We will use oral traditional language as I just quoted above, as a direct way of reframing the psychic field attendant to the global warming crisis. Our research group has been working at converting these observations into a methodology and ultimately protocols that would relanguage dissociated thinking so as to reimbue spirit into the polemic on global warming. A major tool will be using oral traditional language structure to construct a meta-language for reassociating a dissociated Western psyche.
2 These protocols will be developed and field tested with scientists, politicians, environmentalists, corporate executives and others to determine the degree to which this approach is effective in treating the dissociation of the dominant culture.

3 Before and after outcome measures will determine the degree of behavioural change on the part of subjects. These will include comparative brain wave studies.

Notes

1 'Conundrum may refer to: A riddle whose answer is or involves a pun or unexpected twist. . .A logical postulation that evades resolution, an intricate and difficult problem' (Conundrum, 2015).

2 The linguist Robert Blust has pointed out that 'mana' means 'thunder, storm, or wind' in some languages, and has hypothesised that the term originally meant 'powerful forces of nature such as thunder and storm winds that were conceived as the expression of an unseen supernatural agency. As Oceanic-speaking peoples spread eastward, the notion of an unseen supernatural agency became detached from the physical forces of nature that had inspired it and assumed a life of its own' (Mana, 2015).

References

Bernstein, J. (2000) 'On the Borderland.' *IONS Noetic Sciences Review*, 53: 8–13, 44–6.

Bernstein, J. (2005) *Living in the Borderland: The Evolution of Consciousness and the Challenge of Healing Trauma.* New York: Routledge.

Cajete, G. (1999) *Native Science: Natural Laws of Interdependence.* Santa Fe, NM: Clear Light Publishers.

'Conundrum' (2015) *Wikipedia*, wiki article. Available at: https://en.wikipedia.org/wiki/Conundrum (accessed 8 July 2015).

Deloria, P. (1999) *Playing Indian.* New Haven, CT: Yale University Press.

Gillis, J. (2014) 'U.N. panel issues its starkest warning yet on global warming.' *New York Times*, 2 November, A8.

Jung, C. G. (1929) 'Commentary on "The secret of the golden flower".' *CW*13.

Jung, C. G. (1961) 'Symbols and the interpretation of dreams.' *CW*18.

'Mana' (2015) *Wikipedia*, wiki article. Available at: https://en.wikipedia.org/wiki/Mana (accessed 8 July 2015).

Whorf, B. L. (1964) *Language, Thought, and Reality: Selected Writings of Benjamin Lee Whorf*, edited by J. B. Carroll. Cambridge, MA: The MIT Press.

21

PSYCHOLOGICAL RELIEF WORK AFTER THE 11 MARCH 2011 EARTHQUAKE IN JAPAN

Jungian perspectives and the shadow of activism

Toshio Kawai

Activism is meant, especially in the case of social activity, to serve an ideal purpose with goodwill.

The Great East Japan Earthquake on 11 March 2011 was the most powerful earthquake ever to be recorded in Japanese history, with a magnitude of 9.0. The huge tsunami triggered by the earthquake, with a wave height of 30 metres, caused especially heavy damage. It destroyed many cities and villages near the coast and took many lives. Nearly 16,000 people were killed; 3,000 are still missing. Huge material loss is still on its long way to recovery, and radioactively polluted soil near Fukushima will need decades to recover.

After this disaster, not only material loss and its recovery but also psychological loss and relief work have been equally highlighted. Immediately after the earthquake, various kinds of psychological relief work teams were organised and sent to the stricken areas. Afterwards, the psychological relief work was coordinated and supported officially by the government and voluntary organisations. The Association of Jungian Analysts, Japan (AJAJ) and the Japanese Association for Sandplay Therapy (JAST) set up a joint working committee for the psychological relief work. I have been serving as Chair of this committee. Here I would like to thank again the International Association for Analytical Psychology (IAAP) and our colleagues for supporting our activity financially with donations.

Our work was based on the four following concepts.

First, we started to work in places where each of our members had a personal contact. For example, a house of one of our member's parents was near Fukushima power plant; another colleague's parents' house was near Sendai airport, which was devastated by the tsunami. His parents had been missing for a week before they were discovered safely. In my case, Kumiko Tanaka, the wife of my colleague Yasuhiro Tanaka, is from Ishinomaki port city, which was terribly hit by the tsunami. I visited Ishinomaki every two months with my colleague, Yasuhiro. As a small organisation, we cannot cover the whole region equally so we started by contacting those related to persons in stricken areas and asked what kind of needs they had. This may be a valid approach according to network theory.

Secondly, we wanted to respect the needs and the initiative of the victims. Our main activity is listening to what they say to us. Psychological relief work tends to impose its own method on the victims and, as a result, sometimes causes more confusion and stress than relief. We want to avoid this problem and try to exercise a kind of passive activism, inviting the active participation of the victims.

Thirdly, as we had our own work and could not be permanently in the stricken areas, we focused on the work of caregivers such as psychotherapists, teachers and nurses, who are supposed to be able to endure psychological difficulties for a certain period of time without discharging them immediately. On the other hand, they are burdened by the heavy sufferings and stories of the victims, which should be released in the protected circle of our regular visits. So our project became a rather reflective action.

Fourthly, we focused on children and images, especially using sandplay, because of our methodological advantage. We sent a school counsellor to a stricken area when the school principal, who had been a teacher of my colleague's wife in the past, asked us for help. We introduced sandplay there.

I have published three papers in English concerning this activity. The first one is based on a preliminary report I presented in the November 2011 international workshop on disaster in Lisbon (Kawai, 2015). The second one was presented in the 2012 IAAP/ISJS joint conference and rather focused on the concrete psychological relief work (Kawai, 2014), and the topic of the third paper is the change of world view triggered by this earthquake (Kawai, 2013).

In this chapter I would like to limit the discussion to several points concerning activism and its shadow.

1. The importance of natural process

In the case of psychological relief work the importance of immediate intervention is often stressed. That is why many psychotherapists and psychiatrists were sent to the stricken areas right after the earthquake. It looked as though people could not survive without professional psychological support. However, children's pictures drawn in a school three times in a series, brought an interesting process to light. The freely drawn pictures of the first-grade classes showed a clear disturbance of the structure after the earthquake in comparison with those drawn before the earthquake, which indicated that the psychic structure of the children was fundamentally shaken and threatened by the shock of the natural disaster. The pictures drawn three months after the earthquake regained a normal structure and suggested that almost all children had recovered from the first shock. This points at the resilience of the human psyche and means that the shaken psychic structure can recover within the natural course of time, probably if there is enough containment by family and community.

Time seems to be an important factor in terms of psychological recovery. After three or four months – exactly the same period described above with the children's drawings suggesting psychic recovery – many adults started to talk about their terrible experiences on the day of the earthquake and reported that they had had nightmares recently. This can be regarded as an indication that the psyche had started its work of reflection and digestion of the disaster. However, telling of painful experiences and reporting nightmares did not necessarily mean the onset of traumatic complications and the need for treatment by psychotherapy. Very often, after reporting these experiences, people were able to close their critical period and return to their daily life. Some people reported a repetition of the same experience and flashbacks, but in most cases a psychological intervention was not necessary and could even have caused a complication. So it is important to discern what is the natural process of crisis and recovery and what is pathological.

After the beginning of reflection, the complaint and the symptom became very individual. Those who came to psychotherapy did not necessarily talk about matters related to the loss and damages caused directly by the earthquake but focused on their specific problems of relationships in the family, school or workplace and so forth.

In some cases we were surprised to notice that the children could make use of the crisis caused by the earthquake for their own psychological development. Sachiko Taki-Reece's case study after the earthquake in Northridge is a good example of such a process, and she uses the expression 'emergence of a new self' in the study's title (Taki-Reece, 2004).

We were impressed to find (1) how vulnerable the human psyche is to physical shock; (2) how the psyche recovers from the shock over a certain period of time; and (3) how the psyche reflects on the shock and creates something new. The third phase can continue for a long time. However, active intervention can disturb a natural recovery and even impose pathology on the victims. Although important, the treatment of trauma can result in an artificially created trauma. So we must be aware of the shadow of active intervention for the victims of a natural disaster.

2. Conflict with the administrative system

The Japanese government invested a huge amount of its budget not only for the reconstruction of damaged infrastructure of the land and destroyed buildings and houses but also for psychological care. For example, a project was financed for sending a school counsellor once a week to every school in the stricken areas. Prior to the earthquake, only each middle school had had a school counsellor who was also responsible for elementary schools in the area. The arrangement was assigned to the Japanese umbrella organisation of psychotherapists, which had more than 20,000 members. However, as it was impossible to find the same person to come regularly from other areas of Japan to a school in a stricken area, school counsellors changed almost every week. It was a typical example of the difficulty in implementing a global idea in concrete practice.

The principal of the elementary school in Ishinomaki that Yasuhiro and I visited regularly did not want a new school counsellor every week, so he asked our working committee to send the same school counsellor every week. We found a person who was originally from Tohoku region and tried to get a financial support from the government within the framework of the mentioned project. To our surprise, our request was rejected. The administration could not allow for a special case, thus disturbing the principle of equality; it preferred an equal but overall bad situation to having one good case. The administration was very defensive and anxious, and was afraid of being criticised.

Our plan to send a school counsellor had to be officially approved at least by the prefecture and the city, making the negotiation with various administrative organs more stressful than the psychological work with teachers and psychotherapists on site. It would be politically more effective to take up and support bottom-up initiatives and activities like ours than to distribute money equally from above and waste it.

This is not the shadow of activism, but rather the shadow and irrationality of politics, which activism necessarily encounters. Politics is inevitably collective, top-down, and its concern is the sum: how much to budget for a certain item, certain project. People are compelled to take a passive attitude and receive only what is offered. Activism, as I understand it, is opposed to such an idea of politics and tries to work from the bottom up, actively and individually using network. In this sense activism emerges out of the shadow of politics.

3. Personal and collective level

Coping with the administration, as hinted already, was made difficult by the discrepancy between the personal and the collective level. In the course of our activity, the psychological relief work moves to the personal level. People no longer talk about their experiences of the earthquake and their sufferings from personal loss but are interested in their actual problems, for example in human relationships. We can even say that those people who remain identified with the loss and damage caused by the earthquake have difficulty in recovering psychologically. So, if one is stuck in the collective level of disaster, the psychological prospective is rather negative. The healing or recovery depends on transferring the collective, big problem to the personal, small one, which is a kind of transference neurosis.

However, the question that arises is how does the psychological relief work affect the collective level, or if there *is* in fact a collective level of healing or change of world view after the recent terrible earthquake. In the case of the Jogan earthquake, or the 869 Sanriku earthquake that occurred almost in the same place and with the same power as that in 2011, the Gion festival in Kyoto started as an answer to this earthquake. This festival became and still is one of the most important festivals in Kyoto. It involves the ritual of driving away bad spirits and it has become, so to speak, a general healing ritual on a national level.

Since the 2011 earthquake, various religious groups, musicians and artists have been trying to organise rituals, festivals, performances and works of art to offer a kind of collective healing. Among them there are some impressive ones. But it is doubtful if such types of ritual and healing can be shared on the collective level today. This is a dilemma and one of the shadow aspects of activism concerning psychological relief work after the earthquake.

4. The problem of volunteer work

Our psychological relief work is based on volunteer activity. In the case of my group, we visit schools during the day and give group supervisions for psychotherapists in the evening. We need two days for each visit every two months. Our travel expenses and accommodation are paid by the working committee, which was supported by the donations from our members and partially by members of IAAP, but other expenses are paid by us and the supervision is, of course, free of charge.

At the beginning, such a framework was necessary in the face of a national disaster. But in the long run it could become problematic.

I frequently heard from school principals that they were embarrassed by the mismatched material support they received. Sometimes they were given too many pencils, other times too many soccer balls. People offered them what they did not necessarily need. It was also tiresome for the school principals to meet and thank visitors who came to encourage them. A lot of famous sports people, pop stars and movie stars visited schools in stricken areas. In this sense, even our school visits for a kind of consultation and supervision could also become annoying for the school staff if our visits no longer matched the need of the school.

One school made use of our visits very effectively. Teachers, a school social worker and a school counsellor would tell us about the pupils they found problematic and had difficulty coping with. In the first year there were eight such pupils, who did not attend the school. Now there are no pupils who do not attend. It is highly interesting and also moving to hear how some pupils have changed and developed dramatically. However, in the case of another school it was no longer clear why we visited, and talked only with the principal. The predecessor of the current principal was very much interested in psychological relief work and invited a school counsellor from our organisation. We began to wonder if our visits to this school were still really meaningful.

In the aftermath of the Kobe earthquake in 1995, temporary housing became controversial. It was necessary to offer temporary accommodation to people who had lost their homes. However, over time, staying in the temporary housing for some people became a matter of course, as the comfortable conditions prevented them from taking their own initiative. Also, after the earthquake in Tohoku, many people did not start to look for jobs, because they received sufficient subsidy.

In a similar way, group supervision free of charge can become meaningless if it is taken for granted. On the other hand, it is also possible that some people may feel obliged to attend the free-of-charge group supervision even if they find it annoying.

As our activity is based on personal contact and acquaintance, the time to stop our visits may be when our contact person changes his or her workplace. With regards to group supervision, we have now started to ask the supervisees for a symbolic monetary contribution, four years after the earthquake. Although we supervisors are not paid, their contributions can partially cover our travel expenses so that our activity can be supported for longer. Also, as the supervisees now do pay their contributions they can decide to stop paying and come to the group supervision if and when they find it necessary. It seems important to introduce personal involvement instead of giving help and care automatically.

5. Reflection on motivation for activism

I live in Kobe, which was hit terribly by the huge earthquake in 1995. The earthquake killed more than 6,400 people, most of whom were crushed to death. At that time I was not directly involved in the psychological relief work with the victims. I was completely occupied with the care of my own patients in the stricken area, my students at the University of Konan in Kobe and also my family. My colleagues and I were embarrassed to observe that some psychologists who had had little to do with psychotherapy became very active in the psychological care of the victims and were regarded as specialists.

Again, this is also a shadow of activism. We have to be aware of our own motivation for activism. Otherwise, the activity becomes our need to gain personal satisfaction, to make ourselves famous, to prove and spread our theory. As I mentioned, a lot of celebrities visited schools in stricken areas. Although some were moved by their heartfelt concern and goodwill, some seemed, however, to be motivated by their own propaganda.

For myself, I am aware that the classical form of psychotherapy, of waiting in one's office for the patients coming of their own accord, is changing. Psychotherapy is becoming more and more an outreach model, which is offered like a social service. I felt spontaneously compelled to do this job in the face of a national disaster and because of my position and my international contacts. But I am always asking myself what is my motivation now.

References

Kawai, T. (2013) 'The 2011 earthquake in Japan: Psychotherapeutic interventions and change of worldview.' *Spring*, 88: 47–60.

Kawai, T. (2014) 'Big stories and small stories in the psychological relief work after the earthquake disaster: Life and death.' In L. Huskinson and M. Stein (eds), *Analytical Psychology in a Changing World: The Search for Self, Identity and Community*. London and New York: Routledge Taylor & Francis Group, pp. 23–41.

Kawai, T. (2015) 'Big stories and small stories after a traumatic natural disaster from a psychotherapeutic point of view.' In I. Capeloa and C. Wulf (eds), *Hazardous Future: Disaster, Representation and Assessment of Risk*. Berlin/Munich/Boston: De Gruyter, pp. 95–107.

Taki-Reece, S. (2004) 'Sandplay after a catastrophic encounter: From traumatic experience to emergence of a new self.' *Archives of Sandplay Therapy*, 17: 65–75.

22

A JUNGIAN SPOKE IN THE TOWN AND COUNTRY PLANNING WHEEL

It's the alchemy, stupid!

Ann Kutek

In 2010 a Conservative-led coalition may have lent impetus to a recently demerged company of developers to set its predatory sights on an economically declining exhibition and concert venue in West London known as Earls Court 1[1] and 2. Unbeknown to the local people,[2] in the first decade of the century, a competition was run and a 'wise old man' of architecture picked to design a 'masterplan' of regeneration, not only on the site of the iconic exhibition halls with their existing dedicated public transport links (and perversely, with the prospect of a third airport runway to the West of London), but also involving the acquisition and emptying of three public/social housing estates where over 3,000 people live, as well as demolishing hundreds of small businesses, many run by immigrant families. The plan is to regenerate 80 acres at the heart of London into four 'villages' of tower blocks comprising 7,500 residential units, the vast majority available only to private investors, and a new retail high street, even if it is common knowledge that the concept of the high street is all but dead, with a 'lost river park' to green up the setting (see www.myearlscourt.com). (See Plate 11, which is taken from the public consultation for the Earls Court Masterplan undertaken by the Royal Borough of Kensington and Chelsea and the London Borough of Hammersmith & Fulham.)

In considering this planning story, my contention is that intervening in the English planning system is political. The explosion of *outsourcing* – or *segmentation*, as I prefer to call it – in modern economies brings about added complexity to the existing social and technical intricacies. Moreover, Jung's study of alchemy, and his *theory of Archetypes*, has yet to be applied to the built environment, that is to say to the processes of urban development, including town planning and regeneration, to reveal a specific example of what Andrew Samuels has called 'psyche-in-matter and matter-in-psyche' (Samuels, 1993). I hope this necessarily cursory examination will go some way to show how the complexities of town planning can be said to reflect some of Jung's discoveries and analogies and how alchemical and archetypal forces arguably come into play in this very political field.

Jung the builder

Readers of his work hardly need reminding that Carl Jung was particularly sensitive to space, buildings and their symbolic significance.

As he reports in *Memories, Dreams, Reflections* (1963), already as a child, his earliest archetypal dream is powerfully architectural. On discovering a stone-lined hole in the ground, in the middle of a meadow, and upon entering it, he specifies: 'I saw before me in the dim light a rectangular chamber about thirty feet long. The ceiling was arched and of hewn stone. The floor was laid with flagstones, and in the centre a red carpet ran from the entrance to a low platform' (p. 12). Then he comments about the lighting again: 'It was fairly light in the room, although there were no windows and no apparent source of light' (ibid.). His much later interpretation of the hole in the ground was that it probably represented a grave. He continues, 'the grave itself was an underground temple whose green curtain symbolised the *meadow*, in other words the mystery of Earth with her covering of green vegetation. The carpet was *blood red*' (p. 13).

In parallel to his work as a psychologist, Jung was throughout his life engaged in craftsmanship and building. In the 1920s he was on the lookout for a place to concentrate on his own self-realisation. He wanted not a country retreat nor an architect-designed bourgeois summerhouse, but a refuge to be constructed with his own hands. Due to local opposition, unable to buy an island on Upper Lake Zurich, where the family used to camp, Jung acquired a parcel of land in Bollingen on Lake Zurich (see Figure 22.1).

FIGURE 22.1
Jung, circa 1920, camping on the island, prior to the construction of Bollingen

He followed his own design with the help of only two local workmen as mason's assistants, and picked up stone-cutting skills by working in the Bollingen quarries. The construction of the tower with its circular foundation was an expression in stone of his becoming himself.

> From the beginning I felt the Tower as in some way a place of maturation – a maternal womb or a maternal figure in which I could become what I was, what I am and will be.
>
> (Jung, 1963, p. 225)

The Bollingen project lasted from 1923 to its completion in 1956.

Town planning – a stable mate of alchemy?

Archaeology suggests that urban settlement started at the dawn of time in the Indus valley. Subsequently, Greek and Etruscan engineering skills were passed to the Romans (Tatham, 1998).

Town planning, as we understand it in much of Western Europe, evolved out of town charters in early medieval times. One of the most notable milestones was under Otto I in the tenth-century Holy Roman Empire when privileges were set out for townsfolk that included an early form of urbanisation in the German town of Magdeburg. Monarchs subsequently adopted this across Europe. The effects of the *Magdeburg Law* can be seen in thousands of towns and villages to this day. These civic developments were exactly contemporaneous with the then preoccupation with alchemy.

In his decades-long examination of alchemy, Jung formed the view that it was a parallel to psychological transformation. Whereas alchemy with its biological and mystical roots was eventually supplanted by the rationalism and empiricism of modern science, it has not gone away as a template for mankind's search for self-realisation and self-expression. And what bolder manifestation of self-expression can there be than our relationship with the earth and, throughout human history, with the creation of the farmed and built environment?

Mankind's early remodelling of the environment was not only to build shelters, but also an expression of imagination, projection and aspiration. Initially, this would seem to be linked to the after-life, as in the examples of Silbury Hill and Stonehenge in Wiltshire, UK, or the Egyptian pyramids.

Scroll on to the modern era and note that the building of cathedrals throughout Western Christendom is tied up with very ancient craft pathways, handed down to us through secretive freemasonry, with roots pre-dating Christianity. They communicate through gargoyles and bosses on cathedral ceilings and in the ubiquity of the green man, and the occasional green woman too, a reminder of Earth's bounty. The siting and dimensions of these structures would seem to be informed by *sacred geometry*, a branch of alchemy. Note that the roofs of Gothic cathedrals and ancient churches are reminiscent of a massive ribcage or the upturned hull of a boat, a container that floats on the sea, the sea of the unconscious.

Contrast this with the marvels of the Alhambra palace, southern Spain. This shows the late flowering of Moorish culture and its dedication to the study of alchemy through mathematics and geometry, which unlock the patterns in nature, and a built environment based upon the *Golden Ratio*. Its courtyards are bedecked with fragrant plants and reverberate to the sound of constantly flowing water, not traffic! It is the only place on Earth that has all 17 instances of the Wallpaper Group; that is, all the mathematically possible designs for friezes.

Perhaps the recipes for mixing limes and mortars that have lasted for centuries are kindred to the mixes of alchemy. As a reminder, here, in brief, are the principal alchemical phases that can be allied to planning phases in England:

1. *Nigredo*: a phase of blackening of the base substance, confounding dangerous poison fumes and confronting the shadow.

   In planning terms, on gaining planning permission, this leads to arresting activity and life within, emptying and demolishing buildings, uprooting vegetation with the risk of 'planning blight'.
2. *Albedo*: in this phase there is whitening, an integration of soul image, with emergence of anima or animus.

   In planning terms, this could be negotiating with objectors to the proposed plans through the planning authority, agreeing building methodology to take account of neighbours and mitigating public hazards and adjusting architectural detail. *Planning gain* in major developments is a method of *quid pro quo* whereby private developers are obliged to benefit the existing community by providing some public housing and/or facilities.
3. *Rubedo* or *citrinitas*: the phase of reddening or yellowing – turning the base substance into gold. Beset with errors and obstacles, the process is finished insofar as it ever can be.

   In planning terms, this is the delivery of the completed project, sometimes decades later, as in the case of medieval cathedrals!

Modern town-planning theory

Modern town-planning theory recognises approaches like:

- *Master-planning*, as the name implies, centrally planned and as practised in Dubai and Qatar by those with the political clout and access to funds.
- *Collaborative planning*, a method favoured by Prince Charles, involving all 'stakeholders', resulting in projects like Poundbury in Dorset, UK.
- *'Arcology'*, a combination of architecture and ecology, which seeks a harmonious and sustainable future for all the inhabitants: human, animal and botanical.

Town planning in England

Town and country planning is part of English land law and concerns land use planning with the aim of ensuring sustainable economic development and a better environment.

One of the ostensible benefits of the current English planning system (each member country of the UK has its own planning process) is that every planning authority, the locally elected council, is bound to consult with local residents and businesses – whether electors or not – about their views on proposed planning applications to alter the built environment in their immediate neighbourhood. Strictly, it is not an invitation to activism, but the process can involve lobbying and protests, within a designated time frame. Any views submitted to a planning process automatically enter the public domain.

The decision to agree, to reject or to modify a planning proposal made by a planning committee is guided as to matters of procedure by council officials, but the final granting of permission (or not) is in light of the political aims of the majority party of the council, informed by planning law. However, planning law as it currently stands, and its enforcement, is being outpaced by growing complexity and is now arguably ill fitted to the task, as confirmed by the local Member of Parliament.[3]

In the case of controversial and unusually large developments in London, decisions may be referred to the office of the Mayor of London. The ultimate potential decision-maker is the Secretary of State for the Environment. Very occasionally, the discovery of a unique plant or animal on the verge of extinction has been able to divert the proposed route of a motorway, as happened with the M40 motorway in the 1960s. All this makes for a complicated and protracted system; the planning wheel turns slowly and affords a lucrative opportunity for lawyers and consultants who advise their developer clients.

The Thatcher years, which deregulated much banking and commerce, gave a boost to the economy that was reflected in the rise in London house prices and in the reversal of population decline. A further hiccup occurred with the technology bubble in the late 90s followed by the banking crash in 2007/8. Still, London has continued to build and transform, attracting ever more overseas investment capital and making house price inflation a severe deterrent to ordinary people becoming owner-occupiers. Property commentator Jonas Crosland (2014) summed up the situation as follows:

> The London property scene is leading the renaissance that is currently spreading across the rest of the country . . . Is it a case of London becoming frothy while the rest of the country is still playing catch up? One effect of the relentless compression on yields brought about by capital appreciation outstripping rental growth is a steady ripple effect on property values outside central London. This looks set to continue. Traditional property companies have already moved de-risking further up the agenda, thus squeezing

investments on the development side as emphasis switches to building up rental income on existing assets.

This means acquiring assets that will appreciate when demand continues to outstrip supply. It also means converting assets by applying for *change of use* under planning law, which can have profound social and economic implications for the built environment and city life generally. Current effects are for ordinary wage earners to be squeezed out of modernised or regenerated areas, while rich investors *buy to leave*. Hence the dark and expensive streets guarded by private security, where hardly anybody lives.

We can only marvel at the processes that must have taken place in the construction of the Egyptian pyramids, unaided by our technologies and untrammelled by our health and safety requirements, and yet I am willing to bet that a time traveller would recognise quite analogous forces at work now and 5,000 years ago. We cannot eavesdrop on the preparatory outlines given by our Egyptian forebears, but language for today's developers is key to success, or the sugar on the pill. They refer to 'opportunity areas'. They talk of masterplans, no gender bias here, and 'planning gain', which is paying a very high social price for someone's vanity in a grand design.

The regeneration of Earls Court – waking in *nigredo*

While the two boroughs in the frame and City Hall, meaning the Mayor of London, were singing from the same political hymn sheet, the momentum seemed impervious to appeal of any kind. The developer vision suggests we could be in Brasília, or a prairie in the USA or even on the South African veldt, such has been the élan for ploughing up 80 acres of West London, never mind who lives and works there.

On the fringe of the regeneration zone, alongside a railway line, there is barely an acre of wetland, a vestige from Counter's Creek, a tributary of the Thames, which became a canal in the late eighteenth century. When the railways came, mid-nineteenth century, the canal was drained, but the populations of flora and fauna survived. A hundred and forty species of flora were identified as recently as 2009. The current drastic disturbance and uprooting will have done for the biodiversity, which awaits eventual landscaping as part of the planned 'lost river park'.

Planned segmentation – an archetype?

Segmentation, otherwise outsourcing, applies to the chain of command as well as to the supply chain in the development process. Doubtless, the reason is pragmatic, to drive down on-costs and, temporarily, to bring in specialists, consultants, etc. Yet it also serves obfuscation, plays for time and disappears corporate responsibility in a mesh of complexity, while retaining power through the food/payment chain. This ubiquitous model, facilitated paradoxically by both deregulation and regulation, has been particularly evident in the secretive global banking sector.

Planning is a complex process based on the premise that its sister, Inertia, accompanies complexity (see Stevens (1982/2015) on Whitmont's definition of psychic inertia). Most people do not vote in local elections and most people do not comment or even object to planning applications. Wholesale demolition followed by construction of the built environment in the English planning process can be, arguably, a variant of *participation mystique* (Winborn, 2014).

A hint of *albedo*?

In May 2014, one of the parties to the political collaboration across borough boundaries was unexpectedly wiped off the scene. A long-held Conservative majority in Hammersmith & Fulham borough overnight became a Labour win, on the back, it is said, of hospital closures. A review of contracts was ordered and there was a partial pause in the 'masterplan'. However, much of the project is tied down by complex legal contracts, too difficult for poorly resourced local planning officials or residents to contend with, despite sustained local and international opposition and protest (Save Earls Court campaign, 2012–15).

There is some 'consultation' with local 'stake holders', businesses and residents, but it refers purely to the detail of things like lorry movements and keeping within permissible working hours and noise scales. What will emerge, years later, in the *rubedo*, will be the result of errors, accidents and adjustments and compromises, controlled not by one mind but by a hierarchy of interest groups, with rather less than adequate planning law enforcement. It is mobilised by the concept of maximising capital appreciation in the hands of a few by means of land banking and asset purchase and despatching hundreds of small businesses and residents, who once benefited from the commerce that trickled down from the Earls Court exhibition centre and surrounding businesses.

At Bollingen, Jung mused about a hut as might be used by native communities: 'A dwelling place corresponding to a person's primitive consciousness, it should impart the feeling of being born – not only in the physical but also the psychic sense.' He urged, 'find within yourselves the philosopher's stone, prepare it by recasting your nature'. He did not get round to examining mankind's archetypal urge to build and remodel his environment. He lived it.

Notes

1 Earls Court Exhibition centre was designed in Art Moderne style by the noted Detroit theatre architect, C. Howard Crane and completed in 1937, one of only two examples of his work in Europe.

2 Since 2006, the landowners of Earls Court have twice applied for and gained certification against 'Listing' of a site of architectural interest, hence the race to demolish.

3 Andrew Slaughter, MP for Hammersmith, intervening in a parliamentary debate on 9 September 2014, columns 864 and 865, eloquently summarised the Earls Court planning proposals, by the by beyond the capacities and resources of the designated local planning officials – a clear case of the Trickster archetype! http://www.publications.parliament.uk/pa/cm201415/cmhansrd/cm140909/debtext/140909-0003.htm#14090974000002.

References

Crosland, J. (2014) 'On property.' *Investor's Chronicle*, 12 September.

Earls Court developers' website: www.myearlscourt.com.

Jung, C. G. (1963) *Memories, Dreams, Reflections*. London: Collins and Routledge Kegan Paul.

London Borough of Hammersmith & Fulham, and Royal Borough of Kensington & Chelsea Planning Departments: http://www.lbhf.gov.uk/Directory/Environment_and_Planning/Planning/Planning_applications/Planning_advice/161179_Earls_Court_Planning_Application.asp.

Sacred Geometry: https://en.wikipedia.org/wiki/Sacred_geometry.

Samuels, A. (1993) *The Political Psyche*. London: Routledge.

Save Earls Court campaign: http://www.saveearlscourt.com/.

Stevens, A. (1982/2015) *Archetype: A Natural History of the Self*. London: Routledge.

Tatham, P. (1998) *The Makings of Maleness: Men, Women, and the Flight of Daedalus*. London: Karnac Books for SAP.

Wehr, G. (1987) *Jung: A Biography*. Dorset: Shambhala.

Winborn, M. (ed.) (2014) *Shared Realities: Participation Mystique and Beyond*. Skiatook: Fisher King Press.

23

NATURE

Truth and reconciliation

Mary-Jayne Rust

Introduction

On Remembrance Day 2015 I was staying with my parents, who lived through World War Two. Together we watched the ceremony at the cenotaph in Whitehall, central London, which honours the heroes and the dead of the two World Wars. As I watched the ceremony I fell into a reverie in search of a Remembrance Day that I would like to be part of. The following dream/vision unfolded:

> I'm in Whitehall, it's many decades into the future, and I'm part of a huge parade of peoples and creatures from all over the world. At the centre of the ceremony there is no more cenotaph, but instead a huge gnarled tree. Hundreds of plants and animals are carved into its trunk to remember the mass extinction of species, alongside the faces of many diverse peoples who worked tirelessly to care for the earth during the Age of Ecocide.

This Remembrance Day marks the time when Truth and Reconciliation with Nature began, the time of making amends with the earth, a radical shift in world view when humans began to see the rest of nature as subjects, rather than a bunch of objects apparently devoid of soul, to be used as 'resources' with no thought of reciprocity.

'I have a dream'

Many activists are inspired by a dream of making a better world, and then campaign for political change. But as we know from history, the inner work of social change (as in racism and sexism, for example) is complex and very lengthy. Those holding the power are challenged to take back their projections of unwanted parts of the self onto 'the other' and the oppressed must free themselves from these internalised projections. Anthropocentrism, the belief that humans are superior to all other beings on the planet, can be seen as a parallel situation to White superiority over Black, to men over women, and calls for a similar revolution in understanding and psychological process.

In this chapter I will describe a series of inspiring projects that aim at social and ecological change, discussing their success and difficulties. I will be suggesting that there are two main cultural narratives alive at the present moment, which appear to be going in opposite directions. The familiar narrative of mainstream culture, emerging out of a very long and complex history of Western culture, tells a story about a heroic fight *against* nature, through domination and control, to make a better and safer world. Freedom is found by separating from 'mother' earth, transcending the messiness of being embodied, to find an apparently safe and reliable world of the intellectual mind. In Jungian terms this is favouring one function over the three others rooted in the body: feeling, sensation and intuition. This has brought us to a place of living by the rational function alone, as Jung describes:

> [T]he exaggerated rationalization of consciousness . . . seeking to control nature, isolates itself from her and so robs man of his own natural history. He finds himself transplanted into a limited present . . . The limitation creates a feeling that he is a haphazard creature without meaning. . . Hemmed round by rationalistic walls, we are cut off from the eternity of nature.
>
> (Jung, 1927, para 739)

The other more recently emerging narrative, in response to ecological crisis, is a story about humans being equal to all other lifeforms and bound into the web of life, which is both matter and psyche, or, psychoid. Freedom is finding our way back into relationship with the larger whole, listening to 'the other', learning how the four functions work together, and learning interdependence – how to hold the tension between being 'one with' and being 'separate from'.

Most people working for change are searching for various forms of the new story about humans as part of nature; yet the first story is alive and well, and appears again and again as resistance to successful eco-projects.

I will start with the rainmaker story, a story that Jung loved to tell. It is a story relevant to climate change, and illustrates what Meredith Sabini calls 'introverted activism' (Sabini, 2011, p. 94). It is a story about working with nature.

> *The rainmaker story*
>
> There was a great drought (in a village in Northern China). For months there had not been a drop of rain and the situation became catastrophic . . . Finally the Chinese said: 'We will fetch the rainmaker.' And from another province, a dried-up old man appeared. The only thing he asked for was a quiet little house somewhere, and there he locked himself in for three days. On the fourth day clouds gathered and there was a great snowstorm at the

> time of the year when no snow was expected. . . and the town was so full of rumours about the wonderful rainmaker that Richard Wilhelm went to ask the man how he did it. In true European fashion he said, 'They call you the rainmaker, will you tell me how you made the snow?' And the little Chinese man said, 'I did not make the snow, I am not responsible.' 'But what have you done these three days?' 'Oh, I can explain that. I come from another country where things are in order. Here they are out of order, they are not as they should be by the ordnance of heaven. Therefore, the whole country is not in Tao, and I am also not in the natural order of things because I am in a disordered country. So I had to wait three days until I was back in Tao, and then naturally the rain came.
>
> (Jung, 1955–6, para 604, n. 211)

This story illustrates how change within one individual can have ripple effects on the world around, not only on other individuals, but on the whole ecosystem. Arguably humans have changed the climate as a result of becoming out of Tao; what would it take to reverse that change? What would this form of introverted activism look like in our modern lives? The following project is such an attempt.

The Natural Change Project

In 2004 I began to co-facilitate one-week courses together with outdoor educator Dave Key, in Knoydart on the West Coast of Scotland. Both of us were concerned about the seriousness of the ecological crisis, but we did not believe that giving more alarmist information was the way to inspire people to take action. Rather, we wanted to create a space for deepening conversations about, and experiences of, our relationship with the land, with the other-than-human-world and with our own wild nature. Our experiences told us that spending time in wild nature (as close to wilderness as we could find in the UK) was a reliable and powerful way to come back into balance. As Jung writes (1984, p. 142): 'Walking in the woods, lying on the grass, taking a bathe in the sea, are from the outside; entering the unconscious, entering yourself through dreams, is touching nature from the inside and this is the same thing. Things are put right again.'

At the core of the week is a solo day: participants go off in silence at dawn to find a spot to stay in, until dusk. The task is to stay within a four-metre radius and to simply 'be', to watch and to notice the connections between outside and inside. It is inviting people to have an experience of 'finding their way back in' to the web of life, as a living psychic whole.

The next day is devoted to telling their stories, which are always a mix of fear, excitement, boredom, as well as blissful experiences of oneness, timelessness and a longing to return to something original. This is a whole-body experience. As all the senses become heightened, the thinking mind begins to empty. There is more room for the functions of instinct, intuition and sensation to become balanced with intellect.

The experience of 'I' expands. Jung describes this in *Memories, Dreams, Reflections*: 'At times I feel like I am spread out over the landscape and inside things, and am myself living in every tree, in the splashing of the waves, in the clouds and the animals that come and go, in the procession of the seasons' (Jung, 1961 p. 252).

Rationalistic walls crumble, opening the door to an experience of eternity. The vast open spaces of wilderness, the majesty of the mountains, the power of the sea, the rain and the wind can humble the 'I'. 'I' am now a tiny speck in the universe. Raw nature puts us in our place. For some this humility might trigger feelings of humiliation.

Sometimes inner and outer nature can mirror one another in the most uncanny way. A woman who was in a tender state of grief after recently losing her mother had found her way to her spot on the beach. After half an hour of relaxation she realised she was in the presence of a goat and kid who stayed with her all day. Synchronicities are abundant.

Other people describe numinous experiences such as merging into rock, conversations with plants or animals, or hearing the heartbeat of the earth. It is these kinds of experiences of living by a different law inexplicable to the Western mind-set, which can dramatically shift a participant's world view. Often this is the first time that people have shared such experiences in a group, and the witnessing can be profound.

What is most striking is the deep love that arises for the earth. Most are left fumbling for words in the presence of such awe and beauty, often overwhelmed by tears of relief at the sense of 'coming home'. This can trigger a deep grief and mourning about what we, collectively, are doing to our larger body, the body of the earth; it is a reminder that the experience of becoming embodied can be painful. What can also emerge is a natural generosity to give back to the earth: to take action, not from a place of 'should' but from a place of love.

Great care is taken with reintegration. It might take some months, or even years, to allow the experiences to settle, to share them with others, to see how they might inform lifestyles and work.

It quickly became obvious that one-week courses were just an introduction to this work. So in 2008 the Natural Change Project was set up by Dave Key and Scottish psychotherapist Margaret Kerr. It offered six-month courses and was funded by a large green NGO. They selected community leaders from the health, education, private, youth, arts and NGO sectors in Scotland. When they were recruited to the project, none of these participants was active in the field of sustainability; one woman said at the start, 'I thought nature was the gap between Harvey Nichols and the taxi door' (Macdonald, 2009).

The course consisted of a series of residentials and weekends exploring the nature of change from different angles such as personal change, organisational change, lifestyle change. The solo days in the wilds of nature remained a central part of the course, but there was also a chance to experience a solo day in the city.

The director of the NGO said it had been their most successful project and campaign. It inspired leaders in the community to understand sustainability at a deep level, integrating feelings and practical action, bringing a deep connection with the rest of nature back into mainstream culture via the ripples into all participant organisations. (See Key and Kerr, 2011, 2013.)

Resistance

Yet despite such success, funding was discontinued. Why? I suspect that this project included too much emotional process for such a traditional green NGO, which would typically view the process of delving into the inner world as a distraction from effective practical action and at worst self-indulgent and manipulative. In Arnstein's 'Ladder of Citizen Participation' (Arnstein, 1969) 'therapy' is placed on the second to bottom rung of the ladder of citizen participation; at the bottom is 'manipulation'! This chart is still used in teaching on participation in NGOs today. This split between action and reflection has its roots in the cultural narrative about fighting against nature; in this case it is about fighting our own nature, as if exploring feelings would lead us astray rather than liberating energy for action in the world.

On the other hand, the psychotherapy profession has been guilty at times of interpreting political action as a displacement from the 'real' inner concerns, at worst an 'acting out'. In the middle lies a necessary movement between action and reflection.

Awareness of these two cultural narratives helps to bring insight into the resistance against new green initiatives. Here is another example of what I mean. Professor of Landscape Architecture Clare Cooper Marcus has spent decades trying to persuade architects to include gardens and green views in the design of hospitals. Research shows that spending time in gardens, parks or wild nature speeds up the healing process; even just a green view is healing (Cooper Marcus & Barnes, 1999). This would save hospitals huge amounts of time and money. Yet hospitals are moving in the other direction, towards germ-free, high-rise blocks with non-opening windows. Clearly this is a move away from nature; the outdoors is seen as dangerous rather than a healing environment. Ironically this old fashioned 'germ-free' method is now fostering superbugs! This is one of many examples of how innovative eco-activism may be sabotaged by an outdated cultural narrative despite new methods that have ample proven research to back up their effectiveness.

Super-quarry: a community campaign

My third example is about a successful campaign which helped a Scottish community to dialogue between two clashing world views: Earth as utility and Earth as sacred. In the early 1990s a concrete-manufacturing company called Lafarge proposed building a super-quarry in a mountain on the Isle of Harris, a National Scenic area of NW Scotland. Scottish activist and human ecologist Alastair McIntosh campaigned against this proposal for the biggest road-stone quarry in the world. He believed that right relationship with place is central to a sustainable livelihood. He writes:

> The cornerstone of the case to be argued was reverence. Thus I would suggest to the inquiry that to be reverent means to be concerned with the integrity of a thing or person; to value it for itself. . .to work with it in celebration of its being. . .not with a graceless spirit of mere utility.
>
> (McIntosh, 1996)

McIntosh invited two witnesses from very different backgrounds to support him in this case: Rev. Macleod, a native Gaelic preacher, and Stone Eagle, a Native American warrior chief who had been involved in campaigning against a super-quarry in his homeland of Nova Scotia. Both men argued that the land should be shown reverence because it is sacred. It would be an act of desecration to mine the mountain. This caught the imagination of the general public and soon there were newspaper articles and radio programmes about this campaign, which then became international news.

After a very long and protracted fight, the plans for the quarry were rejected. Part of that success was due to the voices of those who articulated to the community a different narrative, counteracting the idea that land is mere utility. The idea that land is sacred, that our relationship with it nourishes the soul, is a difficult case to argue. Frequently this voice is either absent altogether or drowned out by the argument that 'development' is economically beneficial to the community and therefore the necessary route.

In Jungian terms, how does archaic mind find the language to communicate itself to modern mind, which is so bound by reason and intellect?

Reflections

I have so far discussed the making conscious of two opposing narratives in understanding the process of change, and the resistance to change, in the work of eco-activism. But where is psychotherapy itself situated in relation to these narratives?

On the one hand, as I have pointed to earlier, psychotherapy is part of the newly emerging story because it is an exploration of emotional process; it therefore challenges the existing story about the dominance of the rational mind. On the other hand, psychotherapy has always been, and still remains, an exploration of *human* relationships with no reference to our environment, as if the other-than-human world is of no relevance to our trauma and healing, as if human development takes place in some kind of vacuum. How can this be? We are all born into land and we have relationships with animals, plants, elements and place that are, like human relationships, carried through the generations.

While C. G. Jung is one of the few psychotherapists to write extensively about our human relationship with the rest of nature (Sabini, 2002), there are, in my experience, few in the Jungian community who have continued this exploration in theory or practice (see e.g. Baring & Cashford, 1991; Hillman & Ventura, 1993; Bernstein, 2006; Tacey, 2009).

It has taken me many years to know what it means to listen to my client *with the earth in mind*. This might include: how to work with ecological issues that clients bring to sessions (Rust, 2008); the links between ecological health and mental health (Roszak et al., 1996); exploring human development in relation to the other-than-human world (Louv, 2005); taking psychotherapy outdoors (see Grut and Linden, 2002; Totton, 2011; Jordan, 2014; Siddons-Heginworth, 2011); groupwork in the community to facilitate dialogue about the ecological and social crisis (Macy & Young-Brown, 1998; Seed et al., 1988).

This work is about healing the split relationship with nature, which is echoed in the two cultural narratives I have been describing. Underlying these two narratives is a fear of nature (biophobia) and a love of nature (biophilia). Nature is both idealised and denigrated, along with those peoples who have become associated with nature (e.g. women, Black Africans and indigenous peoples). How do we hold the tension between 'defending against/fear of' and 'opening out towards' the other?

In this light the old cultural narrative becomes an exaggerated form of defence. However, our societal structures have been built on this defence. Capitalism relies on seeing the rest of nature as a collection of objects to be used. Becoming 'part of the greater whole' is allied with communism, feared as part of social control, associated (consciously or unconsciously) with, for example, the Nazi Party. It is at these deeper levels that we find the greatest resistance to moving into a greener world. However, if humans refuse to make this shift, it seems that nature is on course for a revolution that cannot be resisted.

References

Arnstein, S. R. (1969) 'A Ladder of Citizen Participation.' *Journal of the American Planning Association*, 35(4): 216–24.

Baring, A. and Cashford, J. (1991) *The Myth of the Goddess: The Evolution of an Image*. Harmondsworth: Penguin.

Bernstein, J. (2006) *Living in the Borderland: The Evolution of Consciousness and the Challenge of Healing Trauma*. London: Routledge.

Cooper Marcus, M. and Barnes, M. (eds) (1999) *Healing Gardens: Therapeutic Benefits and Design Recommendations*. London: Wiley.

Grut, J. and Linden, S. (2002) *The Healing Fields: Working with Psychotherapy and Nature to Rebuild Shattered Lives*. London: Frances Lincoln.

Hillman, J. and Ventura, M. (1993) *We've Had a Hundred Years of Psychotherapy and the World is Getting Worse*. San Francisco, CA: Harper.

Jordan, M. (2014) *Nature and Therapy: Understanding Counselling and Therapy in Outdoor Spaces*. London: Routledge.

Jung, C. G. (1927) 'Analytical Psychology and "Weltanschauung".' *CW*8.

Jung, C. G. (1955–6) *Mysterium Coniunctionis*. *CW*14.

Jung, C. G. (1961) *Memories, Dreams, Reflections*. New York: Pantheon Books

Jung, C. G. (1984) *Dream Analysis: Notes of the Seminars Given in 1928–1930 by C. G. Jung*, edited by W. McGuire. Princetown, NJ: Princetown University Press.

Key, D. and Kerr, M. (2011) *The Natural Change Report*. Scotland: WWF.

Key, D. and Kerr, M. (2013) 'The Natural Change Project.' In M. J. Rust and N. Totton (eds), *Vital Signs: Psychological Responses to Ecological Crisis*. London: Karnac.

Louv, R. (2005) *Last Child in the Woods: Saving our Children from Nature-deficit Disorder*. Chapel Hill, NC: Algonquin Books.

Macdonald, L. M. (2009) 'Changes and gifts: Taking stock.' Blog article from the WWF Natural Change Project, posted 3 February. Currently archived offline. Natural Change Foundation: Edinburgh. http://www.aislingmagazine.com/aislingmagazine/articles/TAM19/Superquarry.html.

Macy, J. and Young-Brown, M. (1998) *Coming Back to Life: Practices to Reconnect Our Lives*. Victoria, BC: New Society Press.

McIntosh, A. (1996) 'Theology, rocks, superquarry project.' *Ailing Magazine*, 19.

Roszak, T., Kanner, A. and Gomes, M. (1996) *Ecopsychology: Restoring the Earth, Healing the Mind*. San Francisco, CA: Sierra Club Books.

Rust, M.-J. (2008) 'Nature hunger eating problems and consuming the Earth.' *Counselling Psychology Review*, 23(2).

Sabini, M. (2002) *The Earth Has a Soul: C. G. Jung's Writings on Nature, Technology and Modern Life*. Berkeley, CA: North Atlantic Books.

Sabini, M. (2011) 'Jung as Nature Mystic.' In K. Bulkeley and C. Weldon (eds), *Teaching Jung*. Oxford: Oxford University Press.

Seed, J., Macy, J., Fleming, P. and Naess, A. (1988) *Thinking Like a Mountain*. Victoria, BC: New Society Publishing.

Siddons-Heginworth, I. (2011) *Environmental Arts Therapy and the Tree of Life*. Exeter: Spirits Rest Press.

Tacey, D. (2009) *The Edge of the Sacred: Jung, Psyche, Earth*. Einsiedeln: Daimon Verlag.

Totton, N. (2011) *Wild Therapy: Undomesticating our Inner and Outer Worlds*. Hay-on-Wye: PCCS Books.

INDEX

Note: bold page numbers indicate figures; bold numbers preceded by **Pl** indicate colour plates; numbers in brackets preceded by *n* indicate chapter endnotes.